THE HIDDEN HUXLEY

Brave New World (1932) has become a byword for the horrors of totalitarianism and the nightmarish potential of genetic engineering. More than any other work, it has established Aldous Huxley as an icon of the liberal tradition. Yet at the time he wrote his classic novel, Huxley was a proponent of eugenics and an outspoken champion of anti-democratic government. For the past sixty years this Huxley has remained entirely unknown.

The Hidden Huxley presents a selection of his hitherto undocumented articles and broadcasts from this period. They reveal a complex figure, who was both typical of his era in his abhorrence for mass civilization, and unique in that his contempt gradually gave way to a sympathetic affinity with ordinary men and women. By 1937, when Huxley left Europe for the United States, the cultural elitist had been firmly displaced by the legendary humanist.

Huxley's fascinating progress from a scourge of the masses to their compassionate spokesman – a volte-face which took him down coal-mines, into factories and to a New Forest camp for the unemployed – is here exposed for the first time.

David Bradshaw is a University Lecturer in English and a Fellow of Worcester College, Oxford. He has written on Conrad, T. S. Eliot, Lawrence and Yeats, and is currently preparing a major critical biography of Aldous Huxley.

THE
HIDDEN HUXLEY

Edited by David Bradshaw

faber and faber
LONDON · BOSTON

For Barbara, Rory
and Georgia

First published in Great Britain in 1994
by Faber and Faber Limited
3 Queen Square London WC1N 3AU

This paperback edition first published in 1995

Photoset by Parker Typesetting Service, Leicester
Printed in England by Clays Ltd, St Ives plc

All Texts by Aldous Huxley © A. L. Huxley Estate,
c/o Reece Halsey Agency, 1994
Editorial Matter and annotations © David Bradshaw, 1994

David Bradshaw is hereby identified as editor of this work in accordance
with Section 77 of the Copyright, Designs and Patents Act 1988

A CIP record for this book is available from the British
Library

ISBN 0-571-17260-1

2 4 6 8 10 9 7 5 3 1

Contents

Note: Titles for Chapters 8, 9, 10, 12, 13, 22 and 23 are supplied by the editor; all other titles are taken from the newspapers, journals, etc, in which the essays first appeared.

Introduction

Aldous Huxley's departure for Florence in the summer of 1923 marked the beginning of his long, balmy exile from England. In 1928 he moved to Paris and in 1930 he bought a house at Sanary on the French Riviera. Seven years later Huxley set sail for the United States and spent his remaining twenty-six years in California.

His exotic choice of habitat, and his reputation as a cynical *habitué* of the 'condemned playground'[1] of inter-war letters, have helped promote the idea that Huxley turned a lofty blind eye to the upheavals which shook his native land in the 1930s. If the Huxley of this period occupies a place in the mind of the reading public at all, it is as the disengaged and impassive foil of the ardent and committed George Orwell. By choosing to describe the author of *Brave New World* (1932) as an 'amused, Pyrrhonic aesthete' in his 1946 Foreword to the novel, Huxley has been the principal and unwitting architect of this long-standing misconception of himself. Unfailingly, each time the novel is reprinted, the Foreword is reprinted as well.[2] Moreover, the visual images we have of Huxley between the wars, such as Max Beerbohm's caricature of his bookish tousle, horn-rimmed eyes and rangy frame spiralling wraith-like from the earth, have served only to reinforce our impression of his airy remoteness from the problems of the real world.[3]

Above all, however, the current view of the inter-war Huxley derives from a standard bibliography of his writings which is as incomplete as it is unreliable. Concealed behind the deficiencies of this principal check-list of his work, the authentic 1930s Huxley has languished misunderstood and unread for over fifty years.[4]

Although early in 1929 Huxley told the *Little Review* that 'detach-ment' was both his weakest and his strongest characteristic, and the quality he liked least and most in himself,[5] by the early months of 1931 Huxley was anything but an aloof and absentee observer of Britain's problems. In fact, he became more intensely ravelled in the chronic social and political crisis which unfolded in the wake of the Wall Street Crash of October 1929 than any other British writer of his generation, and as the 1930s progressed he made frequent sallies across the Channel in order to monitor the effects of the Slump at first hand. By the middle of the decade, the belief in cultural hierarchy and the contempt for mass society which so dominate Huxley's outlook in the 1920s had been superseded by a more humanitarian, even 'socialist' philosophy, and a heartfelt con-cern for ordinary men and women.[6] At present, however, both the depth of Huxley's distaste for mass society and parliamentary democracy, and his later mutation into a fugleman of the anti-fascist intelligentsia and a spokesman for the dispossessed, are completely undocumented.

Huxley's tendency to vacilate between political activism and highbrow nebulosity is evident as early as August 1915, when, as an undergraduate at Balliol College, Oxford, he teased one of his women friends for 'attending the Socialist beanfeast presided over by [G. D. H.] Cole – all in the wrong spirit adds my informant!' The 'beanfeast' in question was most likely the summer conference of the Oxford University Socialist Society. Huxley continued his letter:

It must have been rather instructive. My own politics are, by nature, a sturdy *m'en fichisme* – with acquired sympathies for all creeds – the best system, I take it, for the merely theoretic politician – whose business it is to be universally and sunnily smiling, not ravenously focussed to a point, as should be the active politician.[7]

Even at this stage, however, Huxley's dissociation from politics was less sturdily carefree than he makes out in this letter, and at the beginning of the following term he was enrolled as a Full

Member of the Balliol Fabian Group by Rajani Palme Dutt (1896–1974), a fellow undergraduate at his college and destined to be a commanding figure in the Communist Party of Great Britain from the 1920s to the 1960s. 'A Full Member,' Dutt later explained, 'as distinct from an Associate, had to sign a document known as the Basis . . . affirming acceptance of the principles of socialism.' Dutt continued:

I recall the picture of [Huxley] scrutinising most precisely, with the aid of a magnifying glass he used to aid his eyesight, the small print of the Basis, and then declaring his satisfaction and signing, but adding that he did not want to be 'an economic type of Socialist', since he hated economics, and supported socialism for the same reasons as Oscar Wilde had done.[8]

It seems likely that Huxley's undergraduate commitment to socialism was sincere but less than fanatical. The only surviving record of his activities is an entry in the minute-book of the Balliol, Queen's and New College Group of the Oxford University Socialist Society which records that Huxley was one of those who opened the discussion following Dutt's 'excellent' paper on 'Second Thoughts for Nationalists' on 6 November 1915. In view of Huxley's later attraction to the ideas of H. G. Wells, and his ambivalent projection of a Wellsian World State in *Brave New World*, the secretary's résumé of Dutt's Wells-inspired talk is intriguing:

After showing to what a state of intellectual and political bankruptcy the present political organisation of society had brought us, he urged that the only way out of the difficulty was the substitution of a super-nationalism . . . in which every state would, through force of circumstances, be willing to renounce its sovereignty and to submit to some sort of common higher authority in international affairs.[9]

Among other things, the Fabian Basis reminded members that their movement was dedicated to the 'extinction of private property in Land' and to the disappearance of 'the idle class now living on the labour of others'.[10] Soon after Huxley joined the staff of the

Athenaeum magazine in April 1919, however, an acute concern with the preservation of the leisure class becomes prominent in his work. Huxley had become an eager devotee of the American critic and controversialist Henry Louis Mencken (1880–1956), the so-called 'Sage of Baltimore', and at the time the most celebrated adversary of mass democracy in the English-speaking world. Mencken's vilification of his fellow citizens gave unbridled voice to Huxley's own qualms about Americanization and the levelling advance of mass civilization, fears which had grown increasingly intense during the three years since Huxley had left Oxford in 1916. To date, Mencken's key influence on the early Huxley has been entirely overlooked.

The contempt of the few for the many has a long history, reaching back beyond Horace and Plato to Heraclitus. At the turn of this century, repeated predictions of a population explosion; the lurid forebodings of crowd theorists such as Gustave Le Bon; eugenicist fears about the multiplication of the 'unfit' and the slump in 'national efficiency'; the intelligentsia's aversion to the spread of mass literacy and the looming threat of American materialism, all combined to trigger a resurgence of interest in cultural elitism and a renewed zest for intellectual aristocracy. Yeats was adamant that 'intellectual freedom and social equality are incompatible',[11] and he predicted that the coming age would bring 'an *antithetical* aristocratic civilization in its completed form, every detail of life hierarchical'.[12] Lawrence, too, looked forward to the day when mass democracy would be replaced by a four-tiered ziggurat of power topped by a 'small class of the supreme judges: not merely legal judges, but judges of the destiny of the nation'.[13] Inspired by Mencken's absorption in Nietzsche, Huxley, too, began to extol the virtues of intellectual aristocracy in the early 1920s. Huxley's Menckenian phase lasted until the middle of the decade, but by the time he published *Proper Studies* in 1927, two other anti-democratic notables had begun to exert an influence on his work: the Italian economist and sociologist Vilfredo Pareto (1848–1923) and H. G. Wells.

Pareto has been identified as a precursor of fascism by many commentators.[14] 'In Pareto's work for the first time,' Franz Borkenau wrote in 1936, 'the powerful tendency towards a change of the political machinery and social organization since embodied in Bolshevism, Fascism, National Socialism and a score of similar movements has found clear expression.'[15] Huxley remarked that in Pareto's monumental *Trattato di sociologia generale* (1916) he 'discovered many of [his] own still vague and inchoate notions methodically set down and learnedly documented, together with a host of new ideas and relevant facts'.[16] The *Trattato* provided Huxley with colossal authority for his belief in cultural hierarchy and his scathing disbelief in progress, and convinced him that parliamentary government offered nothing more than a front for plutocracy and a hotbed for wily speculators. So much of Huxley's writing from the mid-1920s to the mid-1930s is shaded by Pareto's *Trattato* that it is worthwhile scanning its essentials.

Pareto claimed that all societies were divisible into a minority 'governing elite' and a governed mass or 'lower stratum'. These two strata do not rest in equilibrium, but are in a state of continuous flux owing to the 'residues' or basic human instincts which exert an irrational pressure on the social psychology. Pareto identified six classes of residues, but the first two of these, the 'instinct for combinations' and the 'persistence of aggregates', are the most important. Individuals are continuously being admitted to and displaced from the governing elite, and under certain circumstances one elite replaces another *en bloc*. Pareto called this process the 'circulation of elites', and it has been described succinctly by Samuel Finer:

The relationship between the governing elite and the governed is determined by the way in which Class I ['instinct for combinations'] and Class II ['persistence of aggregates'] residues are distributed between them. Governing groups with a preponderance of Class I residues tend to be mercantile, materialistic, innovatory, and they rule by guile. Governing groups in which Class II residues preponderate tend to be bureaucratic, idealistic, conservative; they rule by force. The proportion of Class I to Class II residues in the governing elite alternates through time ... So, ultimately, either by infiltration or revolution from below, the governing elite is displaced by a new elite drawn from the ranks of the former governed section of society. This process continues, the new governing elite in time being overthrown, for the same reason.'[17]

'History,' as Pareto puts it, 'is a graveyard of aristocracies.'[18] In the Paretian model, therefore, the governing elite must always be prepared to use force at some point in order to maintain its position. In their renunciation of force, their humanitarian institutions and their encouragement of guileful swindlers and speculators (types which have a pronounced 'instinct for combinations'), parliamentary democracies are profoundly unstable. The strength of a society dominated by men with a 'persistence of aggregates', on the other hand (as Huxley puts it in 'Pareto and Society'), 'lies in its stability and in the violence and the promptitude of the actions dictated by unquestioning faith in an absolute'.

Brave New World was written during a period of unprecedented instability in modern British politics and at a time when Huxley daily expected the country to sink into bloody disorder. Given this context and Huxley's avid reading of Pareto, when, in the third chapter of the novel, Mustapha Mond, the Resident World Controller for Western Europe, lingers momentously over the phrase 'History is bunk', he does more than make a meal of a Fordian cliché before the party of students who hang on his every word.[19] Mond draws his young listeners' and the reader's attention to the fact that elites have long ceased to circulate in the World State. Biological engineering and social conditioning have ensured that history's 'graveyard of aristocracies' is as much a thing of the past as *The Tempest*, darned socks and viviparous mothers.

Steeled by his reading of the *Trattato*, Huxley denounced parliamentary democracy in *Proper Studies* as a system:

whereby confidence tricksters, rich men, and quacks may be given power by the votes of an electorate composed in great part of mental

Peter Pans, whose childishness renders them peculiarly susceptible to the blandishments of demagogues and the tirelessly repeated suggestions of the rich men's newspapers.

Huxley argued that a more 'rational' state would necessitate the 'creation and maintenance of a ruling aristocracy of mind' leading to 'government by those best fitted to govern'.[20]

Proper Studies also contains a 'Note on Eugenics', in which Huxley weighs the pros and cons of special breeding programmes. As early as 1921, in Huxley's first novel, *Crome Yellow*, Scogan predicts that:

An impersonal generation will take the place of Nature's hideous system. In vast state incubators, rows upon rows of gravid bottles will supply the world with the population it requires. The family system will disappear; society, sapped at its very base, will have to find new foundations . . .[21]

And a letter which Huxley wrote to his brother Julian the following year, suggesting likely topics for magazine articles, indicates that he shared his character's fascination with eugenics:

I should think that one on Heredity and perhaps one slightly Wellsian forecast of the possible achievements of biology in the future (pointing out how much more interesting is control of life than control of machinery) would be a good beginning.[22]

In an article published in September 1927 Huxley wrote:

In the future we envisage, eugenics will be practised in order to improve the human breed and the instincts will not be ruthlessly repressed, but, as far as possible, sublimated so as to express themselves in socially harmless ways. Education will not be the same for all individuals. Children of different types will receive different training. Society will be organised as a hierarchy of mental quality and the form of government will be aristocratic in the literal sense of the word – that is to say, the best will rule . . . Our children may look forward to a new caste system based on differences in natural ability, to a Machiavellian system of education designed to give the members of the lower castes only that which it is profitable for the members of the upper castes that they should know.[23]

This adumbration of the future use of eugenics owes much to the work of H. G. Wells, whose stimulus Huxley acknowledged in his Introduction to *Proper Studies*. Huxley had a great deal in common with Wells between the mid-1920s and the mid-1930s, not least his conviction that the state must use eugenic measures to arrest the multiplication of the unfit. As 'The Victory of Art over Humanity' and 'Science and Civilisation' reveal, by the time he wrote the allegedly anti-Wellsian *Brave New World* in 1931, Huxley was no less of an 'Open Conspirator' against parliamentary democracy and a supporter of world government than Wells, the coiner of the term.

Worries about the differential birth-rate, or the tendency of society's supposedly less meritorious members to have more children than parents higher up the social scale, continued to assail Huxley throughout the period covered by this book. He registers his anxiety about the proliferation of mental defectives in 'Babies – State Property' (1930), and, against all the expert advice he had received, Huxley calls for their compulsory sterilization in 'What is Happening to Our Population?' (1934). The following year, in 'The Next 25 Years', Huxley predicts that by 'the early 1950s one person out of every ninety-two [will] be a certifiable half-wit'. By 1960, he continues, Parliament will have passed 'a series of laws embodying all the principles of negative eugenics'. The broad drift of British eugenics in the 1930s was towards a recognition of the role of environment in social hygiene.[24] Huxley's emphasis on heredity and 'national efficiency', on the other hand, highlights the Edwardian complexion of his eugenics.

From a contemporary perspective, Huxley's advocacy of sterilization places him in a distinctly murky light. However, while he was out of step with the leadership of the Eugenics Society in calling for *compulsory* rather than voluntary sterilization, it would be a mistake to suppose that his views reveal Huxley to have been some kind of odious crypto-Nazi. Many progressives envisaged eugenics as a humanitarian means of fast-forwarding to a better world, and the Webbs, Shaw, Naomi Mitchison and Marie Stopes were all deeply involved in the eugenics movement at one time or another. The following statement by the pioneering sexologist Havelock Ellis, which could almost serve as a digest of Huxley's 'What is Happening to Our Population?', was typical of the progressives' point of view:

The superficially sympathetic man flings a coin to the beggar; the more deeply sympathetic man builds an almshouse for him so that he need no longer beg; but perhaps the most radically sympathetic of all is the man who arranges that the beggar shall not be born.[25]

'What a world we live in,' Huxley wrote at the beginning of January 1931:

The human race fills me with a steadily growing dismay. I was staying in the Durham coal-field this autumn, in the heart of English unemployment, and it was awful. If only one could believe that the remedies proposed for the awfulness (Communism etc.) weren't even worse than the disease – in fact weren't the disease itself in another form, with superficially different symptoms. The sad and humiliating conclusion is forced on one that the only thing to do is to flee and hide. Nothing one can do is any good and the doing is liable to infect one with the disease one is trying to treat. So there's nothing for it but to make one's escape while one can, as long as one can.[26]

In October 1930 Huxley had visited the mining village of Willington in County Durham which was then blighted with almost universal male unemployment. His tour of the area had a profound effect on him but, in the event, Huxley resisted the temptation to melt away. From this point onwards another, 'Orwellian' Huxley is at large.

'They're off today to do mines, factories . . . black country; did the docks when they were here; must see England,' Virginia Woolf wrote in her diary on 17 February 1931. Having dined with the Woolfs the previous evening, Huxley and his wife Maria had that morning embarked on a swift reconnaissance of England's centres of heavy industry and even heavier unemployment. As Woolf records, just prior to this sortie to the North and Midlands, Huxley had toured the St Katharine and Royal Albert 'docks' in London. He had also visited a Jewish abattoir in London's East End. His excursions into 'Alien England' now continued with a train journey to Chesterfield, where he and his wife were to 'interview managers'[27] before going on during the ensuing six days to visit a Sheffield steelworks, a Durham coal-mine, Middlesbrough, 'Imperial Chemical Industries' huge factory of synthetic ammonia, sodium and other products' at nearby Billingham, and finally a magneto assembly plant at Birmingham. Although, in retrospect, Huxley complained of having to immerse himself in baths 'round the edges of which are to be found selections from the hairs of all the commercial travellers on the Northern Circuit', and he protested bitterly at the hard beds, icy bedrooms and inedible food he and his wife had had to endure in the overpriced hotels they stayed in, Huxley's own 'Northern Circuit' finally splintered the carapace of his highbrow contempt for the masses. If, as John Carey has suggested, 'Brave New World is the classic denunciation of mass culture in the interwar years',[28] it must also be recognized that at the time he wrote his novel, Huxley published four articles – 'Abroad in England', 'Sight-Seeing in Alien Englands', 'The Victory of Art over Humanity' and 'Greater and Lesser London' – in which the plight of the unemployed masses, and the hardly more enviable lot of those still toiling in factories, steelworks, coal-mines and dockyards, is handled without a trace of condescension.

Foreshadowing the tribute Orwell pays in The Road to Wigan Pier (1937) to the 'most noble bodies' of the miners he encounters in the North-West of England, Huxley writes in 1931 of the 'movingly beautiful' torsos of the miners he meets in the 'monstrous twilight' of a North-East coal-face ('Sight-Seeing in Alien Englands').[29] Similarly, both Old Etonians were made acutely conscious of their status as social outsiders in the North of England. In 1937 Orwell was to emphasize the rigid class barriers which confronted him 'like a wall of stone' in Lancashire and Yorkshire.[30] Huxley deploys the same metaphor in 'Abroad in England' when describing the 'Chinese wall' of class which loomed large and forbidding during his visit to Willington. Finally, like *The Road to Wigan Pier*, Huxley's compassionate dispatches from 'Alien England' are directed most pointedly at a southern, prosperous, metropolitan and potentially hostile readership. Huxley and Orwell had much more in common in the 1930s than is currently acknowledged.

If there is one theme which underpins Huxley's work in the early 1930s it is the threat to social stability posed not just by the gathering legions of the unemployed but also by the unregulated advance of technology, and the lack of any attempt at systematic national planning. 'So long as scientific research goes on,' Huxley warns in 'Science and Civilisation', 'society stands poised above a potential succession of earthquakes.' Later in 1932 he wrote:

A growing body of public opinion is now in favour of the deliberate planning of our social life in all its aspects. It is an ideal which must, it seems to me, appeal to every reasonable man. Viewing the chaos to which a planless individualism has reduced us, we are compelled to be believers in planning.[31]

Brave New World is but one, oblique expression of Huxley's passionate interest in planning and the condition of England. As Huxley saw it in the early 1930s, this country faced a stark choice: 'We must either plan or else go under' ('Abroad in England').

The historian Arnold Toynbee described 1931 as an '*annus terribilis*' during the course of which people 'were seriously contemplating and frankly discussing the possibility that the Western system of society might break down and cease to work'.[32] Huxley was most certainly one of those pessimists, and as the nation's affairs lurched from one crisis to the next (culminating in the formation of Britain's first National Government in late August and the abandonment of the gold standard in late September), so Huxley's exasperation with parliamentary democracy plunged ever deeper. A visit he had made to the House of Commons earlier in the year to attend a critical debate on the economy provided him with conclusive proof that Parliament was little more than a grandiose white elephant, quite incapable of solving the problems over which it presided. In contrast, as 'Abroad in England' and 'Greater and Lesser London' make clear, Huxley was impressed by Oswald Mosley's political vigour and his radical proposals for national renewal. In various speeches distilled in a Manifesto published on 13 December 1930, 'Mosley called for a new parliamentary "machine" to replace the nineteenth century one. Parliament, he said, must become a workshop not a talkshop'. Mosley stressed the need for rapid and effective economic measures to be implemented by a 'strong executive' free from detailed criticism and obstruction and subject only to the 'general control' of Parliament.[33] Mosley's plan, 'though in some respects vague or feeble', also won T. S. Eliot's approval through its blunt recognition 'that the nineteenth century is over, and that a thorough reorganisation of industry and of agriculture is essential'.[34]

However, 'Abroad in England' reveals Huxley to have been much more than a keen adherent of industrial and agricultural rationalisation; he is exposed as a fervid proponent of *Soviet-style* planning. As Huxley put it in an article he wrote at the beginning of September 1931:

We may either persist in our present course, which is disastrous, or we must abandon democracy and allow ourselves to be ruled dictatorially by men who will compel us to do and suffer what a rational foresight demands.

Or, if we preserve the democratic forms, we must invent some psychological technique for inducing the electorate to act before the crash rather than after; we must provide voters with bad emotional reasons for behaving with rational foresight.

Or, finally, we may employ both these last methods together – compel and at the same time use propaganda to make the compulsion appear acceptable.

This is the present Russian method. Refined and improved, it has a good chance of becoming universal.[35]

At one of the darkest moments of modern British history, the figure who has become an icon of the liberal establishment embraced, briefly, the policies he appears to revile in *Brave New World*. Indeed, only a fortnight before he published his novel in January 1932, Huxley advised his wireless audience that: 'Any form of order is better than chaos. Our civilisation is menaced with total collapse. Dictatorship and scientific propaganda may provide the only means for saving humanity from the miseries of anarchy.'

As with Huxley's support for compulsory sterilization, we should be wary of condemning him out of hand for his readiness to sanction an authoritarian solution to the political crisis brought on by the Slump. Faced with its towering ineffectuality, intellectuals of all persuasions more or less despaired of Parliament in the early 1930s, and, whether they championed the corporate state of fascism, the earthly paradise of Soviet communism, the Wellsian World State, or simply the home-grown gradualism of Political and Economic Planning and the Next Five Years' Group, few had any real confidence in the House of Commons, even if they did not work actively for its demise. Whether the free, individualistic and open traditions of democratic society could ever be reconciled with the closed, controlled and stable world of the 'rational state' is a conundrum which Huxley addresses on a number of occasions in this volume.

'Financial speculation is probably the most pernicious game of chance ever invented,' Huxley writes in 'Casino and Bourse'. The bursting of Wall Street's speculative bubble, the Hatry scandal earlier in 1929,[36] and the posthumous revelation, in March 1932, that the legendary wealth of Ivar Kreuger, the Swedish 'Match King', was mostly imaginary, all helped to intensify Huxley's loathing of the speculator.[37] In July 1932 he told his literary agent J. B. Pinker that he was 'working on the scenario of what may be, I think, a rather good play – with a Kreuger-like figure as the central character – linking the story up with general economic ideas, which might be timely, as everyone is bothered about these things'.[38] Huxley called his play *Now More Than Ever* (borrowing half a line from Keats's 'Ode to a Nightingale') and he tried repeatedly to get it produced in the early 1930s.[39]

Soon after the Kreuger scandal broke, Huxley again expressed his astonishment that 'the rulers of highly-organised societies should permit the stability of the mechanism on which the economic prosperity of the community depends, to be compromised by a small group of wealthy gamblers'.[40] The Stavisky affair of December 1933, which for a while threatened to destabilize the Third Republic, was yet another crisis brought on by a speculator's machinations, and it prompted Huxley to redouble his efforts to get *Now More Than Ever* staged. The problem with the play was that its long expository dialogues, which, as far as Huxley was concerned, were its *raison d'être*, also made it a commercial liability. The play's topicality simply could not compensate for its lack of dramatic tension. But, for all its woodenness, in its presentation of the downfall of Arthur Lidgate, 'a financier with a sincere desire to rationalize the world',[41] at the hands of Sir Thomas Lupton, 'a gross, red-faced, greasily-prosperous' speculator and his shady American accomplice Wertheim, *Now More Than Ever* provides yet more evidence of the vital significance which Huxley attributed to planning and his profound concern with national stability in the early 1930s. Huxley re-read Pareto at the end of 1933 and in 'Pareto and Society' he reflects on the Harry, Kreuger and Stavisky scandals from the viewpoint of his Italian master.

As late as July 1933 Huxley could inform a correspondent:

About 99.5% of the entire population of the planet are as stupid and philistine (tho' in different ways) as the great masses of the English. The important thing, it seems to me, is not to attack the 99.5% — except for exercise — but to try to see that the 0.5% survives, keeps its quality up to the highest possible level and, if possible, dominates the rest. The imbecility of the 99.5% is appalling — but, after all, what else can you expect?[42]

Similarly, in his address to a Congress on Intellectual Co-operation three months later, Huxley told his Paris audience: '*Malheureusement la logique a très peu de prise sur les masses. Aux masses, il faut parler en termes d'autorité absolue, comme Jéhovah aux Israélites.*[43]

However, the deteriorating situation within Germany and in Europe as a whole following the appointment of Hitler as German Chancellor in January 1933, and especially after he was proclaimed 'Führer of the German Reich' following the death of Hindenburg in August 1934, led to a sea change in Huxley's attitude to authoritarianism. During the summer of 1933 Huxley tuned in with alarm and dismay to German radio stations and heard reports of book burning and the Jewish Boycott.[44] Later on in the year, German literary refugees such as Thomas Mann and Lion Feuchtwanger began arriving in the South of France, and it was not long before Huxley condemned Nazism as 'a rebellion against Western Civilisation'.[45] Furthermore, in June 1934 Huxley was given a brutal demonstration of the force he had condoned in abstract in 1931 when he witnessed the thuggery of Mosley's black-shirted henchmen at a British Union of Fascists rally in London.[46] By the end of the following year, a radically changed Huxley had opened an exhibition of 'Artists Against Fascism and War' with the declaration that 'any form of dictatorship is intrinsically bad'. Soon afterwards he was installed as the first president of 'For Intellectual Liberty', an anti-fascist organization uniting British intellectuals against tyranny and oppression both at home and abroad. By the time Huxley makes his call for a 'People's Front' in November 1936 (in the first and only bulletin of 'For Intellectual Liberty'), he has long been aware that 'progressives must either hang together or hang separately'.

'Loving one's neighbour is heroic,' says the Oxford-educated communist Walter Clough in *Now More Than Ever.* 'Heroic because it's so damnably difficult, the most difficult thing in the world. I've never been able to do it.' But, though he loathes their pleasures – the movies, jazz, football – Clough believes that with determination 'it is possible to love one's neighbours even though one may have little in common with them'. This was the challenge which Huxley set himself in the 1930s, and as the decade progressed he spoke out more and more vociferously on behalf of those whose lives he had derided or ignored in the previous decade – such as the homeless and impoverished women of London ('The Worth of a Gift') – and whom he now regarded as the powerless victims of a bankrupt political system lumbering towards war. As he put it as early as June 1932, 'All men – and particularly "intellectuals" – are chronically tempted to escape from unpleasant and disturbing particularities into the passionless world of abstraction' ('Dispatches from the Riviera'). Rather than lambasting the 'imbecility' of mass society, Huxley in the mid-1930s dedicated himself to scaling the vast walls which separated, in his own phrase, the 'remote province of the Great Bourgeois Empire inhabited by Literary Men, Professional Thinkers and Amateurs of General Ideas' from the interminable plains of ordinary life.

As late as December 1936, in 'How to Improve the World', Huxley could write of Britain's 'sore need of coherent planning and intelligent reform,' but by now he was also emphasizing the import-ance of diet and holistic medicine in social regeneration. 'At the same time,' he writes, 'all the psychological and chemico-psychical techniques for holiday-making should be carefully investigated', a comment which anticipates his later experiments with mescalin and LSD.

The last two pieces in this volume deal with themes which run through the whole of the section dedicated to Huxley's broadcasts and essays: the menace of unchecked scientific innovation, the misery of long-term unemployment and the tedium and routine of factory work. In 'The Man without a Job' and 'Pioneers of Britain's "New Deal"', Huxley condemns 'Technological progress and the hierarchical authoritarian organisation of industry . . . for taking the satisfaction out of work', and argues in favour of a 'university of common life – a university with colleges and laboratories scattered all over the country, where it should be possible for men and women of all ages to study and experiment with the art of living in all its aspects, personal, social and professional'. After visiting a settlement for unemployed men in the New Forest, Huxley heralded an initiative in which life was envisaged as 'co-operative, and in the fullest sense of the word, communistic'. The consummate highbrow, who had begun his writing career in gloomy dread of the insurgent masses and an Americanized planet, left for the United States in April 1937 convinced that mankind could be saved if only it would renounce conventional politics and live in groups 'between the size of a boat's crew and a rugger team'.

Huxley's early social satires and *Brave New World* will always command a readership, but the more uneven quality of his later novels, in which ideas are more often explicated than embodied, suggests that Huxley's fiction will never rest securely within the canon of the English novel. However, the range, perspicuity, sharpness and prescience of Huxley's non-fictional writings, coupled with the enduring appeal of his first five novels, should ensure his continuing status as a significant figure in the history of twentieth-century thought and culture. The neglected essays and broadcasts gathered together in this present volume, though confined to Huxley's immersion in the social and political morass of the early 1930s, reveal a more troubled, troubling and fascinating writer than we have known hitherto. Though the legendary liberal-humanist does not emerge unscathed from these pages, it may well be that the Huxley who surfaces is a figure even more deserving of our attention.

Worcester College, Oxford
January 1994

NOTES

1   'The condemned playground' was Cyril Connolly's description of the 1930s literary scene. Cyril Connolly, *The Condemned Playground: Essays 1927–1944*, London: Routledge, 1945, vi.

2   Foreword, *Brave New World*, New York: Harpers, 1946, ix.

3 Max Beerbohm, *Things New and Old*, London: William Heinemann, 1923, plate 14, 'Mr Aldous Huxley'.

4 Claire John Eschelbach and Joyce Lee Shober, *Aldous Huxley: A Bibliography 1916–1959*, Berkeley and Los Angeles: University of California Press, 1961. This has now been augmented by David Bradshaw, 'A New Bibliography of Aldous Huxley's Work and its Reception, 1912–1937', *Bulletin of Bibliography*, li, September 1994, 237–55.

   The vast majority of quotations from Huxley's writings in this present volume are from hitherto unpublished letters and undocumented articles, broadcasts and reviews. Unless indicated otherwise, London is the original place of publication.

5 'Questionnaire', *Little Review* [Chicago], xii, May 1929, 48–9.

6 Huxley stated that 'in the economic sphere' the goal of the pacifist must be 'socialism'. '100,000 Say No!', *Nash's Pall Mall Magazine*, xcvii, July 1936, 76–81.

7 Letter to Frances Petersen, Department of Special Collections, University Research Library, University of California at Los Angeles (UCLA), n.d. [early August 1915].

8 Copy of a letter from R. Palme Dutt to Sybille Bedford, 28 May 1968, Chatto & Windus Archive, University of Reading. For Dutt, see John Callaghan, *Rajani Palme Dutt: A Study in British Stalinism* (1993). For Wilde's idiosyncratic socialism, see his 'The Soul of Man under Socialism' (1891).

9 Bodleian Library, Oxford, MS. Top. Oxon. d.467, fol.14.

10 The Fabian Basis is reprinted as an Appendix to Margaret Cole's *The Story of Fabian Socialism*, London: Heinemann, 1961, 336–41.

11 W. B. Yeats, *Autobiographies*, London: Macmillan, 1977, 229.

12 W. B. Yeats, *A Vision*, London: Macmillan, 1938, 277.

13 D. H. Lawrence, 'Education of the People', in Michael Herbert, ed., *Reflections on the Death of a Porcupine and Other Essays*, Cambridge: Cambridge University Press, 1988, 87–166. Quote from p.107.

14 See, for example, Raymond Aron, 'Pareto's Politics', in James H. Meisel, ed., *Pareto and Mosca*, Englewood Cliffs, New Jersey: Prentice Hall, 1965, 115–20. See also Robert A. Nye, *The Anti-Democratic Sources of Elite Theory: Pareto, Mosca, Michels* (1977). More recently, however, Renato Cirillo has argued that Pareto's fascist leanings have been exaggerated and that he should more properly be regarded as a 'radical libertarian'. Renato Cirillo, 'Was Vilfredo Pareto Really a Precursor of Fascism?', in Mark Blaug, ed., *Vilfredo Pareto (1848–1923)*, Aldershot: Edward Elgar, 1992, 239–45. See also Alan Sica, *Weber, Irrationality and Social Order* (1988).

15 Franz Borkenau, *Pareto*, London: Chapman & Hall, 1936, 168.

16 *Proper Studies*, London: Chatto & Windus, 1927, xviii. It is likely that Huxley was introduced to Pareto's work by James Strachey Barnes, the brother of Mary Hutchinson, a close friend of the Huxleys. Barnes was Secretary-General of the International Centre for Fascist Studies in Lausanne from 1927 to 1929. He pays tribute to Pareto's 'masterly' *Trattato* in *The Universal Aspects of Fascism*, which he wrote in 1926 at the same time that Huxley was preparing *Proper Studies* (James Strachey Barnes, *The Universal Aspects of Fascism*, London: Williams & Norgate, 1928, 10). See also Richard Griffiths, *Fellow Travellers of the Right: British Enthusiasts for Nazi Germany 1933–9*, Oxford: Oxford University Press, 1983, 16.

17 S. E. Finer, Introduction to *Vilfredo Pareto: Sociological Writings*, trans. Derick Mirfin, London: Pall Mall Press, 1966, 14–15.

18 Vilfredo Pareto, *The Mind and Society*, trans. Andrew Bongiorno and Arthur Livingston, ed. Arthur Livingston, 4 vols., London: Jonathan Cape, 1935, vol. iii, 1430.

19 *Brave New World*, London: Chatto & Windus, 1932, 38.

20 'Aristocracy', *Proper Studies*, 157–64.

21 *Crome Yellow*, London: Chatto & Windus, 1921, 47.

22 Letter in the possession of Lady Huxley, 7 June 1922.

23 'The Future of the Past', *Vanity Fair* [New York], xxix, September 1927, 72, 102.

24 See, for example, 'Reform Eugenics, Population Research, and Family Planning, 1930–1939', in Richard A. Soloway, *Demography and Degeneration: Eugenics and the Declining Birthrate in Twentieth-Century Britain*, Chapel Hill and London: University of North Carolina Press, 1990, 193–225.

25 Quoted in Daniel Jo Kevles, *In the Name of Eugenics: Genetics and the Uses of Human Heredity*, Harmondsworth: Penguin, 1986, 90. See also Diane Paul, 'Eugenics and the Left', *Journal of the History of Ideas*, xlv, October 1984, 567–90.

26 Grover Smith, ed., *The Letters of Aldous Huxley*, London: Chatto & Windus, 1969, 345. Hereafter, *Letters*.

27 Anne Olivier Bell and Andrew McNeillie, eds., *The Diary of Virginia Woolf*, vol. iv: 1931–5, London: Hogarth Press, 1982, 11–12.

28 John Carey, *The Intellectuals and the Masses: Pride and Prejudice among the Literary Intelligentsia 1880–1939*, London: Faber and Faber, 1992, 86.

29 George Orwell, *The Road to Wigan Pier*, London: Victor Gollancz, 1937, 23.

30 Ibid., 188.

31 'Man Proposes', *Chicago Herald and Examiner*, 24 September 1932, 9.

32 Quoted in Robert Skidelsky, *Politicians and the Slump: The Labour Government of 1929–1931*, Harmondsworth: Penguin, 1970, 313.

33   Robert Skidelsky, *Oswald Mosley*, London: Macmillan, 1975, 227, 237.

34   T. S. Eliot, 'A Commentary', *The Criterion*, x, April 1931, 481–90.

35   'Forewarned is not Forearmed', *Chicago Herald and Examiner*, 18 November 1931, 9. Reprinted in *Nash's Pall Mall Magazine*, lxxxix, July 1932, 50.

36   Clarence Hatry (1888–1965) was the leading figure in a massive Stock Exchange scandal. For a fuller account of his misdeeds, see his obituary, *The Times*, 12 June 1965, 12. Huxley followed Hatry's trial in 1930: see *Letters*, 327. The eponymous speculator and 'large scale, Napoleonic crook' of 'Chawdron' is clearly based on Hatry. *Life and Letters*, iv, April 1930, 255–302. Reprinted in *Brief Candles* (1930).

37   By the time of his suicide in March 1932, the wealth and power of 'The Match King' – Kreuger's sobriquet derived from his monopoly of global production – were legendary. It was soon discovered, however, that Kreuger's assets were largely bogus. Kreuger was the original of Erik Krogh in Graham Greene's *England Made Me* (1935).

      Pareto wrote that a society in which speculators predominate 'lacks stability, lives in a state of shaky equilibrium that may be upset by a slight accident from within or without'. *The Mind and Society*, iv, 1555.

38   Harry Ransom Humanities Research Center, University of Texas at Austin, 24 July 1932.

39   The 92-page typescript of Huxley's play is owned by the Harry Ransom Humanities Research Center. It is being edited by David Bradshaw and James Sexton.

40   'Notes on the Way', *Time and Tide*, 7 May 1932, 516.

41   From a Huxley letter of 27 August 1932, quoted in Leon M. Lion, *The Surprise of My Life: The Lesser Half of an Autobiography*, London: Hutchinson, 1948, 115.

42   Letter to J. Glyn Roberts in the L. J. Roberts and J. Glyn Roberts Papers, Correspondence File, ff.55–6, National Library of Wales, 19 July 1933.

43   'L'Avenir de l'esprit européen', *Coopération intellectuelle*, no. 38, March 1934, 77–9.

44   'German Bonfires', *Chicago Herald and Examiner*, 29 September 1933, 9.

45   'Alypius in a Brown Shirt', *American Spectator*, ii, April 1934, 1.

46   'Vindicator' [i.e. Victor Gollancz], *Fascists at Olympia: A Record of Eyewitnesses and Victims*, London: Victor Gollancz, 1934, 21.

Chroniclers of Folly:
Huxley and H. L. Mencken 1920–26

In the spring of 1921, Huxley wrote to J. C. Squire, editor of the *London Mercury*, turning down Squire's suggestion that he write an article on the Tudor poet John Skelton for the magazine and enquiring about the possibility of contributing something else instead. 'Send along anything, whatever its kind,' Squire replied. *'The Political Creed of a Literary Man* does not sound so likely as the rest from our point of view, but we should like to see it.'[1] Huxley's article has not survived, but if it was, or was to be, a statement of his current ideological bearings, one thing is certain: 'The Political Creed of a Literary Man' would have savoured strongly of Henry Louis Mencken's corrosive rhetoric.

Mencken was the most famous critic of his day in the United States and a tireless foe of mass democracy. His pungent onslaughts on the American people (the most timorous, sniveling, poltroonish, ignominious mob of serfs and goose-steppers ever gathered under one flag in Christendom since the end of the Middle Ages')[2] had roused Huxley to such an extent over the previous fifteen months that he had even begun to imitate Mencken's majestic and billowy prose. In no time at all, Huxley was strafing Britain's masses (and its humdrum poets, painters and composers) with the same Olympian gusto with which Mencken targeted the *'Boobus americanus'*.[3]

In addition to being stimulated by Mencken's publications, which he puffed with rapt enthusiasm as an assistant editor of the *Athenaeum* magazine, Huxley also received at least eleven personal letters from Mencken, though ten of these perished in the fire which destroyed Huxley's Los Angeles home in 1961.[4] However, to the two letters from Huxley to Mencken which Grover Smith published in his edition of Huxley's *Letters* in 1969, we can add ten letters and two postcards which have hitherto lain neglected in American libraries.[5] Huxley's correspondence with Mencken and his reviews of Mencken's books chart the course of his political novitiate.

Mencken's denunciations of his native land quickened Huxley's fears of American cultural expansionism. In a letter to his brother Julian of August 1918, for instance, Huxley peered beyond the imminent armistice and predicted the cultural changes which would attend an Allied victory:

I dread the inevitable acceleration of American world domination which will be the ultimate result of it all. It was a thing that had got to come in time, but this will hasten its arrival by a century. We shall all be colonised; Europe will no longer be Europe. . . .[6]

His anxiety about the future of European civilization helps to account for the extravagant relish with which Huxley hailed Mencken's exposure of 'the extraordinary and fantastic spectacle which is contemporary American life' in his initialled review of Mencken's first volume of *Prejudices*:

It passes before him, a circus parade – vast ponderous elephants, lions, shy gazelles, apes, performing horses – and he comments upon it, laughingly, in that brilliant, masterfully vulgar style of which he knows the strange secret. All the animals interest him, graceful and ugly alike, noble and repulsive; but by preference he lingers, fascinated no doubt by the fabulous grotesqueness of their swollen shapes, among the solemn mammoths of stupidity, mountain-bodied and mouse-brained, slow-moving, prehistoric. They exist everywhere, these monsters; but it is surely in America that they reach their greatest growth. Puritanism there swells into Comstockism;[7] our harmless little European uplift becomes a sinister, rapacious, philanthropic beast; religions pullulate, strange and improbable as the saurians of the Mesozoic age. Mr. Mencken contemplates them with a civilized man's astonishment and horror, then sets his pen in rest and charges upon them. His pen is sharp, his aim unerring, and the punctured monsters collapse with a dolorous whistling of escaping gas. It is a wonderful display. Admiring his skill, one thinks of what Dryden said of himself in his Essay on Satire: 'There is still a vast difference between the slovenly butchering of a man and the finesse of a stroke that separates the head from the body and leaves it standing in its place. A man may be capable, as Jack Ketch's wife said of his servant, of a plain piece of work, a bare hanging; but to make a malefactor die sweetly was only belonging to her husband.'[8] Mr. Mencken is a worthy apprentice of this great Jack Ketch of literature … [and] we should welcome his appearance among us here; for we have sore need of critics who hate humbug, who are not afraid of putting out their tongues at pretentiousness however noble an aspect it may wear, who do not mind being vulgar at need, and who, finally, know not only how to make us think, but how to make us laugh as well.[9]

Mencken's inveterate *Prejudices* lent strident voice to Huxley's emergent convictions, and it is clear that in the early 1920s Huxley himself attempted to fill the critical role he identifies in his last sentence. For the remainder of the decade, the issue of how to protect Europe from the spectre of Americanization and the need to re-configure mass democracy as intellectual hierarchy remained the central concerns of Huxley's work.

In his courteous first letter to Mencken, Huxley amplifies his high-flown praise of *Prejudices*:

Dear Sir,
May I be allowed, as a humble fellow critic, to express my great admiration for 'Prejudices', which I had the pleasure of reviewing recently for 'The Athenaeum'.

I only wish we had a few more people in this country capable of producing anything as good and, at need, as destructive in the way of criticism.

Some day I hope I may have the opportunity of thanking you in person for the pleasure I have derived from your book.

Yours Truly,
Aldous L. Huxley[10]

It has been claimed that Huxley's grandfather, Thomas Henry Huxley, wielded the greatest single influence on Mencken's life and work.[11] This is more than likely since Mencken considered T. H. Huxley 'perhaps the greatest Englishman of all time. When one thinks of him, one thinks of him inevitably in terms of such men as Goethe and Aristotle . . . He was, in almost every way, the perfected flower of *Homo sapiens*, the superlatively admirable all-round man.'[12] Not surprisingly, Mencken was intrigued by Huxley's letter and determined to find out if his admirer was a scion of his hero. 'The other day I had a note from Aldous L. Huxley, full of lofty compliments,' he wrote to a colleague:

My *Prejudices* seems to bemuse [sic] him. He wrote the Athenaeum notice. Who is he? Somehow, I have a notion that he is a grandson of old T. H. Huxley. What has he done on his own account?[13]

His hunch confirmed, Mencken replied to Huxley straight away, dispatching a selection of his recent publications immediately afterwards. Huxley responded eagerly:

Dear Mr. Mencken,

I was very happy to get your letter and the books which followed it have just arrived. I look forward to some very pleasant hours in reading them. As a reprisal I venture to enclose a little volume of my own which has just come out, in the hope that it may amuse you. I believe there is to be an American edition with Doran; but my publishers are still in negotiation.

I have no control over the *Athenaeum*, but I am sure the editor, Middleton Murry, would be only too glad to give hospitality to any article of yours on the American literary situation. Things are pretty bad here, but I fancy they have not come to quite such a pass as with you.

I very much hope that when you come to England, whether in the spring or later on, you will let me know: I would arrange for the local menagerie to show its paces.

Thank you again for the books. I look forward to the autumn and your new *Prejudices*.

Yours sincerely,
Aldous Huxley[14]

The book which Huxley enclosed was *Limbo*, his first collection of short stories. It is inscribed: 'To H. L. Mencken. A token of sincere admiration from Aldous Huxley.'[15]

The three books which Mencken sent to Huxley were almost certainly *Heliogabalus* and *The American Credo*, Mencken's two collaborative efforts with George J. Nathan, and his translation of Nietzsche's *Der Antichrist*. Huxley devoted a brief *Athenaeum* notice to *Heliogabalus* on 12 March 1920,[16] and the following month he reviewed *The American Credo*. Under his *nom de plume* of 'Autolycus', Huxley wrote:

There are some people to whom the most difficult to obey of all the commandments is that which enjoins us to suffer fools gladly. The prevalence of folly, its invariable triumph over intelligence are phenomena which they cannot contemplate without experiencing a passion of righteous indignation or, at the least, of ill-temper. Sages like Anatole France, who can probe and anatomise human stupidity and still remain serenely detached are rare. These reflections were suggested by a book recently, published in New York and entitled 'The American Credo'. The authors of this work are those *enfants terribles* of American criticism, Messrs. H. L. Mencken and George Jean Nathan. They have compiled a list of four hundred and eighty-eight articles of faith which form the fundamental Credo of the American people, prefacing them with a very entertaining essay on the national mind:

Truth shifts and changes like a cataract of diamonds; its aspect is never precisely the same at two successive moments. But error flows down the channel of history like some great stream of lava or infinitely lethargic glacier. It is the one relatively fixed thing in a world of chaos.

To look through the articles of the Credo is to realise that there is a good deal of truth in this statement.[17]

Huxley's ecstatic reception of Mencken's work in England was more than matched by Mencken's wildly laudatory welcome of Huxley's books in the United States. Between 1914 and 1923 Mencken co-edited the *Smart Set* with Nathan, and he used the magazine to promote Huxley's work in America just as vigorously as Huxley exploited his position on the *Athenaeum* to draw the attention of British readers to Mencken's writings. Although *Limbo* was listed last when Mencken reviewed it in the *Smart Set* in August 1920 (along with Scott Fitzgerald's *This Side of Paradise*, A. P. Herbert's *The Secret Battle*, Conrad's *The Rescue* and other volumes), Mencken was quick to deny that there was any significance in this:

The order in which the titles are given is by no means an order of relative virtue. As a matter of fact, it seems to me that one story in the Huxley volume, by name 'Happily Ever After', is the best thing in fiction, barring the Conrad book, that I have read in six months. It is, indeed, an almost perfect piece of work – superbly designed and beautifully executed – really first-rate irony. The rest of Huxley I like less, but in the worst of him there is always the mark of a genuinely competent artist. He is one of the young Englishmen who will be heard of long after many of the present heroes of the blurb writers are forgotten. He writes sound and colorful English, he has unusual ideas, and his work is full of a charming personality.[18]

Mencken had previously written to Huxley about *Limbo*, and Huxley felt sufficiently encouraged by his comments to send him two further examples of his work, a play entitled 'Among the Nightingales', and eight short fictional pieces gathered under the title of 'From a Lyrical Notebook', in the hope that Mencken 'might find one or other suitable for the *Smart Set*', as he put it in the letter which accompanied them. 'I have some more stories simmering on the hob which I should like to send you when they are thoroughly cooked and finished.'[19] The play appeared in the *Smart Set* later that year,[20] but a reference to the pyjamas worn by the narrator's female companion in 'From a Lyrical Notebook' made Mencken chary of publishing Huxley's prose offering.[21] He wrote to London explaining his predicament and Huxley reacted promptly:

Dear Mr Mencken,

Many thanks for your letter. It certainly astonishes me that even [the] Purity League should take offence at my poor pink pyjamas.[22] But you know the mentality of the smuthounds – I bless you for the gift of that enchanting word – better than I. We are, at the moment, doing quite well here; for we have the Guitry company of French players in London doing Sacha Guitry's plays, so that it is actually possible to hear *cocuage* discussed upon the stage in a proper comic spirit.[23] And our audiences really enjoy it just because it's 'so French': though they wouldn't of course tolerate anything of the same character in English, nor would the Lord Chamberlain suffer it to see the footlights.

I think the best solution will be simply to omit the offending passage. It is simply a touch of romantic picturesqueness, the removal of which will make no material difference to the sense or spirit of the thing. If any other emasculations require to be made I rely on you to perform the operation.

I met recently one Mr. Smith of the Century Magazine who told me that he knew you; and, further, that Mr. Nathan proposes to come over here this summer. I should be very happy to meet him if he does.

Yours sincerely,
Aldous Huxley[24]

Huxley doubtless had this experience in mind when he inveighed against America towards the end of the year in a review of *The Melting Pot* by Israel Zangwill:

How inexpressibly unreal it all seems – this rhetoric about the Great Free Republic, the Land of Hope and the Future, Cradle of the Superman, crucible of the nations treated by the fires of love! Inexpressibly unreal when one thinks of the actual America of 1920 – a land where there is probably less personal freedom than in any other country in the world, with the possible exception of Bolshevik Russia: a country where the busy-bodies who love to exercise power by making other people uncomfortable flourish as they have never flourished anywhere or at any time; the home of Komstockery [sic] and the Purity Leaguers (or Smuthounds, as Mr. H. L. Mencken, that most brilliant of Transatlantic critics, has beautifully christened them); of Prohibition and inquisitorial philanthropy; the land where they propose to make the wearing of high heels illegal, where the system of postal censorship was carried during the late war to unparalleled lengths . . .[25]

In the same month Huxley paid this passing tribute to Mencken, Scott Fitzgerald described the American critic as his 'current idol'.[26] However, in another letter from the same period, Fitzgerald adverted to the concern with intellectual aristocracy which is conspicuous in all four of the books Mencken published in 1920: his second salvo of *Prejudices*, his translation of *Der Antichrist*, *Heliogabalus* and *The American Credo*:

Why has no one mentioned to him or of him that he is an intolerably muddled syllogism with several excluded middles on the question of aristocracy? What on earth does he mean by it? Every aristocrat of every race has come in for scathing comment yet he holds out the word as a universal panacea for art.[27]

As Mencken put it in his essay on Thorstein Veblen:[28]

There is, in America, no orderly and thorough working out of the fundamental problems of our society ... In all fields, from politics to pedagogics and from theology to public hygiene, there is a constant emotional obscuration of the true issues, a violent combat of credulities, an inane debasement of scientific curiosity to the level of mob gaping.

The thing to blame, of course, is our lack of an intellectual aristocracy – sound in its formation, skeptical in its habit of mind, and, above all, secure in its position and authority. Every other civilized country has such an aristocracy. It is the natural corrective of enthusiasms from below. It is hospitable to ideas, but as adamant against crazes ... But in America there is nothing of the sort. On the one hand there is the populace – perhaps more powerful here, more capable of putting its idiotic ideas into execution, than anywhere else – and surely more eager to follow platitudinous messiahs. On the other hand there is the ruling plutocracy – ignorant, hostile to inquiry, tyrannical in the exercise of its power, suspicious of ideas of whatever sort.[29]

Significantly, Huxley did not share Scott Fitzgerald's reservation about Mencken's hobby-horse. Indeed, when reviewing the volume, he even singled out Mencken's article on Veblen as 'the most brilliantly conducted' of all the essays in the first series of *Prejudices*. Moreover, 'Professor Veblen' was almost certainly the inspiration behind Huxley's own vindication of an aristocratic elite which becomes the dominant theme of his literary journalism during the latter half of 1920.

In August 1919 Huxley had signed a contract with Constable to write a study of Balzac and in connection with this project he had read *Les Paysans*, Balzac's tale of how General Montcornet is so systematically persecuted by his villeins that they succeed in driving him away from Les Aigues, his ancestral home. For Huxley, Balzac's novel was 'one of the most sombrely prophetic books of the nineteenth century', in that it foreshadowed the contemporary political and demographic forces which were threatening to destroy the vestigial enclaves of aristocratic privilege once and for all. In one of many recapitulations of his argument at this time, Mencken attributed America's cultural malaise to 'the lack of a civilized aristocracy' and Huxley alluded to this *Yale Review* article in the *Athenaeum* piece which he devoted to reflections on the contemporary relevance of *Les Paysans*. Mencken had claimed that: 'It is the instinct of a true aristocracy, not to punish eccentricity by expulsion, but to throw a mantle of protection about it – to safeguard it from the suspicions and resentments of the lower orders',[30] and, as the following quotation reveals, Huxley absorbed Mencken's opinions wholesale:

Balzac was not a democrat. His royalistic conservatism was due partly to his upbringing, partly to his native snobbishness. But chiefly he desired to preserve the old aristocratic order of things for the sake of what an aristocracy makes possible, namely culture, civilisation. When General Montcornet is forced to abandon Les Aigues the peasants fall upon the property and divide it up among themselves. The great old house is pulled down, and what were once the gardens and the noble park become a patchwork of small holdings. Something grand and splendid is destroyed, and something sordid and small takes its place. Balzac feared and hated democracy because he loved culture and art and grandeur and the other luxuries of the leisured rich. Culture and the beautiful amenities of civilisation have always been paid for by slavery in one form or another. Balzac, who heartily despised the philanthropists of his age, considered that the price was not excessive, and that it was right that a lower class should exist and work in order that culture might concomitantly exist in the higher class. The guerilla fighting of 1840 has become an open class war, and the many, as was inevitable, are steadily gaining ground against the few. Les Aigues and its inhabitants, with all their peculiar culture, are doomed, as Balzac foresaw. It remains to be seen what new form of culture, if any, will take its place.

The most important function of an aristocracy is to be so secure in its position that it is impervious to general public opinion, so secure that it can afford to tolerate eccentricity and be hospitable to new and unusual ideas. The American plutocracy is not an aristocracy because its position is precarious. It cannot afford to tolerate eccentricity; heresy means excommunication. But in Europe the tradition of eccentricity still survives, though with ever decreasing strength, in the leisured class. Its members do not risk serious persecution for nonconformity; their secure position protects them from ordinary public opinion, so that they can think, and to a great extent act, how they like with impunity. Not many of them do, of course; but that there should at least be an attitude of tolerance to heresy is of prime importance. Moreover, they actually extend their protection to eccentric and heretical members of other classes. The aristocracy is a sort of Red Indian Reservation, where the savages of the mind are permitted to live in their own way, untroubled and relatively free from persecution. In a little while the advancing armies of democracy will sweep across their borders and these happy sanctuaries will be no more. Les Aigues – the big house, the gardens, the park, the spacious and leisured life, the polite conversations and platonic passion between the literary man and the lady of the manor – will utterly disappear, and the small holder will inherit the land. And eccentricity, new ideas, culture – one doesn't see much room in the new world for these occupations of prigs and madmen. The prospect is melancholy, dims one's liberal ardours.[31]

Huxley goes on to discuss Mencken's *Yale Review* article, dwelling despondently on Mencken's account of the American intelligentsia: 'Hemmed in on one side by the plutocracy and on the other side by the mob'.

Later in the year Huxley again chose the demise of aristocratic privilege as his topic:

It is now two years since the world was made safe for democracy or whatever other name you choose to call that delicious blend of mob rule and irresponsible tyranny now universally current. Never has the old traditional ruling class been less powerful; it has no hand in the mob rule and very little in the tyranny. It subsists, this once all-powerful class, a phantom of its former self. It is still socially distinct from the rest of the population, it still preserves the traditional attitude towards life, evolved by long generations of serene and undisturbed supremacy. But now it has lost that supremacy we shall soon see the disappearance of the characteristically aristocratic gesture and attitude and the extinction of the class. The aristocrat lives on in our world made safe for democracy like the Red Indian in his reservation. His tenure is hideously insecure. At any moment the surrounding hordes of white colonists – so infinitely colonial! – may tear down the barriers of his little park, sweep in and utterly submerge him. At any moment. He is helpless.[32]

It seems certain that these anxieties were to have shaped 'The Political Creed of a Literary Man'. However, after receiving Squire's discouraging letter, Huxley channelled his fears into the Peacockian milieu of *Crome Yellow*, which he wrote during the seven months he spent in Italy from March to September 1921. In view of the novel's Menckenian matrix, the burgeoning size of Crome's annual Charity Fair, for example, may be seen to figure the gradual encroachment of the 'white colonists' of mass democracy on to the aristocratic demesne:

Beginning as a sort of glorified church bazaar, Crome's yearly Charity Fair had grown into a noisy thing of merry-go-rounds, cocoanut shies, and miscellaneous side shows – a real genuine fair on the grand scale. It was the local St. Bartholomew, and the people of all the neighbouring villages, with even a contingent from the county town, flocked into the park for their Bank Holiday amusement.[33]

Although in appearance Scogan in *Crome Yellow* is modelled on the saurian Bertrand Russell, in some of his opinions he is clearly Mencken's surrogate. This is most evident in Scogan's defence of eccentricity in Chapter II:

It's the justification of all aristocracies. It justifies leisured classes and inherited wealth and privilege and endowments and all the other injustices of that sort. If you're to do anything reasonable in this world, you must have a class of people who are secure, safe from public opinion, safe from poverty, leisured, not compelled to waste their time in the imbecile routines that go by the name of Honest Work. You must have a class of which the members can think and, within the obvious limits, do what they please. You must have a class in which eccentricity in general will be tolerated and understood. That's the most important thing about an aristocracy. Not only is it eccentric itself – often grandiosely so; it also tolerates and even encourages eccentricity in others . . . It is a sort of Red Indian Reservation planted in the midst of a vast horde of poor Whites – colonials at that . . . After the social revolution there will be no Reservations; the Redskins will be drowned in the great sea of Poor Whites. (pp.106–7)

At first glance *Crome Yellow* may appear to be Huxley's celebration of this doomed way of life. But, if civilization is threatened from without by social and political forces beyond its control, the antics of those within Crome's 'Redskin' sanctuary suggest that Huxley's complaint in the *Athenaeum* that the 'old traditional ruling class [is] a phantom of its former self' is not without foundation. The 'polite conversations and platonic passion between the literary man and the lady of the manor', for instance (which Huxley had idealized as the perfect creative arrangement in the *Athenaeum*), have bottomed out in Priscilla Wimbush's hankering for Barbecue-Smith's frothy humbug. His 'automatic writing' is a shameless parody of the literary imagination.[34] Henry Wimbush, if anything, is even more empty-headed. After nearly thirty years' work on his *History of Crome*, Wimbush's sense of achievement on completing it is ludicrously misplaced: '. . . I have some genuinely new light to throw on the introduction of the three-pronged fork,' he announces to the assembled nonentities with whom he is to share his table in Chapter 13. His guests include an untalented novelist *manqué*, a blatantly copy-cat painter and Ivor Lombard, who:

had a beautiful untrained tenor voice; he could improvise with a starting brilliance, rapidly and loudly on the piano. He was a good amateur medium and telepathist, and had a considerable first-hand knowledge of the next world. He could write rhymed verses with an extraordinary rapidity. For painting symbolical pictures he had a dashing style, and if the drawing was sometimes a little weak, the colour was always pyrotechnical. He excelled in amateur theatricals and, when occasion offered, he could cook with genius. He resembled Shakespeare in knowing little Latin and less Greek. For a mind like his, education seemed supererogatory. Training would only have destroyed his natural aptitudes. (p.167)

At Crome, civilized eccentricity has degenerated into the egocentric crotcheteering of the Wimbushes and their house party of fatuous ciphers. Their eagerness to jig along to the American jazz-tunes which the vacant Henry Wimbush treads out on his pianola high-lights the moribundity of the aristocratic tradition.

With the hereditary aristocracy in such bizarre disarray, the need for intellectual aristocracy becomes all the more urgent if civilization is to be saved. That Mencken was in part the original of Scogan is even more obvious in Scogan's advocacy of cultural hierarchy; Scogan's ideas are derived directly from the figure whose influence is felt on every page of Mencken's work: Friedrich Nietzsche.

From his earliest writings to his last, Nietzsche was adamant that culture could flourish only where the many have been subjugated to the few. In 'The Greek State' (1871), Nietzsche wrote:

In order that there may be a broad, deep and fruitful soil for the development of art, the enormous majority must, in the service of a minority, be slavishly subjected to life's struggle, to a *greater* degree than their own wants necessitate . . . Accordingly we must accept this cruel sounding truth, that *slavery is of the essence of Culture* . . . The misery of toiling men must still increase in order to make the production of the world of art possible to a small number of Olympian men.[35]

In *Human, All-Too-Human* (1878), Nietzsche insists again on the strict segregation of 'the caste of compulsory labour and the caste of free labour' in any society where a 'higher culture' is to be preserved or attained.[36] Nietzsche's emphasis on caste is stressed by Mencken in his *The Philosophy of Friedrich Nietzsche* (1908) and in his compilation of *The Gist of Nietzsche* (1910), and it is significant that in both books Mencken identifies a passage from *The Antichrist* (1895) as the kernel of Nietzsche's philosophy. Indeed, Mencken considered *The Antichrist* to be so important that he made his own translation of it. Huxley's review of Mencken's 'lively and energetic' version of *The Antichrist* drew attention to Mencken's Introduction, in particular, as a 'happy example of his critical writing'.[37] In it, Mencken pinpoints *The Antichrist* as 'a statement of some of [Nietzsche's] most salient ideas in their final form'. What Nietzsche 'feared most', according to Mencken, 'was the pollution and crippling of the superior minority by intellectual disease from below'. Christian dogma and humanitarian ethics were anathema to Nietzsche because they represented 'a democratic effort to curb the egoism of the strong – a conspiracy of the *chandala* against the free functioning of their superiors, nay, against the free progress of mankind'.[38]

It seems certain that the 'Rational State' Scogan outlines in Chapter 22 of *Crome Yellow* has its most immediate source in this same section of *The Antichrist* which Mencken identified as the crux of Nietzsche's philosophy. 'The *order of castes*,' Nietzsche declared,

the highest, the dominating law, is merely the ratification of an *order of nature*, of a natural law of the first rank, over which no arbitrary fiat, no 'modern idea', can exert any influence. In every healthy society there are three physiological types, gravitating toward differentiation but mutually conditioning one another, and each of these has its own hygiene, its own sphere of work, its own special mastery and feeling of perfection. It is *not* Manu but nature that sets off in one class those who are chiefly intellectual, in another those who are marked by muscular strength and temperament, and in a third those who are distinguished in neither one way or the other, but show only mediocrity – the last named represents the great majority, and the first two the select.[39]

Scogan's 'Rational State', like Nietzsche's 'order of castes', would be governed by an elite corps of 'Directing Intelligences' (p.243) who would in turn control an executive consisting of 'Men of Faith' (p.243), groomed through 'a long process of suggestion' (p.244) to implement their policies. These, in their turn, would govern a vast subservient 'Herd' reared in the belief that 'there is no happiness to be found except in work and obedience' (p.246). Beneath its patina of whimsy and its deft social comedy, the central, sombre theme of Huxley's sardonic first novel is that only an 'order of castes', or an 'intellectual aristocracy', or a 'Rational State' of the kind outlined by Nietzsche, invoked by Mencken and propounded by Scogan, can preserve civilization from transatlantic adulteration and the advancing hordes of democracy.

Mencken re-fashioned his *Yale Review* article into 'The National Letters', a more lengthy excoriation of the banality of American literature, which was subsequently incorporated into his second series of *Prejudices*. This, like its predecessor, Mencken sent to Huxley when it was published in October 1920. On 16 March 1921 Huxley wrote:

Dear Mencken,

The arrival of your letter to-day brought violently to the surface a remorse that has been festering in my mind for months past. For I have owed you a letter for I hardly know how long, and what is more, a letter of thanks for the second series of Prejudices, which were a real pleasure to me. The first essay, on Contemporary Letters in America, was really admirable – and I have been meaning ever since before Christmas to write and tell you so, but have not succeeded; partly because I have been horribly busy earning my livelihood, which is no excuse at all, partly because I have been lazy, which is more adequate as a justification.

I wish I had a new book to send you in revenge; but I have had neither the time nor the energy to do anything but the quotidian journalism – reviews, literary articles, dramatic criticism and the most fantastic hack-work (happily well paid) for an American fungoid growth which has established itself over here recently, called 'House and Garden'. How-ever, I am not sorry that these last months have been so intolerable, for they have brought the whole thing to a head, reduced the journalism business to the absurd. And I am now engaged in burning my boats preparatory to starting in a week's time for Italy, where money looks four times as plentiful as it does here and where, even though the principal industry of the country is the manufacture of paper money, it is still possible to live fairly cheaply. There I shall spend the next few months writing to amuse myself and seeing if I can make the process pay. If so, good; if not, then back here to journalism. My wife has gone before me to prepare my way and on Easter morning I shall enter the City of Florence in triumph, resurrected from this tomb of darkness . . . .

You speak of Lawrence. Rumour assigns a pleasing reason for his writing so badly now. It is said that he was psycho-analysed last year and that with the scotching of his numerous complexes and resultant sanity – for he used to be a bit of a sexual maniac – he has entirely lost the power of writing novels and is only at home when he is pouring forth little lucubrations about baa lambs and daffodils. He is living in Sicily at present, where I shall not go and visit him; for he and his Prussian wife, *geboren* Von Richthoven [sic], are the most formidable couple I have ever known – or were, at any rate, before the psycho-analysis, since when, of course, it is possible they have become as tame as Anglicans. Am I right in supposing that his book, 'Women in Love,' written about four years ago, has been published by subscription or privately or something of the sort in America? If so you should read it. It contains some quite incredibly grotesque things, including some stupendous chapters about an old friend of mine, Lady Ottoline Morrell, who is represented as attempting to murder Lawrence with a lapis lazuli paper weight and only failing to do so because the nimble L. takes cover under a volume of Thucydides which he happens at the moment to be reading. It's all just like Ouida. What an odd thing it is in a man who has done such exceedingly good things!

There is not much history here. The perishing of the Athenaeum as an independent paper and its incorporation with the Nation is the most significant and most melancholy literary event.

What other news? Mr. Clutton-Brock is now known to write his sermon-leaders in the Times Literary Supplement by means of automatic writing; he sits still and his pen disgorges the excrements of his brain at the rate of eighteen hundred words an hour. Result: vast salary for Brock and ever increasing popularity and esteem. I can think of nothing else very epoch making.

I will write again from Italy and possibly send something which you might like to print in the Smart Set. Meanwhile, farewell. I suppose there is no prospect of your visiting These Shores during the course of the summer?

Yours sincerely,
Aldous Huxley[40]

Six months later, with his return to London imminent, Huxley told Mencken:

I have been industrious here, completing a comic novel in the manner, vaguely, of Peacock. It is an agreeable form; and besides, at the moment, I lack the courage and the patience to sit down and turn out eighty thousand words of realismus.[41]

Huxley had instructed his publishers to send Mencken a copy of *Crome Yellow* on its publication in November 1921, but he discovered three months later that this had not been done. Huxley hastened to rectify 'this defect of courtesy, with the hope that the thing may amuse you a little', inscribing the copy of *Crome Yellow* he sent from London 'with homages'. Huxley continued his accompanying letter:

I am back in this decaying Metropolis, functioning chiefly on the great Mr. Condé Nast's publications which, tho' not inordinately high i' the brow, pay adequately – which no literary journal does.[42]

When I have hoarded a few pence I shall flit off once more to some cheap Dago state for rest and refreshment. But meanwhile I am pretty well fixed here.

And you – is there any prospect of your early arrival? I have been seeing an acquaintance of yours in H. B. Liveright who has been here astonishing the natives and whom I liked very much.[43]

Reviewing *Crome Yellow* in the *St Paul Daily News*, Scott Fitzgerald lauded Huxley's novel as 'the highest point so far attained by Anglo-Saxon sophistication',[44] and Mencken himself soon acclaimed it even more rapturously in the *Smart Set*. Since Scogan's views on the role of the aristocracy are identical to Mencken's, it is surprising that Fitzgerald reviewed *Crome Yellow* so radiantly. For the same reason it is not difficult to understand why Mencken's reception of the novel was so unashamedly eulogistic. Mencken even went so far as to claim that Huxley surpassed his grandfather in worldly wisdom:

If it does not make you yell with joy, then I throw off the prophetical robes for ever. It is a piece of buffoonery that sweeps the whole range from the most delicate and suggestive tickling to the most violent thumping of the ribs. It has made me laugh as I have not laughed since I read the Inaugural Harangue of Dr. Harding.[45]

This Huxley, in truth, is a fellow of the utmost shrewdness, ingenuity, sophistication, impudence, waggishness, and contumacy – a literary atheist who is forever driving herds of sheep, hogs, camels, calves and jackasses into the most sacred temples of his people. He represents the extreme swing of the reaction against everything that a respectable Englishman holds to be true and holy … Here, in brief, is a civilized man's *reductio ad absurdum* of his age – his contemptuous kicking of its pantaloons. Here, in a short space, delicately, ingratiatingly and irresistibly, whole categories and archipelagoes of contemporary imbecility are brought to the trial by wit. In some dull review or other I have encountered the news that all the characters of the fable are real people and that the author himself is Denis … Nonsense! Huxley, if he is there at all, is Scogan, the chorus to the whole drama, with his astounding common sense, his acidulous humor, and his incomparable heresies.[46]

'I doubt that I'll see any literati in London, save perhaps [Hugh] Walpole and Huxley,' Mencken wrote to Sinclair Lewis in August 1922 while *en route* from New York to Plymouth.[47] Mencken, who must have written to Huxley with a view to arranging a meeting, was unaware that his disciple would be abroad during his stay in London, covering the Salzburg music festival for the *Weekly West-minster Gazette*. From Salzburg, Mencken received this reply to his forwarded letter:

I hear from various sources that you are now or will shortly be in England … I wish I were there to see you: but I am taking a beer cure in Salzburg and listening to Mozart, going on to Italy for a few weeks tomorrow. Do let me know … how long you will be in Europe and if there will be a hope of seeing you.[48]

Mencken described Huxley's next book, *Mortal Coils*, as 'entertainment of the first order'. Stating that one of the five pieces in the volume, 'Permutations Among the Nightingales', had already been published in the *Smart Set*, Mencken continued:

Another, a superb short story called 'Nuns at Luncheon', would have got into these pages also if it had not been for the Comstocks. Since the manuscript paid its visit to this office Huxley has denatureized it a bit, and, rather strangely, greatly improved it. It is, as it stands, a truly excellent short story – sparing in words, but extremely vivid and ingenious. Two others in the quintet are quite as good: 'The Gioconda Smile' and 'The Tillotson Banquet'. The fifth, 'Green Tunnels', I like a great deal less. But what would you? Here is a man who prints a book of which four-fifths is capital stuff – novel in content, bold in handling, and superbly written. This Huxley I have much confidence in. He keeps himself clear of the bow-wow manner. He has fine humor and a crackling wit. He writes a pellucid and colorful English. He has novel and amusing ideas. No more genuine original has emerged from the fogs of London for years. Go get all of his books and enjoy yourself in a civilized manner: 'Limbo', 'Chrome Yellow' [sic], 'Leda' and 'Mortal Coils'.[49]

Huxley's next letter to Mencken, written from London in December 1922, is particularly interesting in that it records not only his sense of a widening chasm between the cultured elite and mass society, but also the degree to which Huxley had absorbed his mentor's idiolect:

Dear Mencken,

... How goes life in the Great West? Here we are made daily conscious of a steady increase in imbecility. The Press and now the Wireless Telephone are doing wonders in the way of spreading darkness, vulgarity, fifteenth-rateness, folly, mental idleness, cant, confusion, waste of energy: one can see the results at once. The gulf between the populace and those engaged in any intelligent occupation of whatever kind steadily widens. In twenty years time a man of science or a serious artist will need an interpreter in order to talk to a cinema proprietor or a member of his audience. However, perhaps it's all for the best: who knows. In any case the Consolations of Philosophy will never fail us here

in England so long as the Upper House retains its present 2/3 majority
of titled brewers and distillers.

The seasonal benedictions.

Yours,
Aldous Huxley[50]

In the early months of 1923 Huxley sent Mencken a postcard
depicting a statue of Neptune inscribed: 'You somewhere, some
time'.[51] In April of that year 'Over the Telephone', a short story by
Huxley, appeared in the *Smart Set*.[52] But by the time Mencken
reviewed *Antic Hay* in March 1924, his estimation of Huxley's talent
seems to have cooled a little. Mencken considered Huxley's second
novel alongside James Branch Cabell's *The High Place* and *The Blind
Bow-Boy* by Carl Van Vechten. In his opinion, Cabell's book showed
'the most adept workmanship', and Van Vechten's was 'the most
novel in plan', while Van Vechten's and Huxley's novels demon-
strated 'the fact that the burlesque modern novel is very hard to
write – that the slightest letting down reduces it to mere whimsi-
cality and tediousness'. Even so, wrote Mencken:

Both tales are full of fine gusto and neither ever grows dull, even when it
grows thin. Human life is here depicted as ... gay, senseless and
orgiastic. Is this realism, too? Is it, in fact, a more penetrating and
accurate realism than that of the orthodox realists? There are days when
I so suspect.[53]

Although at one point in *Those Barren Leaves* (1925) Francis
Chelifer muses that in 'a few generations it may well be that the
whole planet will be covered by one vast American-speaking tribe,
composed of innumerable individuals, all thinking and acting in the
same way', like the characters in a novel by Sinclair Lewis',[54] Huxley
claimed that the main theme of his third novel was 'the undercutting of everything by a sort of despairing scepticism and then the
undercutting of that by mysticism'.[55] However, Huxley's disen-
chantment with *Those Barren Leaves* was almost immediate; he
condemned it as 'jejune and shallow and off the point. All I've

written so far has been off the point. And I've taken such enormous pains to get off it; that's the stupidity.'[56] In the light of this confession, it seems probable that Huxley's decision to journey to India later in 1925 was motivated in part by his desire to achieve a more profound insight into the mystical life. That he was no less disillusioned by his travels in the Far East is evident in the letter he wrote to Mencken on his subsequent arrival in San Francisco in May 1926:

Dear H.L. Mencken,

I am entering the U.S.A. by the back door – tho' I suppose they call it the front in California – from the Orient, where I have been spending some months to satisfy myself empirically that all this rigmarole of Light from the East, etc, is genuinely nonsense. Having done so, I am now on my way home – *orientis partibus adventavit Asinus*, as they used to sing in the blasphemous *Messe de l'Ane* – and passing through your continent.[57] Will there be a hope of seeing you? My wife and I will be spending some three weeks or so in New York from about mid-May onwards . . . It will be a great delight if you're visible.

I regaled myself during two or three days of this voyage with your fourth Prejudices. Very magnificent. You ought to have some of your best passages recorded for the gramophone – you read so well aloud; there are really Ciceronian thunders. Have it bawled by some sonorous comedian like Hackett or Forbes Robertson into the phonograph and then circulate it to do its missionary work among phonograph owners.[58] The majority of people in our modern world are not educated up to the point of understanding what they read in books. But they can understand a thing when it is spoken *viva voce*. E.g. the soldiers in The War, who had to have the Army textbooks read out to them, lectured into their brains, instead of reading for themselves. A 12-inch disk of Prejudice would penetrate further than a book.[59]

Huxley and Mencken met for the first time soon afterwards at Moneta's restaurant in New York, where Mencken had invited the Huxleys to dine with him. 'Mencken gave us so much to drink,' wrote Maria Huxley, 'and I felt so sick I enjoyed it less than I might have':

He was very amusing and looks like Belloc or like a travelling salesman or a farmer who now lives in the town. Also present his lady friend, a vulgar and hideous blonde who made worshipping and hideous eyes at A. I could see no excuse for her but A. suggested that she is probably allright in bed. I suppose that can be enough for some people. A dreary reason for one's life though. Drinks are always very sickening but of course it would be offensive not to accept them as they have to be purchased with much money and trouble.[60]

While he was in New York, Huxley was asked by a journalist for his impressions of America. Huxley's comments were reported under the caption: 'We're "Immense" to Aldous Huxley'. Alongside the vast scale of the Grand Canyon and the huge emptiness of the Midwest, Huxley stationed his first guru:

Mr. Huxley is a great admirer of Henry L. Mencken, who he thinks is 'immense' too. He said there was no writer in England who compared even remotely with Mr. Mencken adding that if Mencken were English and wrote about England as he did about America he would be 'doused cold' by the English critics, 'who would not appreciate him'. He said Mencken would have no trouble finding buncombe and fallacy in England as he had in America.[61]

Ironically, this first meeting between Huxley and Mencken in May 1926 was their only encounter and the high point of their relationship. When Mencken reviewed Huxley's *Two or Three Graces* in September 1926 (along with *Nigger Heaven* by Van Vechten and *Show Boat* by Edna Ferber) his last review of a book by Huxley was still warm but plainly circumscribed:

All these stories, it seems to me, fail below the high marks of their authors; nevertheless, every one of them shows sound work and every-one is interesting … Mr. Huxley's story is extremely slight: a rococo anecdote of a man who is always losing his best girl to other men — nay, acting as procurer for them. But all his sure and delicate skill gets into the telling of it. It is rich with searching and frolicsome humors. It is a capital piece of writing.[62]

The following month Huxley published his mordant impressions of the United States in *Jesting Pilate*. Soon afterwards he was sent a copy of *American Soundings* (1926) by John St Loe Strachey. In that the seeds of *Brave New World* were sown during Huxley's first visit to America, his response to Strachey is worth quoting in full:

Dear Mr. Strachey,

I have been reading the book you were so very kind as to send me with great enjoyment. What a country it is! You approach it, it seems to me, in the right spirit – with gusto; as Dryden approached Chaucer: 'Here is God's plenty.' Or the devil's plenty. It is a matter of taste. Perhaps I should have put in a little more of the devil than you do. But the real point, in any case, is the plenty, and the fabulous, the supernatural quality of it.

I wish you had seen California. It is pure Rabelais, a chronic kermesse. Materially, the nearest approach to Utopia yet seen on our planet. After twenty-four hours of it, you begin to pine for the slums of Dostoievsky's St Petersburg!

And then the great Middle Western plains! Endless, and the sparse towns and villages uglier than anything you have ever seen. No wonder they take to curious religions in those regions. It is the only thing, now that drink has been abolished, that is left to them. Talking about curious religions – I notice that you attribute no importance to the Tennessee anti-evolution business. So did I, until recently, when I received a pamphlet from an organisation called the Science League of America. One state and quite a number of education boards in individual cities, from Georgia to California, have followed the example of Tennessee. All states are being organised by the Fundamentalists for Federal and State anti-evolution laws. Funds for this purpose are freely forthcoming. Anti-evolution bills are promised in numerous state legislatures during 1927. California and Texas have ordered the elimination of evolutionary doctrines from the text books of tax supported schools and colleges. And so on and so forth. Altogether, it looks as though the movement were no joke. In any case, the Science League of America, which has a most eminent and respectable committee of scientific men, seems to take it very seriously. Their pamphlet is quite blood-curdling.

I wonder if you are not a little too generous to the American universities. They are fine, certainly; and it is an excellent thing that the contemporary rich should salve their guilty consciences by founding colleges as their ancestors did by endowing monasteries. But there is a reverse to the medal. To begin with, the standard of scholastic attainment in a great many of these universities is incredibly low. (If you remember, Mr. Babbitt was a university graduate.[63] And I have met plenty of Americans with resounding degrees, who were fabulously ignorant of the subjects in which they had graduated.) In the second place, one must remember the rather sinister influence exercised on universities by the rich business men who endow them and who, in practically all cases, are the trustees and governors of American seats of learning. The persecution of unpopular political opinions is almost universal. Veblen's book on the Higher Learning in America and Upton Sinclair's rather lurid, but (according to so knowledgeable an authority as Dr. Harvey Robinson) very well documented book, 'The Goose Step' make rather disagreeable reading for anyone who has been brought up in the English love of free speech and fair play.

Thank you once more for your 'Soundings'. I hope to have the pleasure of discussing the inexhaustible and extraordinary subject of the book personally when I am in London next.[64]

Huxley and Mencken appear to have stopped corresponding after 1926. They may have met once more, when Huxley returned to New York in 1933, but, according to Mencken, a meeting which Huxley tried to set up did not come off.[65] The following year Huxley wrote to Mencken to say that he had given his cousin Gervas a letter of introduction to him:

Is there any chance of seeing you on this side of the Atlantic? . . . I wish I could make out what was happening in those United States – and doubtless many of its inhabitants wish the same. Here the English are engaged in telling themselves that they are well off – which appears to be the same thing as being well off.

I'm glad to see that Pareto's *Sociology* has been translated and is coming out in New York. Such a monument of common sense.[66]

When Scott Fitzgerald sent Mencken a copy of *This Side of Paradise* in March 1920 he confessed in his inscription: 'As a matter of fact Mr. Mencken, I stuck your name in on page 224 in the last proof – partly I suppose as a vague bootlick and partly because I have *adopted* a great many of your views.'[67] Fitzgerald's next two novels, *The Beautiful and the Damned* (1922) and *The Great Gatsby* (1925), reveal the truth of this admission, and Mencken had an equally tell-tale influence on the work of other American novelists such as Sinclair Lewis and Theodore Dreiser. Yet his imprint on *Crome Yellow*, and his formative influence on the early Huxley in general, were no less bold. Mencken's full-blooded goading of the American public, and his Nietzsche-inspired exaltation of the few, provided Huxley with a rumbustious model of cultural criticism which he assimilated both through an avid reading of Mencken's publications and what must have been a kind of correspondence course in the art of scorn.

NOTES

1 Squire to Huxley, 2 March 1921. J. C. Squire Papers, Department of Special Collections, University Research Library, UCLA.

2 H. L. Mencken, 'On Being an American', *Prejudices: Third Series*, New York: Knopf, 1922; London: Jonathan Cape, 1923, 9–64. Quote from p.10.

3 George Jean Nathan and H. L. Mencken, *The American Credo: A Contribution Toward the Interpretation of the National Mind*, New York: Knopf, 1920, 100. A good example of the Menckenian tenor of Huxley's work at this time is 'The Cry for a Messiah in the Arts', *The Patrician*, iii, January 1922, 57, and *Vanity Fair* [New York], xvii, January 1922, 57.

4 According to the inventory prepared by Jacob Zeitlin in collaboration with Huxley after the fire, and enclosed in a letter from Zeitlin to Huxley, Department of Special Collections, University Research Library, UCLA, 6 June 1961.

5 Eight letters and two postcards are deposited in the Rare Books and Manuscripts Division of The New York Public Library, and the remaining four letters, including the two published ones, are held by the Enoch Pratt Free Library in Baltimore. There is one letter from Mencken to Huxley in The New York Public Library.

6 *Letters*, 160.

7 That is, moralistic censorship. The term derives from Anthony Comstock (1844–1915), an indefatigable crusader against obscenity in literature and,

in 1873, founder of the New York Society for the Suppression of Vice.

8   'Jack Ketch' was the byname of John Ketch (died November 1686), an English
    executioner notorious for his bungling ineptitude. In 1685, for instance, he took
    at least eight strokes of the axe to behead the Duke of Monmouth. His name
    became a generic term for all executioners.

9   Review of *Prejudices: First Series* by H. L. Mencken, *Athenaeum*, 2 January 1920,
    10. Huxley's anonymous contributions to the *Athenaeum* have been identified
    through reference to the marked copies of the magazine now housed in the
    Centre for Interactive Systems Research, Department of Information Science,
    City University, London. Huxley's earlier brief notice of this book (*Athenaeum*,
    28 November 1919, 1273) is included in the standard bibliography. Huxley's
    other reviews of Mencken's books are undocumented.

10 H. L. Mencken Papers, Rare Books and Manuscripts Division, New York
    Public Library, 10 January 1919 [i.e. 10 January 1920].

11 Charles A. Fecher, *Mencken: A Study of his Thought*, New York: Knopf, 1978,
    64.

12 Quoted in Isaac Goldberg, *The Man Mencken: A Biographical and Critical Survey*,
    New York: Simon & Schuster, 1925, 91–2.

13 Guy J. Forgué, *Letters of H. L. Mencken*, New York: Knopf, 1961, 175, 4 Feb-
    ruary 1920. Mencken recalls his delight on discovering that the appreciative
    Aldous was indeed the grandson of T. H. Huxley, and provides a cameo of their
    relationship in the early 1920s in his posthumous *My Life as Author and Editor*,
    ed. Jonathan Yardley, New York: Knopf, 1993, [308]–11.

14 Rare Books and Manuscripts Division, New York Public Library, 13 February
    1920.

15 It is deposited in the Enoch Pratt Free Library in Baltimore.

16 *Athenaeum*, 12 March 1920, 354.

17 'Marginalia', *Athenaeum*, 30 April 1920, 574–5.

18 'Books More or Less Amusing II', *Smart Set*, lxii, August 1920, 140.

19 Rare Books and Manuscripts Division, New York Public Library, 12 April
    1920. In *My Life as Author and Editor* Mencken misdates this letter 12 *March*
    [1920].

20 *Smart Set*, lxiii, November 1920, 71–88.

21 Eventually, only the second part, 'In the Teashop', was published in the *Smart
    Set*, lxvii, January 1920, 3.

22 The pyjamas were originally purple. See 'From a Lyrical Note-Book', *Palatine
    Review* [Oxford], no. 5, 1917, 11–16.

23   Sacha Guitry (1885–1957) was a French playwright, actor and film director. He
     wrote over 100 pieces, mostly witty comedies – including *Nono* (1905), *Un Beau
     Mariage* (1911) and *L'Amour masqué* (1923) – and acted in the majority of them.
     Cocuage: cuckoldry.

24   Rare Books and Manuscripts Division, New York Public Library, 26 May 1920.
     It is not known if Huxley met Nathan.

25   *The Westminster Gazette*, 9 December 1920, 6.

26   Andrew Turnbull, ed., *The Letters of F. Scott Fitzgerald*, London: John Lane/
     The Bodley Head, 1964, 466.

27   Ibid, 463.

28   Thorstein Veblen (1857–1929), American economist and social scientist. In his
     Theory of the Leisure Class (1899) he coined the phrases 'conspicuous consump-
     tion' and 'pecuniary emulation'.

29   H. L. Mencken, 'Professor Veblen', *Prejudices: First Series*, New York: Knopf,
     1919; London: Jonathan Cape, 1921, 59–82. Quote from pp. 80–81.

30   'The National Literature', *Yale Review*, NS ix, July 1920, 804–17.

31   'Marginalia', *Athenaeum*, 27 August 1920, 274.

32   *Athenaeum*, 10 December 1920, 812. At the end of the month yet another
     'Marginalia' article was entirely devoted to the aristocracy's tolerance of eccent-
     ricity:. *Athenaeum*, 31 December 1920, 893.

33   *Crome Yellow*, London: Chatto & Windus, 1921, 267. Subsequent page refer-
     ences are embodied in the text.

34   Huxley's letter to Mencken of 16 March 1921, quoted below, reveals that
     Barbecue-Smith was based on Arthur Clutton-Brock (1868–1924), author of,
     among other volumes, *Thoughts on the War* (1914), *More Thoughts on the War*
     (1915) and *What is the Kingdom of Heaven?* (1919). Clutton-Brock was a regular
     contributor to the *Times Literary Supplement* between 1908 and his death.

35   Reprinted in *Early Greek Philosophy and Other Essays*, vol. ii of Oscar Levy, ed.,
     The Complete Works of Friedrich Nietzsche, trans. Maximilian A. Mügge, London
     and Edinburgh: T. N. Foulis, 1911, 1–18.

36   Reprinted in *Human, All-Too-Human: A Book for Free Spirits (Part 1)*, vol. iii of
     Oscar Levy, ed., *Complete Works*, trans. Helen Zimmern, London and Edin-
     burgh: T. N. Foulis, 1909, 319.

37   *Athenaeum*, 23 April 1920, 557.

38   H. L. Mencken, Introduction to F. W. Nietzsche, *The Antichrist*, trans. H. L.
     Mencken, New York: Knopf, 1920. Quotes from pp. 18, 210.

39   *The Antichrist*, 163–4. See also Bruce Detwiler, *Nietzsche and the Politics of
     Aristocratic Radicalism* (1990).

40 Rare Book and Manuscripts Division, New York Public Library; Huxley was soon to be no less 'stupendously' hurtful to Lady Ottoline Morrell by incorporating her into *Crome Yellow* as the ridiculous Priscilla Wimbush. During the war both Lawrence and Huxley had been given sanctuary at Lady Ottoline's Garsington Manor in Oxfordshire.

41 *Letters*, 203.

42 Huxley was writing for *Vogue*, *House and Garden* and *The Patrician* at this time, and contributing to *Vanity Fair*, the New York equivalent of *The Patrician*.

43 This letter of 5 February 1922 and the inscribed copy of *Crome Yellow* are both in the Enoch Pratt Free Library, Baltimore. For Liveright see Walker Gilmer, *Horace Liveright: Publisher of the Twenties* (1970).

44 Quoted in Donald Watt, ed., *Aldous Huxley: The Critical Heritage*, London and Boston: Routledge & Kegan Paul, 1975, 72–4.

45 Warren G. Harding (1865–1923) was the twenty-ninth President of the United States, 1921–3.

46 'Scherzo for the Bassoon', *Smart Set*, lxviii, May 1922, 142–3. Reprinted in William H. Nolte, ed., *H. L. Mencken's 'Smart Set' Criticism*, Ithaca, New York: Cornell University Press, 1968, 322–3. In 1975 Donald Watt quoted from another review of *Crome Yellow* by Mencken, but confessed that he had been unable to locate its original place of publication. This review, if that is what it was, has still not come to light. *Aldous Huxley: The Critical Heritage*, 8, 35.

47 Forgué, 238.

48 Postcard, Rare Books and Manuscripts Division, New York Public Library, 16 August 1922.

   Huxley also adopted Mencken as his model in his music criticism. For instance, the tone of Huxley's account of a concert given by the Portuguese cellist Guilhermina Suggia, which culminated in her performance of Léon Boëllmann's *Variations symphoniques*, is distinctly Menckenian: 'One thinks of the waste of the performer's talent and time (not to mention the waste of our time and the price of our tickets); one thinks of the minds of the people who like this sort of thing; one thinks of all the lovely works one might be hearing and isn't; one thinks of the spiritual hierarchy of man and makes the melancholy constatation that there are a great many Sudras in the world.' ('Bad Music', *Weekly Westminster Gazette*, i, no. 45, 23 December 1922, 14.) Also, compare 'Some Easter Music', *Weekly Westminster Gazette*, i, no. 10, 22 April 1922, 13, and 'The Criticism of Music', *Weekly Westminster Gazette*, i, no. 15, 27 May 1922, 14, with Mencken's 'The Allied Arts' in *Prejudices: Second Series*, New York: Knopf, 1920; London: Jonathan Cape, 1921, 192–210.

49 'Chiefly Pathological', *Smart Set*, lxix, November 1922, 144. It seems Mencken was mistaken when he claimed that 'Permutations Among the Nightingales' had already been published in the magazine.

50 Rare Books and Manuscripts Division, New York Public Library, n.d. [December 1922].

51 Rare Books and Manuscripts Division, New York Public Library, n.d. [early 1923].

52 *Smart Set*, lxx, April 1923, 41–5.

53 'Three Gay Stories', *American Mercury*, i, no. 3, March 1924, 380–81.

54 *Those Barren Leaves*, London: Chatto & Windus, 1925, 372.

55 *Letters*, 234.

56 *Letters*, 242.

57 'The Ass arrived from the East.' Huxley is quoting from the thirteenth-century 'Prose of the Ass', a boisterous extension to the *text* of the Mass, performed at Beauvais and other French cathedrals at the feast of the Circumcision (1 January). 'The ceremonial included a drinking bout, the bringing of an ass into the church at the singing of the Prose of the Ass

Orientis partibus
adventavit asinus

and the ending of certain liturgical pieces with a bray.' Karl Young, *The Drama of the Medieval Church*, Oxford: Clarendon Press, 2 vols., 1933, vol. i, 105. Huxley would have been familiar with the 'Prose of the Ass' through the version printed in E. K. Chambers, *The Mediaeval Stage*, vol. ii, Oxford: Clarendon Press, 1903, 280–82.

58 James Henry Hackett (1800–71), American actor. Falstaff was one of his most popular roles, and he was hugely successful in both the United States and England as Nimrod Wildfire in J. K. Paulding's *Lion of the West*, a satire of Davy Crockett. Sir Johnston Forbes-Robertson (1853–1937) was one of the foremost actors of his day. Noted for his Hamlet and his elocution, he retired in 1915.

59 Rare Books and Manuscripts Division, New York Public Library, 5 May 1926.

60 Maria Huxley to Mary Hutchinson, Harry Ransom Humanities Research Center, University of Texas at Austin, 16 May [1926]. Between January 1920 and December 1933, the manufacture, sale or carriage of alcoholic drinks was prohibited throughout the United States by the 18th Amendment to the constitution.

61 *The World* [New York], 19 May 1926, 3.

62 'Three Novels', *American Mercury*, ix, no. 33, September 1926, 127.

63 George Folansbee Babbitt is the solid, home-loving, Republican protagonist of Sinclair Lewis's satirical novel of the same name (1922).

64 House of Lords Records Office, MS. S/33/5/113, 6 January 1927.

65 Rare Books and Manuscripts Division, New York Public Library, 11 May 1933.

66 Enoch Pratt Free Library, Baltimore, 16 October 1934. In his reply of 27 October 1934 Mencken told Huxley that he would be delighted to see his 'brother', but that he would be confined to Baltimore for the foreseeable future in view of his wife's poor health. 'Roosevelt,' Mencken added, 'is going from bad to worse. My guess is that he'll keep on wasting money until the country goes bankrupt and that we'll then have something resembling a Fascist revolution. There is not one chance in a million that the United States will ever go Communist. The Americano is incurably capitalistic in his hopes, if not in his talk.' Rare Books and Manuscripts Division, New York Public Library.

67 Quoted in Matthew J. Bruccoli, *Some Sort of Epic Grandeur: The Life of F. Scott Fitzgerald*, New York: Harcourt Brace Jovanovich, 1981, 106–7.

Open Conspirators:
Huxley and H. G. Wells 1927–35

It has been alleged on a number of occasions that Huxley and H. G. Wells were at loggerheads with one another during the inter-war period. Anthony Burgess once went so far as to dub Huxley 'the greatest anti-Wellsian of them all'.[1] Invariably, though, the evidence which is adduced to highlight their discord comprises little more than Huxley's caustic remarks about Wells's *Men Like Gods* (1923) and Wells's equally pejorative observations on *Brave New World*.

As a dyed-in-the-wool debunker of progress, Huxley found it impossible to square Wells's projection in *Men Like Gods* of a cheery distant future, where the problem of over-population has long been solved, where there are no mental defectives, party politics, prisons or police, and where the 'vast majority of Utopians are active, sanguine, inventive, receptive and good-tempered', with his profound sense of cultural deterioration.[2] Even at the end of the decade Huxley could not resist a scoff at 'General Wells and the New Salvationists' for their heady and unjustified optimism. 'In theory,' Huxley wrote in 1929, 'I am all for man living scientifically, creating his own destiny and so forth. But in practice I doubt whether he can. I doubt whether any great scheme of human regeneration, of large-scale social Salvationism can be carried through.'[3] However, as we shall see, the global chaos which followed the Wall Street Crash (which occurred within a month of him making these sceptical comments) prompted Huxley to adopt a more positive attitude to Wellsian 'Salvationism'. In all but name, Huxley became a card-carrying 'Open Conspirator'.

Wells has long been identified as 'one of the twentieth century's most confirmed antidemocrats':

> In a century which listened to the strictures on democracy of Pareto, Ortega y Gasset, Santayana, Babbitt, Mencken, Shaw, Kipling, Belloc and T. S. Eliot, Wells may not always have been the most audible antidemocrat, but he contributed as much as any of these to the intellectual attack.[4]

Like Huxley, Wells was dismayed by what he perceived as the failings of parliamentary democracy and was convinced that contemporary civilization must be re-configured as an aristocracy of intellect if it was to stand any chance of surviving and improving. Both writers envisaged eugenics being used to hasten the advent of this Scoganite Rational State, and it seems likely that Wells was upset by *Brave New World* because Huxley appeared to be disowning the principles he thought they shared.

To set against his sporadic and well-documented snipes at the progressive utopianism epitomized by *Men Like Gods*, we can marshal new evidence of the acute interest Huxley took in Wells's work throughout the inter-war period and especially in the 1930s. On 11 February 1921, for example, in a review of Wells's and St John Irvine's dramatization of Wells's *The Wonderful Visit* (1895), Huxley wrote of his 'great admiration and respect' for Wells and referred to his 'on the whole amazingly great book' *The Outline of History* (1920), which he later summarized as 'a tract in favour of international and scientific planning'.[5] In 1923 Huxley enthused:

> [Wells] is contemporary, he breathes the same atmosphere as ourselves, his problems are our problems, and though his works may prove, in the words of the old poem, to be 'damnably mouldy a hundred years hence' when *King Lear* will still serenely remain what it is and always has been; though we know very well that, judged by any standard, they compare, to say the least of it, poorly with those of Shakespeare; we are ready, after too long a sojourn in the past, to turn to him with a passionate avidity.[6]

It was with just such a 'passionate avidity' between 1927 and 1935 that Huxley championed the creation of a 'Samurai' caste and promoted the notion of world government, the central plank of Wells's 'Open Conspiracy'.

The 'Open Conspiracy' went through a number of permutations before Wells settled on a stable definition of it in 1928. In the fifth chapter of *Anticipations* (1902), for instance, Wells had asserted that 'a world-wide process of social and moral deliquescence is in progress, and that a really functional body of engineering, managing men, scientifically trained, and having common ideals and interests, is likely to segregate and disentangle itself from our present confusion of aimless and ill-directed lives'.[7] The same chapter concludes:

And so it is I infer that, whether violently as a revolution or quietly and slowly, this grey confusion that is Democracy must pass away inevitably by its own inherent conditions, as the twilight passes, as the embryonic confusion of the cocoon creature passes, into the higher stage, into the higher organism, the world state of the coming years.[8]

When *Anticipations* was re-issued in 1914, Wells added a 'specially-written introduction', in which he confessed that the 'conception of an open conspiracy of intellectuals and wilful people against existing institutions and existing limitations and boundaries is always with me'.[9] This was the first time Wells had used the phrase, but it is clear that the elite *samurai* of *A Modern Utopia* (1905), whose 'widely sustained activities . . . had shaped and established the World State in Utopia', and who control four subservient castes – the 'Poietic', the 'Kinetic', the 'Dull' and the 'Base' – were the Open Conspiracy's avant-garde.[10] Their 'Utopian classification' reflects the *samurai*'s rejection of 'the assumption that men are unclassifiable, because practically homogeneous, which underlies modern democratic methods and the fallacies of our equal justice', but which is alien to the *samurai* mind.[11]

The Open Conspiracy was launched officially in *The World of William Clissold* (1926), a novel in which Wells's mouthpiece sketches the global and hierarchical system of government which must, in his view, supersede mass democracy:

I do not regard the organisation of all mankind into one terrestrial anthill, into Cosmopolis, the greater Athens, the Rome and Paris and London of space and time, as a Utopian dream, as something that fantastically might be. I regard it as the necessary, the only possible, continuation of human history.[12]

Cissold's triple-decker bagginess was condensed into an exposi-tory primer entitled *The Open Conspiracy: Blue Prints for a World Revolution* (1928), in which Wells argued the need for far-reaching, world-wide reform with his customary vim. On its publication in 1928, Wells gave Huxley a presentation copy of *The Open Conspiracy* inscribed to 'Aldous Huxley, these prosaic but necessary statements from H. G. Wells'.[13] In essence, *The Open Conspiracy* called for:

1 The complete assertion, practical as well as theoretical, of the provisional nature of existing governments and of our acquiescence in them;

2 The resolve to minimize by all available means the conflicts of these governments, their military use of individuals and property and their interferences with the establishment of a world economic system;

3 The determination to replace private local or national ownership of at least credit, transport and staple production by a responsible world directorate serving the common ends of the race;

4 The practical recognition of the necessity for world biological con-trols, for example, of population and disease;

5 The support of a minimum standard of individual freedom and welfare in the world; and

6 The supreme duty of subordinating the personal life to the creation of a world directorate capable of these tasks and to the general advancement of human knowledge, capacity and power.[14]

It is not known whether Huxley, like Shaw and Beatrice Webb, wrote to Wells to congratulate him on *The Open Conspiracy*, but, in view of what Huxley wrote during 1927–8, it is likely that his opinion of Wells's book was more favourable than his later 'General Wells' snipe might suggest.

Wells's conspiratorial crusade was not confined to his books. In

1927, a series of articles in the *Sunday Express* had provided him with the opportunity of reaching a wider public. One of these pieces, 'Is Parliament Doomed? – The Farce of Our Elections: New Experiments in Government', attracted Huxley's attention. In his newspaper article Wells asks the reader to 'name a single man of really first-class moral and intellectual quality in British, French, American or German politics today'. Scarcely represented at all in Parliament, Wells claimed, were 'the creative minds that would educate, reorganize and push towards an ampler life of our race'. According to Wells, this was already happening elsewhere in the world:

Russia has a mere pretence of representative government entirely and openly controlled by the Communist Party . . . [and] China, after some parliamentary beginnings in Peking, has cast them aside for that most remarkable students' association, the Kuomintang.

The abolition of democracy in Italy, Spain, Poland, Hungary, Greece and Turkey is noted approvingly before Wells ends his article, unexpectedly, with the view that democracy would work in Britain if only the British would adopt a system of proportional representation.[15] The following Thursday Huxley wrote to Wells:

Thank you for writing the wholly excellent article in the *Sunday Express*. I was saying, 'Them's my sentiments' all the time as I read it. But I wish I'd seen it before meeting you on the boat last Saturday; for then I'd have asked you about the one point which seemed to me obscure in your exposition – about the possible remedy to present chaos in a form of proportional representation. How are you going to make a strong working government from a body of people elected on a great variety of different tickets and not bound together by party ties? It would be easy enough if men were rational beings. But since they are what they are . . . I wish you'd give me an opportunity of asking you one evening next week, if you're in town. Could you have dinner with me here, say Wednesday next, or Thursday?[16]

Whether Wells was able to accept Huxley's invitation is unknown, but his anti-parliamentary diatribes certainly had an immediate impact on the development of Huxley's political ideology. In an article of August 1927 entitled 'The Outlook for American Culture', for instance, Huxley wrote in terms which are almost identical to Wells's:

> The ideal state is one in which there is a material democracy controlled by an aristocracy of intellect – a state in which men and women are guaranteed a decent human existence and are given every opportunity to develop such talents as they possess, and where those with the greatest talent rule. The active and intelligent oligarchies of the ideal state do not yet exist. But the Fascist party in Italy, the Communist party in Russia, the Kuomintang in China are still their inadequate precursors.

Further on in his article, Huxley looks forward to the 'evolution of a new social hierarchy, based on the facts of human nature', a world where 'the humanitarianism that professes to regard all human beings as equally endowed with moral worth and intellectual ability will be looked upon as an archaic absurdity'.[17]

In his introduction to *Proper Studies*, published in November 1927, Huxley acknowledged Wells as one of the 'sociological writers' whom he had 'read with profit',[18] and on 25 October 1928 he told Julian that he had received 'a very nice note from H. G. Wells' after the publication of his next book, *Point Counter Point*.[19] This was despite the fact that Rampion, the character Huxley based on D. H. Lawrence, parodies the Wellsian version of progress in one of his drawings,[20] and that Huxley slots Wells's anti-parliamentary rhetoric into the mouth of the bombastic windbag Everard Webley, leader of the British Brotherhood of Freemen. However, beneath his Ruritanian regalia and tumid rant, Huxley's 'Tinpot Mussolini' (p.55), like Mustapha Mond, is an unlikely spokesman for Huxley's own 'Wellsian' views when he avers that 'there's nothing to be done in these days by Parliamentarianism' (pp.76–7) and that 'we desire the rule by the best, not the most numerous' (p.463).

Warren Wagar has noted that the Open Conspiracy acquired 'a new lease on life after 1930, for which the world business depression deserved most of the credit'.[21] On the face of it, *Brave New World* appears to be a straightforward send-up of the futuristic dispensation sketched out in *The Open Conspiracy* and Wells's other utopian books.[22] But if this is how we wish to read the novel, then we should also acknowledge that the crisis of 1931 led Huxley to call in earnest for the kind of global government with which Wells had become synonymous. In 'The Victory of Art over Humanity', for example, Huxley recognizes that a solution to the economic muddle of the Slump can only be achieved 'by all the principal nations of the world, acting in concert':

There must be a world-wide adjustment of production to consumption, world-wide agreements about the establishment of new industries and the use of new inventions in old ones, a world policy for gold, for fuel, for agriculture – in a word, a general agreement to make some universally valid sense out of our babel of separate and private achievements.

Later on in the article, having inspected warehouses bursting with stored and stockpiled goods from around the world while on a tour of London's dockland, Huxley sees the 'Gargantuan profusion' which surrounds him as:

the symbol and symptom of world-wide poverty. Wool is piled up in mountains – and Australia is bankrupt . . . Everywhere the same disease. And the remedy? Some sort of world-wide plan to co-ordinate the separate plans whose mutual incompatibility is the cause of the present confusion.

This is the genuine voice of a Wellsian fellow-traveller, not 'the greatest anti-Wellsian of them all'.

In October 1931 Huxley wrote to a correspondent:

Poor H. G. does squeak – but I think he's right in supposing that, given a little intelligence now, the world could really be made quite decent . . . also right in fearing that the necessary intelligence will not be applied, but that stupidity, coupled with cupidity, will prevail, as of old, and plunge us deeper in the mire.[23]

Three months later Huxley broadcast a talk entitled 'Science and Civilisation'. During the course of it, he ruminated that if, in the interests of stability, eugenics were to be used by the state to create a caste of stupid, docile, manual labourers, 'this would have to be accompanied by the special breeding and training of a small caste of experts, without whom a scientific civilisation cannot exist':

> … in a scientific civilisation society must be organised on a caste basis. The rulers and their advisory experts will be a kind of Brahmins controlling, in virtue of a special and mysterious knowledge, vast hordes of the intellectual equivalents of Sudras and Untouchables.

These views were aired two weeks before the publication of *Brave New World* in January 1932, a novel which has been interpreted consistently as a forthright condemnation of genetic engineering. At the time of this broadcast and the novel's publication, however, Huxley did not regard the notion of a pyramidal caste system as abhorrent and he was, at the very least, equivocal in his attitude to the state use of eugenics.

The Federation of Progressive Societies and Individuals came into existence later in 1932, principally through the efforts of C. E. M. Joad, 'to promote contact and cooperation between societies and individuals working towards social and economic reconstruction, with a view to increasing the effectiveness of their efforts'.[24] The H. G. Wells Society, the Gymnic Association of Great Britain, the Anti-Fascist Council and the Woodcraft Folk were among the progressive organizations which coalesced in their belief that:

> The chaos of international relations, the failure to balance production and consumption, the nationalist policies pursued by governments with their appeals to fear, greed and self-interest under the guise of patriotism, must, unless arrested, inevitably lead, through social demoralization and tariff and military wars, to the breakdown of civiliza- tion.[25]

A clear statement of the Federation's principles was provided in the first number of its magazine, *Plan*:

In general we stand for a Planned Economy as against Unplanned Muddling; for production for use as against production for profit, with its crowning achievements of unemployment, the armaments ramp, and the destruction of food while thousands starve. We believe that World Government is the only sure way to World Peace. *We believe that Fascism is the greatest menace to it.*[26]

The securing of civil and religious liberties, the rescission of legislation concerning sexual conduct and the pursuit of radical educational reforms were the FPSI's other main policies.

To add some cachet to the Federation, prominent intellectuals, such as Wells, Bertrand Russell, Rebecca West, A. S. Neill, Leonard Woolf and Aldous and Julian Huxley, were co-opted as vice-presidents towards the end of 1933. It has been claimed that 'Wells lost interest almost immediately; and in private he denounced it in effect as a miscellany of dilettantes, which may have been a fair criticism. But by intention, at any rate, the FPSI started its brief career in the spirit of the Open Conspiracy.'[27] Certainly, the function of the FPSI's luminaries seems to have been largely decorative. Huxley's vice-presidential activity, for instance, appears to have been restricted to a weekend conference of the FPSI's Education Group at Digswell Park, Welwyn Garden City, in June 1934 (during which he gave a nude reading of Blake and *The Waste Land* in a cabbage patch[28]) and a Conway Hall lecture on propaganda in 1935.[29]

To further its ends, the FPSI issued, in 1934, a *Manifesto* in which twelve contributors, representing the broad raft of social and political reform with which the FPSI concerned itself, outlined their own positions. Reviewing this *Manifesto* in the July number of *Plan*, Huxley wrote that, while he was willing to endorse many of the 'detailed proposals' contained in the *Manifesto*, he had reservations 'about some of the general principles underlying the proposals':

In his introduction Mr Joad tells us that he 'relies on human reason' and believes that 'if we only argue cogently enough, persuasively enough and patiently enough in support of these aims (of the F.P.S.I.), we can, in the long run, bring other people to share them'. But how long, we may ask, is that run to be? And, meanwhile, what will happen to the world if large masses of people fanatically accept the attractively simple philosophies and one-track programmes of Communism or Fascism? In the world as we know it, there seems to be a certain psychological incompatibility between the faith that moves mountains and the science that understands them, between driving fanaticism and knowledge, between singleness of purpose and breadth of mind. History makes it fairly clear that most people will accept reason only in small doses and (except in matters which do not touch them very closely) only on irrational grounds, generally of a religious nature. Mr. [Olaf] Stapledon, in his essay on education, tries to escape from this rather depressing conclusion by the simple process of loudly declaring that people ought to be different from what they actually are. 'The individual,' he says, 'must be taught to think accurately and to regard all information critically. If possible, he must be given a passion for pioneering in thought, even for piratical adventures against the sanctified beliefs of his teachers. Above all, he must be taught to be relentlessly critical of his own motives . . . In general he must learn to be both receptive and cautious, both imaginative and sceptical, and at the same time both sensitive and self-reliant.' (He might also, while he was about it, learn to be both Mozart and Sir Isaac Newton, both Casanova and Pascal, both Edward Gibbon and Jack Dempsey.)[30]

By 'the individual' Mr. Stapledon presumably means 'all individuals'. But that all individuals should be convertible (at any rate within the next few centuries or millennia) into critical, self-analytical, cautious, self-reliant, sceptical pioneers of thought seems to me, I confess, almost infinitely improbable.

Certain 'Samurai' used to play an important part in the earlier prophetic books of Mr. H. G. Wells. They play no part in the F.P.S.I. Manifesto. The fact, it seems to me, is greatly to be regretted, as well on theoretical as on practical grounds. The Samurai idea is scientifically justified, in as much as it implies a recognition of the irreconcilable differences between human beings and a rejection of that wish-born theory of equality, which Mr. Stapledon has taken from the Encyclopaedists.[31] It is also a programme, a plan of action. The fact that the advocates of a given policy or ethic are disinterested people trained up in habits of austere self-discipline, is in itself no guarantee of the intrinsic excellence of that policy or that ethic. But it does undoubtedly render the policy or ethic more generally acceptable. If people were profoundly stirred by the preachings of the Franciscans, of Savonarola, of the early Jesuits, it was to a great extent because they respected the preachers as being better than themselves. Mr. Joad relies on men's reason; he would, I believe, be better justified by events, if he transferred his reliance to their admiration for disinterested and self-sacrificing good-ness. The creation of a caste of Samurai is a piece of strictly practical politics.

There is even a great deal to be said for the creation of a caste of Brahmins above the Samurai. Their immediate, political, propagandist value would be less than that of the more active Samurai; but ultimately, it seems to me, society can derive nothing but benefit from the existence of such a caste.[32]

As the journalist Alan Campbell Johnson discovered, Huxley was still a proselyte of 'the Samurai idea' as late as November 1935. When he asked Huxley whether in *Brave New World* 'his ultimate sympathies were with the savage's aspirations or with the ideal of conditioned stability', Huxley replied:

'With neither, but I believe some mean between the two is both desir-able and possible and must be our objective' . . . However, the tempta-tion to retire into a shell must be set aside. At one moment he suggested that our efforts might have to be limited to the training of an intellectual aristocracy, and at another he pointed to the lines this training should take.[33]

It is frustrating that Johnson offered no indication of what Huxley had in mind, but his commitment to such a patently Wellsian strategy in the same month that he launched a major anti-fascist exhibition in London reveals the true depth of Huxley's affinity with his fellow writer.

NOTES

1 Anthony Burgess, *The Novel Today: A Student's Guide to Contemporary Fiction*, London: Faber & Faber, 1967, 39.

2 H. G. Wells, *Men Like Gods*, London: Cassell, 1923, 74.

3 'The New Salvation,' *Vanity Fair* [New York], xxxiii, September 1929, 76, 106.

4 Warren Wagar, H. G. *Wells and the World State*, New Haven: Yale University Press, 1961, 169.

5 *The Westminster Gazette*, 11 February 1921, 6. Huxley's later comment about the *Outline* was made in 'Best Sellers', *Chicago Herald and Examiner*, 18 June 1934, 11.

6 'Contemporaneousness', *Weekly Westminster Gazette*, ii, no. 56, 10 March 1923, 14.

7 H. G. Wells, *Anticipations: Of the Reaction of Mechanical and Scientific Progress upon Human Life and Thought*, London: Chapman & Hall, 1902, 143.

8 Ibid., 175.

9 H. G. Wells, *Anticipations: Of the Reaction of Mechanical and Scientific Progress upon Human Life and Thought*, London: Chapman & Hall, 1914, x.

10 H. G. Wells, *A Modern Utopia*, London: Chapman & Hall, 1905, 261.

11 Ibid., 265.

12 H. G. Wells, *The World of William Clissold: A Novel at a New Angle*, 3 vols., London: Ernest Benn, 1926, vol. iii, 613.

13 Further 'signed volumes by H. G. Wells' and 'several letters from H. G. Wells' were destroyed in the disastrous 1961 fire. See page 25 (note 4). Wells also sent Huxley his two-volume *Experiment in Autobiography* in 1934, signed simply 'Aldous Huxley from H. G.' (for Huxley's letter of thanks to 'H. G.', see *Letters*, 38?); and *The Anatomy of Frustration: A Modern Synthesis* in 1936, inscribed to 'Aldous Huxley to steady his mind, from H. G.' Information from *Books from the libraries of Sir James Barrie and Mr. Aldous Huxley together with the personal library of Mary Webb consisting of only 30 volumes*, Elkin Mathews Ltd, Catalogue 73, February 1938, 35. Huxley quotes from the *Anatomy of Frustration* in *Ends and Means* (1937), 178.

14 H. G. Wells, *The Open Conspiracy: Blue Prints for a World Revolution*, London: Victor Gollancz, 1928, 113–14.

15 *Sunday Express*, 20 March 1927, 12, 19. Wells restated his admiration of the Russian Communist Party and the Kuomintang in *Democracy under Revision*, London: Hogarth Press, 1927, 28–9.

16 *Letters*, 285–6.

17 'The Outlook for American Culture: Some Reflections in a Machine Age', *Harper's Magazine*, clv, August 1927, 265–72. Reprinted as *America and the Future*, Austin and New York: Pemberton Press, 1970.

18 *Proper Studies*, xix.

19 *Letters*, 303. Wells's 'note' has not survived.

20 *Point Counter Point*, London: Chatto & Windus, 1928, 290–91. Subsequent quotations are embodied in the text.

21 Wagar, 194.

22 This view has been argued by Mark R. Hillegas, for example, in *The Future as Nightmare: H. G. Wells and the Anti-Utopians*, New York: Oxford University Press, 1967, 111–19.

23 *Letters*, 356.

24 C. E. M. Joad, Allan Young et al., *Manifesto: Being the Book of the Federation of Progressive Societies and Individuals*, ed. C. E. M. Joad, London: George Allen & Unwin, 1934, 21.

25 Ibid, 22.

26 [John W. M. Dudding], 'Editorial', *Plan*, i, April 1934. 2.

27 Wagar, 198.

28 Anne Olivier Bell and Andrew McNeillie, eds, *The Diary of Virginia Woolf*, vol. iv: 1931–5, London: Hogarth Press, 1982, 223. The conference took place on 9–11 June 1934.

29 Huxley read out the lecture he had given to the Paris conference. See the note at the end of 'Ballyhoo for Nations', p. 191.

30 'Jack Dempsey' was the byname of William Harrison Dempsey (1895–1983), otherwise known as the 'Manassa Mauler'. He was world heavyweight boxing champion between 1919 and 1926.

31 The 28-volume *L'Encyclopédie* (1751–72) edited by Diderot and D'Alembert, was one of the chief works of the Philosophes, a body of French intellectuals dedicated to the advancement of rationalism, deism, humanitarianism and the new science. The *Encyclopédistes* included Voltaire, Rousseau and Montesquieu. Five more volumes appeared in 1776–7.

32 *Plan*, i, July 1934, 6–7, 15.

33 Alan Campbell Johnson, 'Peace Psychology', *Peace Offering*, London: Methuen, 1936, 152–64.

ABROAD IN ENGLAND

1930–36

Babies – State Property

After having been for a good many thousand years an institution, the family has now, almost suddenly, become a problem. Why? Let me try to formulate the causes of this occurrence.

The first and principal cause must be looked for in that change in our view of the world, and even in our consciousness, which has taken place in recent times and which is responsible not only for the crisis in the family, but directly or indirectly for almost all the other crises, so numerous and so distressing, in the midst of which we live and have our uncomfortable being.

Briefly, what seems to have happened is this. We have become more aware of ourselves, more consciously individual than our fathers. And at the same time, with the compensating spread of humanitarianism, we have become more conscious of the feelings and the rights of others. In the sphere of the family, as elsewhere, these changes in the mode of consciousness have produced profound effects. To begin with, it is impossible for us as self-conscious individuals to accord the old unquestioning belief to the traditional axioms. The family has ceased to be the divine and inevitable institution it was. And scepticism born of self-conscious individualism is reinforced, in the case of this institution, by humanitarianism. We feel acutely that our children have rights and that we are not justified in imposing upon them too strict a discipline or constraint. Our dread of being tyrannously unfair to our children has rationalised itself in the curious educational doctrine, now so popular, that the sole purpose of education is to guarantee to every child the possibility of complete 'self expression'. More rational in their aims, the old educationists sought to transform and ameliorate the self before permitting it to indulge in expression. The means they employed to achieve this end were barbarously brutal. In our hatred of the means we have failed to see that the ends were good.

But it is not only the attitude of the parents towards their children that has changed; their attitude towards themselves is no longer the same as in the past. Self-consciously individualistic as well as humanitarian, parents feel that they too have rights. They want to 'live their own lives', 'to express themselves', to have some other than a merely parental *raison d'être*. In a word, they resent the weight of family responsibilities. Accordingly, they try to mitigate these responsibilities, first by reducing the size of their families and, secondly, by handing over such children as they do produce to professional educators.

And here we come to the second main cause of the present crisis in family life. The family has decreased in size. Increasing individuality and self-consciousness rendered intolerable the old united family with its three or four generations living under the same roof. From being a banyan the family tree has long since become (at any rate in the West) an oak. Scattered at a distance from the parental stem the acorns grow up into a separate existence. In the past these separate young trees were prolific; but recently the increase of self-conscious individuality has led, for the reasons already given, to a reduction in the number of offspring. (These psychological causes have been reinforced by economic causes – themselves, very often, of psychological origin. Thus families cannot be big because we must keep up the standard of living. But why must we keep up the standard of living? Because conscious individuals cannot put up with conditions which were quite tolerable to the un-self-conscious and imperfectly individualised. The only people who have large families nowadays are the mentally deficient.)

Now, from the point of view of the children, small families are not much good. A big family is the world in miniature; to be brought up in a big family is the world in miniature; to be brought up in a big family is a complete preparation for life. An only child is heavily handicapped. Two children are not very much better off. A family only begins to be really satisfactory when it can count at least four or five members. From the children's point of view very few modern families are satisfactory. Hence the importance in modern life of the professional educator, who forms an artificial family, within which it is possible for children to find psychological satisfaction. 'Advanced' people propose that the family system should be abolished altogether and that the professional educator, paid by the State, should take control from earliest infancy. Indeed, this view threatens to become the orthodoxy of the modern democratic State.

Where there are too many self-conscious individuals the State is always insecure. Humanitarianism is the antidote to excess of individualism. It is in the name of humanitarian democratic principles that the modern State battles with the dangerous individuals who menace it. In England and the other western countries it is a wavering indecisive fight, because neither side has quite clearly formulated the cause for which it is fighting.

The Russians are more logical and explicit. There the Communist leaders have frankly avowed their intention of suppressing individualism in the interests of society. They are hardly less merciful to the family, because of its tendency to create an *imperium in imperio*. The State-paid professional educator is to take the place of the parents. There is an obvious tendency, all over the western world, to follow the lead of Russia – not through any desire to imitate the Soviets but because circumstances are rendering it increasingly necessary for all States to guard against the dangers of insurgent individualism. Human standardisation will become a political necessity.

Psychologists having shown the enormous importance in every human existence of the first years of childhood, the State will obviously try to get hold of its victims as soon as possible. The process of standardisation will begin at the very moment of birth – that is to say, if it does not begin before birth! Which means that both the individual and the family are in for a very bad quarter of an hour. That they will emerge again when the danger is past I have no doubt.

Individuality is something that has grown and waned and grown again throughout recorded history; and the family relationships have always provided such a variety of important psychological satisfactions that it seems impossible that human beings can ever consent to dispense with them permanently. For the moment, however, there seems to be no doubt that the family is on the decline. The institution is disliked, as I have shown, both by the self-conscious individuals and also by the advanced democrats who are the enemies of anything that stands in the way of social solidarity.

Against this double assault the family cannot stand. A single generation has already profoundly modified the character of the institution. In two or three more generations from now it will be unrecognisable; it will perhaps have ceased to exist. But as nobody with a personal experience of family life will then be alive its decease will go unmourned and probably almost unnoticed.

Evening Standard, 21 May 1939, 7

Abroad in England

Abroad in England? Yes, abroad; for in varying degrees we are all foreigners even in our own country. How little of this England of which we are the citizens, how absurdly little, for any one of us, is 'home'! Each of us inhabits his own world, a world whose boundaries are fixed, for him and for those who are like him, by temperament, by upbringing, by opportunity. Fixed almost irrevocably. For the overwhelming majority of men and women there is no possible revision of the treaties they have made with Fate. The frontiers of their various worlds are strictly guarded. Emigration is rare, and even the passage of tourists is relatively infrequent.

The notes which follow are the casual jottings of a tourist – a tourist whose home is that remote province of the Great Bourgeois Empire inhabited by Literary Men, Professional Thinkers and the Amateurs of General Ideas. A pleasant corner, I admit; but even in the pleasantest corners one can grow restless. Curiosity about foreign parts has always been one of my besetting weaknesses. Now, parts can be spiritually as well as geographically foreign. My curiosity has taken me, not only into other continents, but also from time to time across the frontiers of my social and mental province into those neighbouring countries, whose confederation is that largely alien entity called England.

The Great Bourgeois Empire is surrounded by a more than Chinese wall. Class barriers are everywhere high; but in no country of the West are they so high as in England. Differences in economic status create differences in outlook, in ways of living, thinking, feeling and judging. Our English system of education is deliberately designed to accentuate these differences. In France or Germany, for example, the intelligent proletarian who wins scholarships is educated at the same school as the intelligent child of wealthy parents – not to mention their unintelligent child; for money still buys the privilege of higher education for those who do not desire and are quite unfitted to receive it. In England the intelligent children of the poor are not educated in the same schools as the children of the rich and of those who, though not actually rich, are compelled by their social status to behave (at the price of what frightful sacrifices!) as though they were. Hence the wall, the more than Chinese wall.

Lofty and formidably solid, it rose for me the other day in the cloisters of Durham cathedral – rose yet once more with the same old uncompromising insistence. I had been lecturing at a neighbouring mining village and had come in by bus, with two companions, to spend the afternoon in more congenial surroundings.[1] It was a long and dismal ride; but suddenly, after the grimy industrial suburbs, suddenly there was the cathedral, huge on its scarped hill, with the bright autumnal woods descending and the river like black glass beneath. There it was, startlingly, dramatically, the great stone fossil left over from another world. Later, wandering in the twilight of the huge Romanesque arches, we spied the Dean.[2] One of my companions was acquainted with him, spoke to him, and a few minutes later we were being very hospitably entertained to tea among the monastic splendours of the Deanery. And here it was that the Chinese wall began to make its presence felt. The Dean and I were

1 On the evening of Friday 10 October 1930, Huxley gave a lecture on 'Science and Poetry' to a study circle organised by Charles Wilson in the mining village of Willington in County Durham. Wilson was certainly one of the men who accompanied Huxley to Durham city the next day; the other is unidentified. For a more detailed account of Wilson, Huxley's visit to Willington and the profound effect it had on him, see David Bradshaw, 'Huxley's Slump: Planning, Eugenics and the "Ultimate Need" of Stability', in John Batchelor, ed., *The Art of Literary Biography*, Oxford: Oxford University Press, 1995, 151–71.

2 James Edward Cowell Welldon (1854–1937), Dean of Durham 1918–33. An Old Etonian, he had gone on to distinguish himself as a schoolmaster at Harrow.

one side of it, my two companions on the other. In spite of the difference in age, in spite of the separating gulf between our opinions, it was easier for me to establish contact with the ecclesiastical dignitary than with my companions from the mining town. They were men I liked; I found them pleasant, intelligent, well informed; I agreed with their views. But all the same it was easier for me to get on with the Dean. It was a question of upbringing. In Pavlov's phrase, the Dean and I had had our reflexes conditioned in those curious hotbeds of bourgeois imperialism, the Public Schools. My companions had received their training in the state-supported seminaries of the Proletarian Empire. They were the citizens of one country, we of another, an alien and sometimes hostile country. D. H. Lawrence, who was the son of a miner, used to tell me, I remember, that, though he had grown accustomed to bourgeois ways, he could never establish contact with a member of the bourgeoisie, however personally sympathetic to him, as easily as he could with a man or woman who had sprung from the working classes. 'You can't exaggerate the strength and importance of class,' he used to say. The more dealings I have with people on the other side of the Chinese wall, the more completely do I find myself in agreement with him.

Sitting in what had been the refectory of a fourteenth-century Benedictine monastery, I listened (on our side of the wall) to the Dean's spirited conversation. 'Harrow,' he was saying, 'used to be the great Whig school. Eton was always Tory. I don't suppose,' he went on, 'that there are many people nowadays who would hesitate to send their sons to Eton for fear of the Toryism in the air.' I didn't suppose so either. What I did suppose, however, was that there were a great many people who would hesitate a very, very long time before sending their children to a state-supported school. The Chinese wall exists; we take infinite pains to keep it in good repair.

After my lecture an elderly clergyman who had been in the audience, came up and spoke to me. We talked a little on the rather abstruse subjects with which I had been amusing or failing to amuse my audience. (And whatever the general feeling may have been, a number of astonishingly acute and intelligent questions were asked, when I had finished.) Then, my new acquaintance launched into a considerable discourse of his own, a philosophical lucubration, of which I remember (how vividly!) only the concluding words. 'Well,' he wound up, 'my humble opinion is simply this: that this world is entirely without point or design or purpose – and that's an end of it. Good evening, Mr. Huxley.' And having shaken me by the hand, he left me, a little staggered, I must confess, but full of admiration for the Church of England. A Church which permits its ministers so much licence of belief, that some are more Catholic than the Pope, while others, like the gentleman who had just left me, are considerably less deistic than Voltaire – well, I said to myself, it's a most remarkable institution.

Not to be able to see the wood for the trees is proverbially a source of error. But though uncondemned by traditional wisdom, the converse incapacity is surely no less deplorable. Not to be able to see the trees for the wood is a form of imaginative blindness to which the intelligentsia and the bourgeoisie are peculiarly subject. Hence the silence, on this score, of traditional wisdom. For proverbs were not made by or for the intelligentsia and the bourgeoisie (which did not exist, at any rate in its present form, at the time when proverbs were being invented), but by and for the folk. Now the folk run no risk of not seeing the trees for the wood. The difficulty of the unsophisticated mind has always been to realise the existence of woods – of general ideas as opposed to particular facts. For the folk, the trees are so insistently 'there', that they simply cannot conceive how such solid realities can be thought of as mere components of that intangible entity, a wood. Trained to think in terms of the general idea, separated by economic circumstances from whole classes of the particular facts that fill the lives of their less prosperous fellows, bourgeois and intellectual often find it very hard to realise the existence of the trees which compose their generalised and abstract woods. Of all the more or less wealthy and well-educated men and women who – in London drawing-rooms, at the Club, over luncheons in the City, in Government Offices –

discuss the Unemployment Problem, the Shrinking of Dividends, the Dole, the Slump, the Depression in our Basic Industries, how many, I wonder, have ever taken the trouble to come and look for themselves at the particular facts summed up by these convenient generalisations? Uncommonly few. And since most of them have ceased to have any function to perform among the trees, it follows that, unless they take this special trouble, they will for ever remain ignorant of all but the large and highly generalised woods of political economy and sociology.

It was not always so. The divorce between property and management, between ownership and responsibility for the things owned, is historically very recent. Modern industry requires great masses of capital; hence the joint stock company and hence the stockholder. What is a stockholder? A stockholder is a man who has given certain bits of paper in order that he may possess certain other bits of paper, which entitle him to receive a yearly allowance of the first kind of bits of paper. The man who possesses a large number of bits of paper of the second class (that is to say, shares) entitling him to receive a copious and regular supply of the bits of paper of the first class (that is to say, money) is the typical twentieth-century man of property. He is the owner of abstractions, not of things; aware only of the financial wood, never of the mere trees of actual production. In certain cases he does not even know the names of the bits of paper which entitle him to his yearly allowance of money; an Investment Trust keeps him in comfortable ignorance of the sources of his income. More often, however, he does at least know the names of his papers. Some, for example, are called So-and-So Colliery, or Such-and-Such Steelworks; some have the outlandish names of East Indian rubber plantations, or Moroccan deposits of phosphates. But, anyhow, they are always the names of woods, never of trees. The modern man of property has not the faintest notion of how miners work – or alternatively, when his dividend has shrunk, how they don't work, but squat on their hunkers at the corner of the village street, or drift about in the towns looking in at the shop windows.

And how is steel made? What sort of life do the coolies lead on a Sumatra rubber estate? His bits of paper don't tell him. As for knowing what anybody wants with the phosphates that the Moors are so busily scratching up for him under the African sun – why, it has never even occurred to him to ask.

The treaties that we make with Fate are imposed on us; we have to accept their terms, almost unconditionally. On the members of the property-holding classes modern economic conditions have imposed this new kind of abstract, irresponsible ownership. They cannot help themselves. The majority of modern owners must own in this way, because there is no other way in which they can own.

Socialism and communism are political religions, whose principal article of faith is the doctrine that private property is wicked. These political religions have grown to their present importance in the course of the last three generations – that is to say, during the period which has witnessed the growth of joint-stock ownership. The coincidence is not fortuitous. Where property consists in real things, for the manipulation of which the owner is directly or indirectly responsible, ownership as such is not resented, never regarded as immoral. It is only when ownership becomes abstract and irresponsible that the owner is hated and the hatred rationalised in terms of moral indignation. Men whom circumstances do not permit to see the wood for the trees are the natural enemies of men whom circumstances do not permit to see the trees for the wood. My own upbringing and present social and economic status have made me a seer of woods. On the other hand, my curiosity has often taken me exploring among the trees. These notes are written, now from the standpoint of the bird's-eye viewer of sociological generalities, now from that of the wanderer among alien particulars. Two eyes give stereoscopic vision.

Mining villages used to be noisy places – noisy and also melodious; for there was singing in the streets as well as shouting. Today they are remarkable for their silence. This is true to my knowledge not only of these Durham villages, but also of the

Nottinghamshire and Derbyshire colliery towns.[1] There is a slump in singing as well as a slump in coal. That these two slumps are closely correlated is obvious. Men out of work do not often feel an inner urge to burst into song. The only singing unemployed are those who wander through the streets of the great cities singing for alms from a charitable public. But this correlation between the vocal and the economic slump, though close, is not complete. For singing has slumped even where prosperity remains. Even regularly employed men seem to sing a good deal less than they used to. This is true not only of England, but of other countries as well. Nobody who has known Italy at all intimately during the last ten years can have failed to be struck by the decline in Italian singing. What was traditionally a Land of Song has become, musically speaking, as much of a Land of Silence as contemporary England.

What are the reasons for this world-wide slump in singing? Economic depression accentuates it, as we have seen, but does not seem to be a cause; for the musical began before the industrial decline and continues even during periods of prosperity. The gramophone and radio are partly responsible, no doubt, for the slump in singing. Man is a lazy animal, even in his pleasures, and if he can get a machine to amuse him, he will not trouble to amuse himself. Moreover, the machine sings with the voice of a professional and so provides a depressing standard of comparison for the vocal amateur, who is ashamed of displaying the defects in his own performance. Finally, I believe, there is something in the

[1] In late January and February 1928 Maria Huxley typed 'the "worst" bits' of Lawrence's *Lady Chatterley's Lover* for him at Les Diablerets in Switzerland. The following month the Huxleys toured the industrial Midlands of England by car to see for themselves the problems they had read about in the novel and which they had no doubt discussed with its author. 'Nobody who has visited the coal and iron towns of the North can fail to have been struck by the dreadful silence and listlessness of the crowds of unemployed men who shuffle along the streets like walking corpses,' Huxley wrote in 'Magic of London', *Sunday Dispatch*, 16 December 1928, 12. Immediately after returning from Willington in October 1930, Huxley travelled up to Ripley in Derbyshire to visit Lawrence's sister. Lawrence had died at the beginning of the year.

circumstances of modern life and labour which is in some way hostile to singing. The contemporary world is not a world in which many people feel tempted to lift up their hearts in song. It is a pity; but there it is. One cannot get something for nothing. Industrial progress has to be paid for. The suicide rate is rising (in some countries of the West it is five times what it was in 1870); nearly twice as many Englishwomen die in childbirth as died five and twenty years ago; there has probably been a genuine increase in the death-rate from cancer. These are a few items in the price humanity is paying for our particular kind of civilisation. The decline in singing is perhaps another item.

'In the vicinage of each colliery there are extensive rows of small houses, in which the families of the *pit-men* and other workmen reside. These are all built of stone and covered with tiles. All very solid, and very good, and invariably well furnished; hardly one of them without a good chest of drawers and other evidences of good living.' These are the words of William Cobbett, who rode through County Durham in 1832.[1] Pretty queer words they now seem to us. For these 'extensive rows of small houses', all so 'very solid and very good', are simply the rows of two-roomed cottages which still disfigure the outskirts of so many Durham mining villages – which sometimes *are* the village. There they still stand, hundreds of little black stone boxes confronting one another across a roadway dotted at intervals with communal latrines. What Cobbett admired fills the contemporary spectator with horror and indignation. It is a question, as usual, of relativity. Compared with the daub-and-wattle huts in which the peasantry of some of the southern counties were living in Cobbett's day these colliers' dwellings were magnificent. At least they kept the rain out. A steadily growing, ever active humanitarianism has given us, in the course of the last half-century,

---

1   Huxley is quoting from G. D. H. and Margaret Cole's three-volume edition of William Cobbett's *Rural Rides* (1930), vol. ii, 716, which he took with him on his second visit to the Durham coalfield in February 1931 ('Notes on the Way', *Time and Tide*, xvi, 29 June 1935, 974–6).

other standards of comparison. For us, the old reformer's 'very good, very solid' houses are a disgrace to civilisation.

Middlesbrough is a characteristic product of nineteenth-century civilisation. In 1800 the town consisted of three farms and had a population of twenty-five. Then, in the early 'thirties, came the iron works. Middlesbrough grew and flourished like – well, not exactly like a green bay tree: like a fungus, should we say? like staphylococcus in a test-tube of chicken broth? Miles of streets were laid out, thousands of mean and squalid little houses built and instantly overcrowded. Public buildings of an almost unbelievable hideousness were erected. Prosperity had come; and it lasted. The river was dredged, docks constructed, yet more factories put up. Round the iron works the slag heaps grew into mountains and the young salmon coming down the Tees on their way to the open sea died in ever larger and larger quantities as they tried to pass the city. All, in a word, was for the best in the best of all possible worlds. By nineteenth-century standards, Middlesbrough was a fine, progressive, successful town. True, a casual observer might not, at a first glance, have realised the fact – might even have thought that the place was remarkably like his conception of Hell. But then all fine, progressive and successful nineteenth-century towns *were* remarkably like people's conception of Hell. The fact was perhaps unfortunate. But it didn't, of course, prevent all being for the best in the best of all possible worlds.

Even in its palmiest days Middlesbrough cannot have been a very exhilarating or inspiring place. Nineteenth-century industrialism bothered itself very little with beauty, or the good life, or any nonsense of that sort. Business is Business: that was its watchword. For the Middle Ages Business was a branch of Morals and could not be thought of except in terms of general human values. It remained for Protestant Anglo-Saxondom to discover that the economic world was a world apart, unrelated to the rest of human life, obeying laws of its own. So long as they were committed in the name of Economics, the most unspeakable atrocities might be countenanced with a clear conscience. And, in fact, virtuous and pious men did countenance them. It is only during the last thirty or forty years that Protestant Anglo-Saxondom at large has come to realise what such rebellious prophets as Ruskin and Morris had proclaimed: that Business isn't exclusively Business, but a branch of man's social life. The grandchildren and great-grandchildren of the men who perverted the world to the revolting heresy that Business is Business are now the most active missionaries of humanist ortho-doxy. The Anglo-Saxons were the first to go astray; but they have also been among the first to return into the right path.

Meanwhile the products of the Business-is-Business mentality remain with us as a monument to past and a warning against present and future stupidity – as a burden to bear and a problem to be solved. Middlesbrough is a characteristic product of that mentality. Ugly and dismal enough even in its best days, it is now, in the hour of its misfortune, unspeakably gloomy, a sort of city of the dead. Yes, of the dead. For that is the impression they give you, these crowds of unemployed men who fill the streets of Middlesbrough (or for that matter of almost any other big northern town) with their slow interminable procession. Dead men walking, walking from nowhere in particular to nowhere else, aimlessly and in silence.

I have never seen a ghost – only something that afterwards turned out to be the medium artistically draped in butter muslin; but I am sure no ghost could be quite so terrifying as these spectres of flesh and blood who walk the streets of our northern cities. Dead men hopelessly resigned to death. One could wish that they were less resigned, less dumbly patient. But the dole has taken the violence out of their despair. Rebellion is generally a product of hunger. Regarded as a premium against the risk of revolution, the dole has been well worth paying.

The boredom of the idle rich is bad enough, but the boredom of the compulsorily idle poor is much worse. The rich can buy distrac-tions, stimulants, narcotics. Not so the poor; they cannot even afford to drown their boredom in watery beer. Their only devices for the killing of time are walking about, standing at street corners, and looking in at shop windows. A certain proportion of the younger men, at any rate in the mining towns, go in for reading. (Culture is, among other things, an excellent time-killer and narcotic.) But to those of the elder ones who have got quite out of the habit of books (and the majority of men in every rank of society give up all serious reading as soon as they leave school) even this resource is denied. The streets, the sporting news, an occasional visit to the movie and the pub – these are the only things that stand between them and death by boredom. The material results of prolonged unemployment can easily be calculated. But who will ever be able to compute the sum of psychological mischief, for which it has been and is responsible?

In the early 'thirties of last century William Cobbett was in Sheffield. The spectacle of all that highly skilled and specialised industry duly impressed him. Surely, he said to himself, no other nation will ever be able to compete with us in the making of iron and steel. We know too much, we have too long a start. Middlesbrough was as yet non-existent. But if Cobbett's ghost could have ridden along the Tees forty years later, it would have felt justified in drawing the same conclusion as the living Cobbett had drawn at Sheffield in 1832. At the beginning of the 'seventies Middlesbrough and the other English centres of manufacture were producing more iron than all the rest of the world put together. And yet in 1891 the United States had outstripped us; in 1904 our production was less than Germany's; and in 1921 it even fell behind that of France.

The truth is, of course, that the enormous and highly specialised prosperity of England during the nineteenth century was a kind of historical accident. Because we went into the business before anyone else, we were enabled to establish and for some time to preserve a virtual monopoly in the production of certain articles – iron and cotton among manufactured goods, coal among the raw materials. Most of what we produced we were able to export, for the simple and all-sufficient reason that we were the only producers.

Today almost every country is a producer. Many are very efficient producers. Having gone into the business later, they are not burdened with the old-fashioned plant and superannuated business methods bequeathed to us from an earlier generation of manufacturers. (Some of our rivals had what has turned out to be the luck to get their industrial provinces devastated during the War, and so were forced to begin again with a clean slate. A little judicious devastation in northern England, coupled with the discharging of some of the more elderly company directors, might have been the salvation of our basic industries.) Moreover, efficient or inefficient, all these new producers are Protectionists and most of them are, by our standards, underpayers of labour. The surprising thing is not that our export trade should have fallen off, but that it should have remained even as flourishing as it is.

It is sufficiently obvious that the historical accident which gave us our immense prosperity during the nineteenth century can never recur. There is no possibility of our becoming once again either the world's coal merchant or the world's manufacturer of iron and cotton goods. Even if the basic industries were protected – and there seems to me the strongest possible case for giving manufacturers and workers a certain security and stability, either by means of tariffs, or else by the establishment of import boards – even if they were assured the home market, they could never recover the preponderant position which they occupied during the nineteenth century. Large numbers of the men who used to be employed in these industries can never be employed in them again. Can they all be absorbed elsewhere? Probably not. The army of unemployed is destined, no doubt, to remain a standing army. Can we pay for the upkeep of this army? And can we reduce its numbers? Yes; but only by the most careful and systematic national planning. The age of happy accidents is over. Little piecemeal improvements and local tinkerings are inadequate to the modern circumstances. Stability and a measure of assured and permanent prosperity can be achieved only by the nation that has an intelligent national purpose.

Russia has an intelligent national purpose. If her Five-Year Plan succeeds – and many competent foreign observers think that it will succeed, if not in five, then in eight, or ten, or even twelve years – Russia will be in a position to convert the whole world to her way of thinking.[1] So long as it demonstrably doesn't pay, communism can make but little appeal. But a time may come when communism will pay and pay better, for the majority of men and women, than capitalism. If the Five-Year Plan succeeds, and if, in the meantime, capitalism has not worked out as good or better plans in the countries where it is still in force, then communism will pay better, for the majority, than capitalism and so must inevitably win the day. Intelligent national planning is dictated by the most rudimentary considerations of self-interest. We must either plan or else go under. Moreover, it is only by planning that we can hope to make England, or any other highly industrialised country, a place in which it will be possible for the majority of men and women to lead anything like the good life.

There are two national plans at present on the English market – Sir Oswald Mosley's and the rather more fully worked-out plan propounded recently by the *Week-End Review*.[2] Whether either of these plans, or indeed any large-scale plan, could be put rapidly into execution by purely constitutional means, I do not know. It seems to me, I must confess, rather doubtful. The War made it sufficiently clear that rapid large-scale action and the traditional constitutional methods are not compatible.

So long as there exists a gulf between what is, by the highest human standards, desirable and what is actually desired by a majority or even a minority of human beings, force has got to be used. We are using it all the time. Many people desire to take cocaine; but it is not desirable that they should do so. We do our best to prevent them from getting what they want and, if they succeed and we catch them, we punish them severely. Nobody desires, I imagine, to pay income tax; but it is desirable that all whose income is over a certain figure should contribute to the

1   The first Five-Year Plan, covering the years 1928–32, was launched by Stalin.
2   For details of Mosley's plan, see the Introduction, p.xviii. 'A National Plan for Great Britain' was published as a sixteen-page Supplement to the *Week-End Review*, iii, 14 February 1931.

expense of running the community. Force is used to extract the contributions. In the present case, a powerful minority, including almost all those now holding political power, may have strong objections to large-scale national planning. But if national planning is, by the highest human standards, desirable, then the actual desires of this minority will have to be overridden and the desirable thing imposed by force. But as this minority at present controls the governmental machine, it follows that the application of force may have to be done unconstitutionally. Which would doubtless be regrettable; but not so regrettable, I think, as the prolongation of the present state of affairs, with the cheerful prospect of economic breakdown, revolution and a final communist triumph.

Nash's Pall Mall Magazine, lxxxvii, May 1931, 16–19, 84.

Sight-Seeing in Alien Englands

Middlesbrough is a characteristic product of the nineteenth century; Billingham, across the river, of the twentieth. In 1919 Billingham was very much what Middlesbrough was in 1800; it hardly existed. Today, thanks to Imperial Chemical Industries' huge factory of synthetic ammonia, sodium and other products, it is a small town, having, I suppose, about the same population as Middlesbrough had in the early 'forties of last century. But whereas Middlesbrough in the early 'forties must already have begun to look decidedly infernal – a typical Victorian hell-city in the bud – Billingham is a place where one wouldn't object to living oneself. ('One', in this case, is the normally prosperous bourgeois – a person who would feel himself outraged if you asked him to live in any of the working-class quarters of Middlesbrough.)

Middlesbrough in 1840; Billingham in 1931. Two small industrial towns, but between them what a world of difference! What are the reasons for this difference? Partly it is that self-interest has become more enlightened than it was. Industrialists have discovered that it pays to treat even workmen as though they were human beings not so enormously different from themselves, and not as mere instruments for the performance of a function. Better conditions make for better work; it is demonstrably profitable to make them better. Again, the proletariat is now powerful. It can protest effectively against a state of things which, in the past, it could only patiently accept. And finally (for motives are almost always mixed, the higher ennobling the lower, and the lower intervening to make slightly suspect those which proclaim themselves the highest) there has been a genuine progress in humanitarian sentiment and practice, a genuine heightening of our awareness of the other man – of his sufferings and his legitimate claims. But this heightened awareness is not enough; it needs as its instruments intelligence and a directing idea. The chaos of nineteenth-century town planning was informed by no idea. Towns were allowed to grow like cancers – shapelessly, indefinitely, with what appalling results London and the lesser cities of industrial England abundantly testify. The Wen, as Cobbett called even the little London of a hundred years ago, the great Wen and all the lesser warts and tumours of the North remain as a hideous disfigurement to the face of England. It will take long years and much expensive surgery to restore this densely populated country to health and beauty.

Meanwhile we can see to it that the wens grow no bigger, and that all further increases of population shall be accommodated in towns rationally designed to promote industrial efficiency and at the same time to guarantee for their inhabitants the decencies of living. This is no place to discuss the theory and practice of modern town planning. Suffice it to say that the consensus of opinion is in favour of Satellite Towns grouped round a larger centre of population and separated from it by a belt of inviolate country, well provided, however, with means of communication. Each Satellite Town would be an industrially independent entity, not a mere dormitory for a population employed elsewhere.

It would also be, up to a point, culturally independent; that is to say, it would have its own theatres, libraries, schools and the like – though of course it would have to rely for higher education and the more expensive and out-of-the-way forms of entertainment on the larger centre of population to which it was a satellite. Cultural independence, even if it be partial, is only possible in towns having a certain minimum population. You cannot enjoy the amenities of city life in a village. On the other hand, it is possible for the inhabitants of a not very large town, to enjoy many of the amenities of country life without sacrificing their urban advantages. It has been calculated that it is in a town of about forty thousand inhabitants that the individual can most easily make the best of both worlds. About forty thousand is, accordingly, the population aimed at by the promoters of the Garden City schemes at Letchworth and Welwyn.

In time, it is to be hoped, the greater part of our industrial population will be distributed in properly planned towns of this kind. But meanwhile the great Wen and all the little wens continue to grow and grow. True, the new tentacles which they throw out are often presentable enough in themselves. Many of the post-war housing estates on the outskirts of our great cities are excellent. Nevertheless, the whole process of modern urban growth remains in most cases fundamentally unorganised, chaotic, cancerous. There are individual houses; there are whole streets and quarters in the rapidly expanding outer suburbs of London, for example, which are excellent. Nevertheless, regarded as members of the great organism of London, these new outer suburbs are monstrous excrescences, wens on the Wen. By increasing the difficulty of entering or leaving the central areas; by intensifying the traffic congestion all round the circumferences, these new growths threaten to make London almost uninhabitable. The problems of urban growth and new industrial development can only be dealt with adequately on a national scale.

As usual, a plan is needed, and, as usual, there is no plan.

There is no general plan, but there are many particular plans – plans almost unbelievably adequate to the matter with which they are meant to deal and worked out in practice to the last detail. Industrially and financially, we are, at our best, thoroughly scientific and rational, full of sense and foresight; politically – and, of all the strange anomalies of civilised life, this is one of the strangest – we are still pre-scientific; very imperfectly rational, without vision or serious thought of the future. Taken in most of its details, the national behaviour is that of a man of sense; but these particular displays of reasonableness are not co-ordinated, so that, regarded as a whole, the national behaviour is almost imbecile.

Billingham is a triumphant embodiment of particular planning. The great ICI factory is one of those ordered universes that exist as anomalous oases of pure logic in the midst of the larger world of planless incoherence.[1] Considered merely as a spectacle, the process of synthesising ammonia from the atmosphere is profoundly impressive. The visitor privileged to go round the works, passes from one marvel to another. Beginning in the boiler-house, where the steam which provides all the necessary power for the factory is raised in furnaces burning pulverised coal, he passes by way of the dynamo house (the various electrolytic processes carried on in other parts of the factory employ large quantities of current) to the building in which the captured air undergoes its first transformation. Huge fans draw it down from the outer space and force it, in alternation with gusts of steam, across the white hot coke of a series of special ovens. The resultant gases, a mixture of hydrogen, nitrogen, carbon dioxide and carbon monoxide, are led away to another building where they begin to be compressed. The work is done by great turbines, and the steam to drive these softly purring monsters is brought at high pressure from the distant boiler-house along the pipe bridges which run in all directions through the factory site. In the first of the enormous church-like structures which house the machines a series of turbo-compressors take the gas up to ten atmospheres. The resultant heat is used to raise steam and the cooled gas hurries on to the next cathedral. Here another set of turbines geared down to drive a piston-and-cylinder compressing machine raises the compression to fifty atmospheres, and the gas emerges into a series of tall steel towers where a stream of

1 In fact, Billingham was the 'most spectacular victim' of the Slump in the ICI empire. 'The decision to invest £20m. there, taken in 1927, collapsed into ruin at the end of 1929 . . . [because] plant had been put up far in excess of any likely demand. ICI, within three years of its foundation, was flung into crisis: crisis so grave that it might have been mortal.' 'The Impact of the Slump 1929–1931' in W. J. Reader, *Imperial Chemical Industries: A History*, vol. ii: 'The First Quarter Century 1926–1952', London: Oxford University Press, 1975, 116–23. As another commentator has remarked, 'Billingham, far from carrying ICI as had been intended, was a burden for the rest of ICI to carry.' Andrew M. Pettigrew, *The Awakening Giant: Continuity and Change in Imperial Chemical Industries*, Oxford: Basil Blackwell, 1975, 123.

cold water absorbs and carries off the carbon dioxide. (The water issuing from these towers under enormous pressure is made to turn a water wheel, which develops about a thousand horse-power, converted by a dynamo into current.) From the towers, the gas goes back to the place it came from, where another set of machines lifts the compression to two hundred and fifty atmospheres – and the temperature, incidentally, to several hundred degrees above boiling point. And now occurs the final transformation. The scene of it is a huge building, even more impressively ecclesiastical than any of the others, church-like by reason of the silence that reigns there, its solitude and the long line of vast steel cylinders receding, like the columns of a Norman cathedral, into a distant twilight. It is within these cylinders that the mystery is finally consummated. Brought into contact with a catalyst, the hot compressed gases suffer a last sea-change. That which, a quarter of a mile away, was air, emerges from the cylinders as ammonia.

Merely as a spectacle, I repeat, the process is wonderfully impressive. But when one remembers what this dramatic picturesqueness symbolises; when one thinks of all the discoveries in pure science that had to be ingeniously applied, of all the technical difficulties patiently overcome; when one tries to calculate the number of accumulated years of thought, the quantity of ability, learning, industry that have gone into the perfecting of this single process, then indeed one must marvel. A factory like Billingham is a vast co-operative work of art, the joint product of many separate creations, the visible manifestation, in a single co-ordinated whole, of countless individual thoughts. Many technicians and industrialists have spoken to me, in tones that suddenly became almost rapturous, of the moments of intense happiness which had come to them while working on their various problems. Looked at aesthetically, a well-organised factory is a work of art – a poem of which the technicians and administrators are the joint authors. For, artistically, Billingham is nearly perfect. In its own kind it is a magnificent poem. After seeing Billingham – a particularly choice specimen of industrial poetry – I had no difficulty in understanding the raptures of engineers and organisers. For if, I said to myself, I can get an extraordinarily intense pleasure from writing, what is, I am afraid, only a moderately good poem, they may be expected to be at least as happy in helping to create a work of art which, in its own line, is obviously of the first order. The delights of creation are always and everywhere the same.

But what of those who don't create; of those who, even though they may have it in them, are never given an opportunity to create? The technicians and the organisers are the artists of industry. But the workman – what is he? Too often, I am afraid, he is simply part of the material with which the artists work, one of the instruments they are compelled to use.

In that terrifyingly unnatural goblin-world of the mine, to be confronted suddenly – after what seems, to the stranger from the upper sunlight, an age of wandering through stifling labyrinths – by the pale glimmer of the naked human body . . . The impression is overwhelming. How movingly beautiful it is, this body of man. How white and smooth and, in the monstrous twilight at the coal-face, under the menace of the low ceilings of sagging rock, how delicate-looking, how defenceless and frail![1]

Defenceless and frail, I thought again, as I watched the men drawing off the molten steel from one of the furnaces of a Sheffield ironworks. The metal spurted in a long thick jet of incandescence and fell splashing into a gigantic bucket. The sparks went up like spray, and in the hellish glare the men went about their business, frail and defenceless and, at the foot of the towering furnace, by the side of the great bucket, how small! Small as children. Fifty yards

1 It is almost certain that Huxley made his first descent of a coal-mine on Thursday 19 February 1931, possibly the Brancepeth 'C' pit at Willington, Charles Wilson's old mine. Huxley went down another mine in March 1936 in the company of Victor Rothschild. This was probably the Moorgreen pit at East-wood, Nottinghamshire. The late Lord Rothschild recalled: 'We went down a coalmine, to the coal face. We must have looked an odd couple as Aldous was tall and gangly whereas I was square, or at any rate thick set at that time.' Letter from Lord Rothschild to David Bradshaw, 12 March 1984.

away a high pressure boiler was being forged out of a single ingot. Completed, it would be one of those seamless steel cylinders, thirty or forty feet long and with walls five inches thick, which we had seen lying in a corner, waiting to be carried to their final destination. In its present state, it was just an enormous sausage-shaped lump of red-hot steel standing on the platform of the hydraulic press, with a mandrel stuck into a hole at its centre. A tiny man turned a handle. Gently and quite noiselessly the press descended on to the red-hot mass. Under its six-thousand-ton pressure, the metal flattened out squelchily, as though it had been mud. The little man made another movement and the press rose, the red-hot ingot was turned so that a fresh surface was exposed to the press and, in silence, very gently, the process began again.

Small, frail and defenceless. And yet it is the body of man that has laboriously created the underworld of the coal-mine; it is the little body of man that has set up those colossal structures which seem to dwarf it into insignificance. The body of man no less than man's mind is responsible for the marvels of our civilisation. In our admiration for the planning mind, let us not forget the body, without whose aid none of the plans could be put into execution.

'Gardening?' an eminent man of letters once said to me. 'Yes, I love gardening. Nothing I enjoy more than looking on while a good gardener gardens.' Personally, I don't much enjoy even that sort of gardening. Watching other people do work that I should hate to do myself – work that I know I should do very badly, if indeed I could do it at all – this makes me feel rather uncomfortable. My feelings when I visit a factory or go down a mine are mixed. Curiosity and a desire to know and understand struggle with a sense of shame. For the work performed by the overwhelming majority of my fellows seems to me so dreary, so utterly boring, that I feel ashamed, in their presence, for my freedom from it; I want to apologise to them for being a man whose labours are not only thoroughly congenial to him, but also much more profitable than the, to his mind, odious and intolerable business of his less fortunate fellows. Intellectually I enjoy the vicarious practice of gardening – or coal-mining, or motor manufacturing, or artificial silk spinning, or whatever it may be; but morally I suffer. I am ashamed of being a tourist from another world, sight-seeing in the alien Englands of manual labour and routine. My only hope is that the inhabitants of these other Englands don't find their countries quite so awful as I find them. It is the traditional consolation of the prosperous and the free. 'Believe me, my dear, they really *don't* feel as intensely as we do.'

Statistics have a way of contradicting one's personal observations, and it is possible that statistics might conclusively prove that these great centres of population on the Tees and the Tyne are surrounded by market gardens. If so, the market gardens escaped my notice. I do not remember to have seen a single cabbage growing in all the neighbourhood. Presumably such vegetables as these meat-loving Northerners consume come from the Continent. This is, no doubt, one of the blessings of unrestricted Free Trade. Still, in fairness to Free Trade, let me add this corollary. Even if home-grown vegetables were protected and a stable price for them assured, I greatly doubt whether an enormous quantity of them would be grown. The best way of producing vegetables is by intensive cultivation on small holdings. Various schemes for getting people on to the land as owners or tenants of small holdings exist. Those already in operation have not been remarkably successful and I suspect that no such scheme is ever likely to be successful in modern England – for the good reason that the proprietor of a small holding has got to work a great deal harder than most Englishmen are now prepared to work. Those who have lived for any length of time among French or Italian peasants know how prodigiously laborious is the life of these small holders. Eight-hour days are unknown. In Provence I have seen the peasants delving by moonlight.

Very large numbers of the younger French peasantry are finding that *la terre est trop basse* – the ground's too low; there's too much painful stooping to be done. They are leaving the country for the movies, the bars, the bigger money wages and, above all, the eight-hour day of the town. In France itself, the home country of peasant proprietorship, land is steadily falling out of cultivation. Can men who have found the ground 'too low' and the country too dull ever be induced to return to the laborious and solitary life of the small holder? It seems extremely unlikely. Urban entertainments and the eight-hour day are invincible attractions. On the great factory farms of Communist Russia, the agricultural labourer can live and work almost in urban conditions. His home is in a large communised village equipped with all the modern conveniences and his job is to tend machines for eight hours a day. The problem is solved – but not completely. For mechanised farming is possible only on certain types of land and only for the production of certain crops. Vines, most vegetables, even certain cereals, such as rice, cannot be cultivated in a wholesale, mechanical fashion. Neither is the machine of much use in hilly country, nor in places where, for one reason or another, the land has been divided up into small fields. In spite of Mr. Ford, the problem of the small holder remains unsolved. We need the products of intensive cultivation, but men will not stay on the land to cultivate intensively. It may one day be found necessary to impose agricultural conscription. Every able-bodied man will perhaps be compelled to do a couple of years' service on the land. Alternatively, we may be gradually driven to do without the products of intensive cultivation. Garden asparagus might easily become extinct, and wine an unheard-of rarity. Meanwhile, however, in France, Italy and other continental countries, enough small holders remain on the land to keep us supplied with all the vegetables and fruit we might grow ourselves, but don't; partly because, at any rate under the present dispensation, it is not profitable to grow them; but chiefly, I believe, because Britons never, never, never will be slaves – and a small holder who cultivates intensively *is* a slave, bound to the earth he owns as closely as was the serf of a thousand years ago to the land of his master.

In Birmingham, I visited a factory of electrical equipment for motor cars.[1] A very efficient, up-to-date factory. In the room where

1   This was probably the magneto assembly plant of Joseph Lucas Ltd., situated at Acock's Green in Birmingham.

the magnetos were assembled, forty or fifty girls were sitting at a long table. In front of them an endless band slowly crawled along, carrying on its surface the constituent parts of an electrical machine. Each girl had her special function – to insert a rod, to tighten so many screws, to make fast certain wires. When the last girl had done her job, yet another magneto was ready to be fitted to yet another car.[1]

Up to five years ago, the manager told me, the assembling of the magnetos was done by skilled workmen. Each man performed the whole process from start to finish. He knew how a magneto worked and what he himself was doing. But in a well-designed factory, to know what you are doing seems to be quite unnecessary – is even rather a hindrance to really efficient labour. The skilled assemblers of magneto parts were too slow, and therefore too expensive. It was found that fifty girls sitting in front of a moving band, and each performing one small and specialised task, which alone she was expected to understand, could turn out finished magnetos much faster than the skilled assemblers who knew what magnetos were. So the skilled workmen went, and the girls came in. Girls, the manager assured me, are much more efficient on this sort of job than men. Greatly to their credit, as I conceive, men get very bored with such fiddling repetitive work, and so do it badly. Girls cost less and do the job better.

'This monotony' (the monotony of work under mass production conditions), 'does not exist as much in the shops as in the minds of theorists and bookish reformers.' So writes Mr. Henry Ford – and being myself one of these theorists and bookish reformers, I am duly abashed.[2] I should be still more abashed if I did not remember

1 This passage compares interestingly with Huxley's description of the work regime in the 'small factory of lighting-sets for helicopters' which the Savage tours in Chapter 11 of Brave New World.

2 The car magnate Henry Ford (1863–1947) gave innumerable interviews and wrote many articles and four books about his revolutionary industrial methods and ideals. His books were My Life and Work (1922); Today and Tomorrow (1926); My Philosophy of Industry (1929) and Moving Forward (1931), but none contains

another passage in Mr. Ford's published writings, where he frankly confesses that he himself would find the ordinary work in one of his own factories absolutely intolerable.[1] Nobody could accuse Mr. Ford of being a theorist or a bookish reformer; so I suspect that this monotony is not so completely a product of the literary imagination as he would like us to believe. For those, at any rate, whose minds are active – whether they are busy with theories or with the problems of practical life – work in a really well-designed modern factory *is* monotonous. Luckily (and here the traditional consolations of the free and prosperous are confirmed by all the findings of daily experience and scientific psychology) luckily there are very many people whose minds are not active. For these, I suppose, the monotony is less intolerable – perhaps hardly even exists.

The machine, say its panegyrists, is a liberator. Low-level routine work, such as the machine demands from its attendants, sets the mind free. (I am assuming that the tempo of the machines is kept reasonably slow. Speeding-up produces a sense of anxiety, which is felt as the exact opposite of mental freedom.) Working at a machine, you do not have to think of what you are doing. Your mind is free. But free to do what? To think, the optimists reply (speaking, if not for the present, at any rate for a rosier future), about the problems of the Universe, the best that has been thought or said, and other matters of the same kind. But you cannot think about the problems of the Universe unless you know what they are, nor about the best that has been thought or said unless you have first read or heard it. And even if you do know, even if you have read and heard, the chances are that these things bore you. Of all the people who have received a long and elaborate education, how many, having

this precise quotation or the one in 'The Victory of Art over Humanity'. Ford expressed many similar views; e. g. 'The robot . . . is merely the creation of a wholly misinformed literary imagination and is really a childish sort of conception . . . the engineer found society immobile and left it mobile. Yet he is now charged by bookish people with wanting to fix the world in a rigid casting'. *Moving Forward*, London: William Heinemann, 1931, 250–51.

1 Huxley has in mind *My Life and Work*, London: William Heinemann, 1922, 103.

done their academic time, continue to bother their heads with the stuff they have been taught? Certainly not a very large proportion. Then what of the people who have been only briefly and perfunctorily educated? A few of them might be interested in intellectual problems if they had been taught to know what the elements of these problems were. But they have not been taught. We can therefore be absolutely certain that the minds of machine-tenders are not occupied with cosmical or cultural matters. How then do they employ their freedom? With long broodings on the theme of their personal relationships? ('What did Bill mean when he said that? Why did Annie go on like that last Tuesday?') With vague daydreams of an impossible prosperity, or more definite anticipations of the evening's leisure or next Saturday night's amusements. With endless calculations of ways and means. And that, to judge from what I have been able to elicit from those who have minded machines, is about all. This mental freedom turns out to have been but a poor gift. One is left wondering whether, after all, the work which keeps the mind occupied is not better, humanly speaking, than the work which leaves it free.

The Victory of Art over Humanity

English motor factories are not quite so completely rationalised as the corresponding thing in America. It is still possible, at Birmingham or Coventry, to see a man step out of the assembling line for a second or two to fetch some necessary tool or part of the machine which is being put together. In Detroit a higher providence brings everything he needs to the workman's hand; he has no excuse ever to stir from his place. Industrial predestination is not yet so absolute in England. Very nearly, however; the difference is only one of degree, not of kind. Regarded as a pure design, as the embodiment of a faultless, logical process, a motor factory is a wonderfully interesting and even beautiful thing. Regarded as a place to work in, it seems, I confess, pretty depressing. Those machine tools ... The thought of having to spend eight hours a day feeding one of those monsters with bits of steel makes me shudder. But let us listen to what Mr. Ford has to say on the subject. 'If the work goes through the tools, it must be right. It will thus be seen that the burden of creation is on management in designing and selecting the material to be produced by the multiple processes utilised in mass production ... The physical load is shifted off men and placed on machines. The recurrent mental load is shifted from men in production to men in designing.'[1]

The implications of the phrase are terrifying. For what does it imply? It implies that one of the best, the most satisfying things in human life — creation — is too much trouble, is a burden of which, if

1 See 'Sight-Seeing in Alien Englands', Note 2, pp. 74–5.

possible, men and women should be relieved. The truth is, of course, that Mr. Ford is making a virtue of necessity. For, inevitably and by their very nature, all labour-saving devices are also, to a greater or less extent, creation-saving devices. That is the tragedy of the machine; it cannot do good without at the same time doing harm. It is the benefactor of labouring humanity inasmuch as it lifts from the shoulders of common men the intolerable load of mere drudgery. But inasmuch as it 'shifts the recurrent mental load from men in production to men in designing', the machine is our enemy; for it deprives the overwhelming majority of men and women of the possibility, the very hope, of even the most modest creative activity.

Our leisures are now as highly mechanised as our labours; the notion that men can recover, as consumers, what they have lost as producers is quite illusory. In the sphere of play no less than in that of work, creation has become the privilege of a fortunate few. The common man has always had to suffer from lack of money; he is now condemned to psychological poverty as well. However much they may desire to do so, most men and women are simply not permitted to create. Consolingly, Mr. Ford assures them that creation is a burden – a burden which, with Christ-like unselfishness, he offers to bear for them. It remains to be seen whether men and women will believe him; whether they will want him as their saviour; whether it is psychologically possible for the human race to adapt itself to the new creation-saving environment which Mr. Ford and his privileged colleagues are now so busily creating.

Not nature, but, in the word's widest sense, art – this is now man's most formidable enemy; not matter, but his own mind. Nature, it is true, still plays us from time to time some frightful trick or other – sends us an epidemic or a flood, strikes when we least expect with iceberg or avalanche, with earthquake, locusts, lightning, drought. And matter, of course, is still unchangeably matter; stubborn, conservative and, in the teeth of the extravagant antinomianism of our day-dreams and our ideals, bottomlessly lawabiding. Nevertheless, it remains true that civilised man has to a very great extent succeeded in domesticating nature, in compelling recalcitrant matter to serve his own purposes. Nothing succeeds like success; but nothing also, on occasion, so surprisingly fails. In place of the old familiar enemies, with whom, since the beginning of things, he has been fighting, and fighting of late with ever more and more success, triumphant man now finds himself faced with new and unfamiliar foes – the products of his own inventive spirit. The moment of his first great victory over the forces of nature has turned out, ironically enough, to be the moment of his first great defeat in a new campaign against an entirely different enemy. The conqueror of nature has been defeated by art – by the very arts which he himself called into being in order to conquer nature. Humanity is at present staggering under the blows received in the course of this disastrous conflict with the organised forces of its own intelligence. Every one of our major troubles at this present supremely uncomfortable moment of history is due, not to nature, not to matter, but to mind and to those arts and sciences which mind has brought into existence.

Why are there armies of unemployed in every industrial country in the world? Because there is over-production. (Not under-consumption, as Mr. [J. M.] Keynes and other economists would have us believe. During the boom, the Americans consumed more per head of population than any human beings have ever done before in the whole history of the world. This did not prevent the arrival of the Slump.) Why is there over-production? Because those arts of invention, by means of which we have conquered nature, are now, in their turn, conquering us. The rate at which the machinery of production is being improved is far more rapid than the rate at which the consuming population grows, or even than the rate at which appetites can be created and stimulated by advertising and salesmanship. Result: too many goods, consequently too low a price, consequently a panic restriction of production, consequently unemployment. And at the same time and all the time, machines are being steadily made more and more efficient. (For once called into existence, the children of man's inventive mind develop on their own account, as though they were separate organisms, existing apart from their creators – apart and often, as we are now discovering, at war with them.) What is the result of these advances in efficiency? Higher production by fewer producers. More unemployed with less money to buy more goods. A combination of over-production and compulsory under-consumption. In the past it was supposed that this 'technological unemployment', due to improvements in the process of manufacture, could always and automatically be cancelled out by the creation of new demands for the now cheaper article. For the same improvements which turn men out of their jobs reduce the cost of what they were making; lower costs encourage greater demand; and greater demand reinstates the unemployed workers – at any rate, until the next industrial revolution. Such is the theory – a theory which, for some time, the facts confirmed. During the nineteenth century technological unemployment was cancelled out by progressively increasing demand. But then, during the nineteenth century, there were few producers and a rapidly increasing population of consumers. There was also, after 1849, plenty of gold, with consequent rising prices, and a virgin market in the Far East. Today there are many producers, using machinery about ten times as efficient as that of the few producers of last century, and a consuming population whose rate of increase has sharply declined. At the same time, gold is scarce and prices have therefore fallen. And the Far East has become, for political and monetary reasons, a very poor customer. The restoration of normal conditions in China and India, and the release of hoarded gold, would obviously help the manufacturers of the West. But there are now so many manufacturers, and they are all (relatively to nineteenth-century standards) so progressively efficient, that there is really no good reason to suppose that, even during a millennium of easy gold and Chinese customers, the technological unemployed can ever be wholly reabsorbed into industry. Victors over nature, we are vanquished by art.

We are vanquished not only in the factories, but also in the fields; vanquished by our own marvellous art of agriculture. Thanks to the engineers, the chemists, the botanists and entomologists, agriculture has become, for the first time in history, reasonably efficient; two blades of wheat grow where only one grew before. Result: every wheat farmer in Europe, Australia and North and South America is now more or less completely bankrupt. Wheat is burned, or thrown into the sea, or given to the pigs and chickens. (The prosperity of English poultry farming is founded on the ruin of Manitoba and Hungary.) Or else it is stored – millions of tons of it – in gigantic elevators, hoarded up in the pathetic hope that somebody may some day offer to buy it at a price that will cover the costs of production. Once more, in the very moment of our triumph over nature, art has been too much for us.

We know the disease and its causes. What of the remedy? Clearly, the remedy must be homoeopathic. The only cure for too much art and too much mind is not more matter and more nature (which would almost instantly destroy our complicated modern world) but more art and more mind. Art, it is true, is now the enemy. But that is only because we have been artful, so to speak, in patches, never artful all along the line. Man has used his mind to create a thousand separate arts, which are compelled by the very laws of their being to grow and proliferate like living things, independently of their creators. These separate arts require co-ordination; in the interests of all of us, their often monstrous and disproportionate growth must be curbed and regulated. But the art of regulating and co-ordinating remains to be invented. Only the half-formed seeds and rudiments of it exist at present. Its creation will have to be the joint labour of many different classes of men – of politicians co-operating with industrialists and men of science, with financiers and economists and manual workers; the joint labour, I repeat, of many different classes of men, belonging, if possible, to every nationality. For the art of co-ordinating the arts will be only very partially effective if it is not practised by all the principal nations of the world, acting in concert. There must be a world-wide adjustment of production to consumption, world-wide agreements about the establishment of new industries and the use of new inventions in old ones, a world policy for gold, for fuel, for agriculture – in a word, a general agreement to make some universally valid sense out of our babel of separate and private achievements. International agreement on any important issue is hard to reach. Impossible, a pessimist might have said a year or two ago. But necessity makes strange bedfellows. To take but one example, the collapse of wheat prices has already brought such inveterate enemies as Hungary and Romania into conference and a measure of agreement. As I write, Mr. Macdonald's country house party at Chequers is still in the future.[1] It remains to be seen whether anything will come of it, or whether it will end as so many hopeful international and inter-imperial confabulations have ended in mere expressions of a vague friendliness and the formulation of good resolutions which none of the governments represented is able to carry out. It was thus, to take a recent example, that the agricultural conference held in Paris at the end of February depressingly concluded. Delegates from the Central and Eastern European wheat belt met delegates from the industrial countries of the West. Both parties were in a very bad way; why not strike a mutually profitable bargain – so much wheat in exchange for so many manufactured articles? With an appalling lucidity, Mr. Poncet, the president of the conference, explained why this simple and sensible solution of the problem was not possible. 'Most of the states represented at the conference,' he said, 'are countries in which the grain trade is free. The state, the government, is not a corn merchant and the delegates attending the conference are wholly without power to engage themselves as purchasers of such and such quantities or qualities of grain, at such and such a price, because it is not the habit of governments to proceed in this way.'

It is not the habit of governments to proceed in this way.

The heart of the matter is there. All the governments of the world are dear old gentlemen who live by their habits – habits which were

1 Presumably, Huxley was alluding to the forthcoming International Conference of Ministers on the German Financial Situation which took place in London on 20 July 1931. The main item on their agenda was President Hoover's suggestion that there should be a moratorium on German reparation repayments.

formed and fixed, for the most part, between 1830 and 1870: dilatory habits of parliamentarism; habits, in matters of political economy, of *laissez-faire*; habits of nationalism; tortuous and mendacious habits of Metternichian diplomacy;[1] quaintly mediaeval habits of going about armed to the teeth. Dear old gentlemen should never be upset. Their habits are sacred and must be respected – even when it is manifestly obvious that these habits are a danger to civilisation. Only by rejuvenating the dear old gents and breaking them of their century-old habits – only by bringing existing institutions up to date and empowering governments to deal adequately and promptly with the problems of a civilisation at war with its own arts – can we hope to come clear out of our troubles. The art of co-ordinating the separate arts has got to be first invented, then imposed by some strong and intelligent central authority. Yes, imposed. For, as usual, the desirable is not the same as that which is in practice desired – at any rate by an important section of the population. Governments are not the only dear old gentlemen with bad habits who afflict our modern world. Industry, commerce, finance, agriculture – there is a dear old gent in every cupboard. And even when these separate arts are young and active, there still remains an aspect of them which is old and hide-bound by habits inherited from the nineteenth-century individualists. This old man embedded in almost all our youths is in process of dying. But he dies too slowly. The difficult times demand his prompt assassination. There is no one who can kill him except a rejuvenated government, equipped with the necessary institutional weapons, and capable of acting swiftly and with a well-informed and intelligent ruthlessness.

*

1   Klemens Wenzel Nepomuk Lothar Metternich-Winneburg, later Prince von Metternich (1773–1859), Austrian statesman and Minister of Foreign Affairs, 1809–48. As the nineteenth century unfolded, Metternich became synonymous with reaction and repression.

Among the rhinoceros horns and the ivory lay some twenty or thirty enormous tusks, strangely curved and as brown as the teeth of an inveterate smoker. It was not tobacco, however, that had stained them thus; it was five or ten thousand years of cold storage in a frozen tundra. For these were mammoth tusks. Caught by the last ice age or some more recent catastrophic change in their environment, the hairy old jumbos of the North have left their bones and ivory all over Siberia. Their tusks are dug up at the rate of at least a hundred pairs a year. A fair proportion of the fossil ivory finds its way to this particular warehouse in St. Katharine Dock. From a distance at least as far in years as in miles it comes to the London of 1931.

Wholesale prices are low this year, and the time-stained teeth of *Elephas primigenius* are not commercially so valuable as the tusks of his surviving relatives in Africa. With luck you can pick up a hundredweight of fossil ivory for seventy or eighty pounds.

Outside, the sun was shining; the pale sky was tenderly blue and blurred – gauzy with that faint mist of watery smoke which makes every distant object in a London view seem so heartbreakingly remote, which gives such richness to the colours, such a fruity bloom to the lights, such velvety darkness to the shadows; that mist, in a word, which makes of London the most beautiful city, in its own pensive and profoundly melancholy way, of the whole world. The century-old warehouses of St. Katharine Dock are vast and rather splendid buildings. Porticoes of cast-iron Doric columns sustain their bulk; the grimed brick walls rise black and blank and precipitous into the sky and are darkly reflected in the water at their feet. English architecture has often suffered from a certain smallness of scale, a fiddliness, a petty, hole-and-cornery preoccupation with detail. Round about St. Katharine Dock the scale is Egyptian, the naked simplicity that of a mediaeval stronghold.

From ivory we passed, through spices, to wool – tens of thousands of cubic yards of wool; then to an enormous cathedral full of rubber and from there, underground, into the cathedral crypt – seven acres of Norman vaulting upheld by a symmetrical forest of columns. Faint gas jets burned, point after luminous point in long recession down the black aisles. A rich rank perfume haunted the darkness. Raising our torches, we saw that the vaults were festooned with a sooty lace-work of fungi. Innumerable casks lay dozing, as it seemed, between the pillars, their bulging forms rich with a kind of mellow and sleepy sensuality. We were in one of London's wine cellars.

Four miles further down the river, the Royal Albert Dock can accommodate ships of twenty thousand tons. Big liners from South America and the Far East tie up at its quays; the largest of modern cargo boats can come and go with ease. Our sight-seeing here began with meat. In a refrigerator about as big as Westminster Abbey two hundred and fifty thousand carcases were waiting to be devoured. From the top floor, where the meat arrives on an escalator from the unloading ships, we descended by lift into the cold store. In a dim electric twilight (for the cork-lined walls of the store are wholly windowless) we walked in fifteen degrees of frost through an interminable morgue of sheep and oxen. A few muffled workmen came and went with their loads of mutton and beef. There was silence and, in spite of the cold, a faint persistent smell of butchery. I was glad to get out again; profoundly thankful, too, that I could earn my living otherwise than by lugging corpses about in arctic cold and darkness.

The work in the tobacco warehouse a little further up the quay seemed delightful in comparison. At any rate, the smell there was agreeable and the temperature normally English, not Siberian. How many thousand tons of potential smoke were stored in that warehouse? I have forgotten. All I know is that the figures seemed fabulous, larger than life. Yes, larger than life. The world of the Docks is Gargantuan. It would take a Rabelais to describe that fantastic profusion of eatables, drinkables, smokables, wearables and miscellaneous usables assembled from every corner of the earth along this short stretch of tidal river. A Rabelais to describe and, more important, a whole committee of Napoleons to organise their profitable exchange in the permanent interest of consuming and producing humanity. For, at the moment, this Gargantuan pro-fusion at the Docks is the symbol and symptom of world-wide poverty. Wool is piled up in mountains – and Australia is bankrupt. There are cathedrals full of rubber – and the Malayan plantations cannot pay their way. Everywhere the same disease. And the remedy? Some sort of world-wide plan to co-ordinate the separate plans whose mutual incompatibility is the cause of the present confusion. The Docks of London are the best possible advertise-ment for planning. Themselves, not so long ago a flagrant example of planlessness, they have become, under the co-ordinating Port of London Authority, efficient and progressive. It remains for some larger equivalent of the Port of London Authority to deal with the larger chaos of world trade.

Looking down from the roof of the tobacco building over the wide expanse of water, with the great ships tied up at the quays, the warehouses, the cold stores, the silos and, beyond them, to the smoking factory chimneys and all those mud-coloured miles and miles of London, I was suddenly appalled. For any bird's-eye view of man's incessant and ant-like activity *is* rather appalling. All this carting of bits of matter about from one point on the world's surface to another point – don't we overdo it a little? Couldn't we take things a bit more buddhistically, try what it would be like to sit still for a change? When I am on a height or by the sea, my *welt-anschauung* is always apt to turn rather quietistic. But the wind was uncommonly cold; I was driven down again into the aromatic warmth of the warehouse. My quietism evaporated; I hurried on to look at the silos . . . .

---

1   Partly reprinted as 'Pigmalion contra Galatea', *Sur* [Buenos Aires], no. 3, Winter 1931, 85–93.

Greater and Lesser London

Early this spring I attended, for the first time in my life, a parliamentary debate. From the newspapers at next morning's breakfast I learned, somewhat to my surprise, that I had had the luck to be in at an historic occasion. (The historicalness consisted, apparently, in the fact that Mr. Snowden had told the House what every man and woman not mentally deficient must have known for at least a year previously – that the public finances of Great Britain were in a bad way.)[1]

Historic! The papers were full of the rich reverberating word. Over my toast and marmalade I was left uncomfortably wondering what on earth the unhistoric debates could be like.

There is a kind of weariness of the spirit, to which I privately give the name of Septic Boredom. It comes upon me whenever some unlucky chance, *force majeure* or the conventions compel me to be present, for a long time and without the possibility of protesting, at some particularly flagrant manifestation of imbecility. The symptoms of the disease are horrible. A desire to scream, to burst into laughter, or tears, or both together, to rush out of the room shouting curses and obscenities, becomes almost irresistible. One is conscious of it as of a demoniac possession, against which one has to struggle with all the strength of the will. The struggle is exhausting;

---

[1] From his seat in the Strangers' Gallery of the House of Commons, Huxley observed a crucial debate on the national economy on 11 February 1931. Philip Snowden was the Chancellor of the Exchequer in Ramsay MacDonald's second Labour Cabinet, June 1929–August 1931.

but time inexorably prolongs itself, the display of imbecility goes on and on and on; one is filled with a hopeless misery. A sickening discomfort preys upon the vitals. Little by little this discomfort spreads all over the body. The blood seems to be thickening and clotting in one's veins; it is as though one had been bitten by a cobra. Another hour, one says to oneself, and the pulsing stream of life will have gone quite solid, like so much calves' foot jelly. Which will be the end. Waves of self-pity pass over one; but a much larger wave rolls majestically in from the plumbless ocean of imbecility upon whose shore one stands. The little waves of self-pity are swallowed by this greater wave; the end, one decides, will be a blessed relief. If only the blood would cake a little faster!

Four hours in the Strangers' Gallery had brought me to this suicidal stage of Septic Boredom, when a visitant from heaven, a friendly angel, it seemed, appeared at the door and beckoned me out of the torture chamber – out and away, down the more-than-medievally winding staircases of Barry's astounding palace, through the neo-Gothic splendours of its echoing halls, along immense subterranean corridors into – oh, blessed vision! – a glittering dining-room. The clotted blood began to melt; by the time I had finished my soup it was coursing once more quite normally through my veins.

Time has blunted the point and smoothed the jagged edges of that agonising experience. I can look back on it now with equanimity, can make it a subject of dispassionate comment. To begin with, what in heaven's name, in an age of cheap and rapid printing, are we doing with this mediaeval council chamber, where men waste interminable hours very slowly and hesitatingly bawling out aloud things which could be expressed much more completely and, at the same time, much more succinctly, in writing? When the oratory is bad, the hearers are bored – septically bored to the very brink of suicide. When the oratory is good, they find themselves agreeing with the speaker, not for the intrinsic soundness of his arguments, but simply because he happens to have a fine tenor voice and the talents of an actor. Two consummations equally not-to-be-desired. If the general ideas and the particular suggestions of members could be circulated in writing, neither of these undesirable things would happen. Readers would not suffer boredom; a few seconds would suffice them to skim through the imbecilities, which it would take a speaker at least half an hour to get off his chest. They would also run no risk of being swept off their feet by accomplished vocalists and comedians. In a word, they would be in a position (but for the party loyalties, of course) to judge each individual proposal on its merits. Which isn't such a bad idea, when you come to think of it. And then, what a saving of time, temper, energy! What an enormous increase in efficiency!

Meanwhile, however, in the appropriately Gothic hall of the Mother of Parliaments, the old anachronistic bawling continues to reverberate – just as it still reverberates in the lecture rooms of our universities. When the first universities were founded books were worth their weight in silver; the professor had to dictate to his students the substance of works, which they could not possibly afford to buy. Now, in most cases, he merely dictates a chapter from an easily obtainable textbook. Four out of five lectures are now perfectly unnecessary. When I was at Oxford, I never attended more than two lectures a week; I was an industrious young man and didn't want to waste my time. I am still moderately industrious, still have a puritanical objection to fooling around when I might be doing something sensible. Hence my sufferings in the Strangers' Gallery. I have more important things to do than to listen to old or middle-aged gentlemen repeating very, very slowly and with an immense amount of humming and hawing, the less interesting (because more vague and rhetorical) passages in the leading articles of *The Times*, the *Morning Post*, the *Express* or the *Daily Herald*. On the day I was in the House it took four hours for about fifteen of these gentlemen to recite their painfully learned saying-lessons. There were dozens more eager and panting to fire off their bit. The debate must have continued for at least four more hours after my departure. Eight hours, of which, at the most moderate computation, seven were completely and irrevocably wasted.

Even the speech which was supposed to have made the debate so historic was mostly a waste of time. True, one is not bored when Mr. Snowden opens his mouth. He is an admirable speaker and can put more barbs and bitterness into what he says than any man I have ever listened to. As a performance, his speech was superb. It began with twenty minutes of bull baiting. The skill with which he planted his banderillos was masterly. By the time he had done with it, the Conservative bull (or is it, alas, only a very corpulent ox?) looked like a pin-cushion. It was all very amusing, no doubt; but where the interests of England came in – that, I confess, was rather hard to see. The exchange of virulent abuse between the two sides of the House reminded me of my earliest schooldays. 'Hillside', where I received the rudiments of culture, was in a state of deadly and chronic rivalry with 'Branksome', a mile away in the valley. The things we children said to and of one another! The blows we would have exchanged if our masters had not been there to prevent us! Only little boys, I thought, could behave in quite so silly a fashion. But I was mistaken. I had never been to the House of Commons. Prep-school scolding-matches are apparently in the great parliamentary tradition. It is high time, then, that the tradition was altered.

As for the rest of Mr. Snowden's speech – it certainly held the listener's attention. The Chancellor is a virtuoso of the vocal chords. But it contained no information of which any reader of a serious newspaper could possibly be ignorant. Nor was there any hint in it of any suggestion for improving the financial position which it painted in such realistically gloomy colours. The terms of the debate did not permit of any such suggestions being made. Questions of general policy were barred by the rules of the game; the subject of the debate was economy. But economy, in the present circumstances, cannot be discussed apart from general policy. Essentially, this historic debate was just a performance of *Hamlet* without the Prince of Denmark. This fascinating drama had been preceded (I was almost forgetting the fact) by a quite deliciously farcical little curtain-raiser about bone-setters. Should osteopaths have degrees, or should they not have degrees? The question was still being busily debated when I took my seat in the Gallery; *Hamlet* minus Hamlet was not booked to begin till half-past three. Now I have the highest admiration for accomplished bone-setters, I sympathise with them in their misfortunes; but all the same it does seem to me that, in a moment of grave national crisis, the parliament of England has something more urgently important to do than to argue about the rights of bone-setters to call themselves Doctors, or Licentiates, or whatever the coveted title may be. Just as it has something more urgently important to do than to talk for eight hours about public finance apart from the general policy which decrees how money shall be raised and spent. Fiddling while Rome burns is bad enough; but twaddling, it seems to me, is even worse. So long as parliamentary procedure remains what it is, twaddling is unavoidable, prompt and comprehensive action all but impossible. Some such reforms in procedure as those suggested by Sir Oswald Mosley are obviously essential. And no doubt reforms will be made – but, as usual, much too late and not in their desirable entirety.

Sixty-five is the age at which Old Age Pensions are granted, the age at which the employees in most public services and many private businesses are compulsorily retired. After sixty-five subordinate workers are supposed to be too old to be fully efficient; in their own and the public interest they are pensioned off. Now, if it is desirable that subordinates should be retired at sixty-five, it is obviously still more desirable that those who command the subordinates should also be retired. The greater a man's responsibility, the greater the mischief he can do by failing to be efficient. And yet – fantastic and dangerous paradox – we find that the heads of great businesses and the politicians who hold the fate of the country in their hands have no retiring age. I heard recently of the board of directors of an important colliery company. The chairman of this board was eighty-seven; the youngest member, a chicken of seventy-four. Certain English mines are said to be rather old-fashioned in their equipment and management. One is not particularly surprised. Our social system permits the political and economic rulers of the country to ripen, or to moulder, into Grand Old Men. Now Grand Old Men are almost always very picturesque and often, for their age, extraordinarily active, both in mind and body. Still they cannot, since the laws of physiology are inexorable, be so active as even quite un-grand young men. Nor, in the nature of things, is it possible for them to be so intimately aware of the contemporary world as those who have grown up in it. In a period when the present was in all fundamentals very like the past, an aged statesman could not go far wrong and might go very right. The problems he was called upon to solve at eighty were, in their essence, the same as those he had solved at thirty. Habit makes perfect, and he might be expected to do his job better than a less experienced young man. But what of an age, whose present is not at all like its past, and whose future promises to be quite unlike its present? In such an age – and our own is such an age – experience dating from even the relatively recent past, through which an old man has lived, will not only be useless, but actually harmful. What is the use of knowing how things were done in the good old days, when the bad new days have come along and made complete nonsense of your knowledge?

Economically, the good old days were genuinely and objectively good; the bad new days are genuinely bad. Forty years ago the country was prosperous; today it is not prosperous. What more natural than that there should be a tendency among the old to believe in the practices and policies which, in their youth, led to prosperity? What worked then, they argue, must work now. But circumstances have changed. Methods which once made the country rich now make it poor. Young men no older than the new circumstances, and with no prejudices in favour of the old methods, are in a much better position to deal with contemporary problems than older men, to whom the old methods are sacred and the new circumstances alien. Under the present system politicians think they have a divine right to the apotheosis of Grand Old Manhood. Suppose (what is, alas! extremely improbable) that they were to abandon this claim and retire, like any other public servants, at the age of sixty-five. How would this self-denying ordinance affect the existing political world?

Mr. Snowden, Mr. Henderson, Mr. Lansbury would have ceased quite a long time ago to adorn the Government front bench. The Prime Minister would be due for his pension in the autumn of the present year; Mr. Baldwin, some ten months later. Sir Austen Chamberlain would already have retired into private life; so would Lord Brentford.[1] In a word, we should, at one stroke, lose the flower of both Houses of Parliament. Britannia would drop a tear; but I fancy she would also heave a pretty deep sigh of relief.

From a backyard some little way south of the Commercial Road you go up a few steps into a small room of peculiar and rather sinister aspect. The walls are bare, the floor tiled and guttered. There is no furniture; but three or four curious structures of cement stand table-high against the walls. Each of these monolithic counters is pierced by a row of large round holes that lead down, funnel-wise, into a kind of metal drawer, let into the base of the structure. Ovens? you speculate, as you enter the room; washeries? An insipid, yet horribly sickening, smell returns an immediate negative to these suggestions. What then? My companion answered my question by pulling open one of the metal drawers at the base of the nearest block of masonry. It was an inch or two deep in blood.

'But flesh with the life thereon, which is the blood thereof, shall ye not eat', and again, 'Only be sure that thou eat not the blood; for the blood is the life and thou mayest not eat the life with the flesh. Thou shalt not eat it; thou shalt pour it upon the earth as water.' The Mosaic law still runs in Whitechapel and Jews are very partial to poultry. This queer little room off the Commercial Road was a

1 Arthur Henderson was Foreign Secretary in MacDonald's second Cabinet and George Lansbury was Minister of Works. Stanley Baldwin was the Conservative Leader of the Opposition; Austen Chamberlain had been Foreign Secretary during Baldwin's second Cabinet (1924–9), and Sir William Joynson-Hicks, universally known as 'Jix', had been Baldwin's Home Secretary in the same government.

place for the ritual slaughter of chickens. Business, I am happy to say, was not in progress while I was doing my tour of inspection. I had to rely on my companion's description of how the rite was performed. 'We hold the birds like this,' he said. 'We slit their throats, we let the blood from the artery squirt into these holes. On Thursdays the slaughtering goes on all night – in preparation for the Sabbath. These drawers are almost full by the time the morning comes. On Thursday night,' my young friend concluded, 'I come here to help my father. He's in the poultry business.'

We left the little slaughter house and walked slowly back towards the river, talking as we went of modern literature. My young Jewish friend was a communist, and did not forget the fact even when he was discussing books. For example, he judged D. H. Lawrence by the standards of Marxism and found him wanting.

The wood and the trees. Who sees the one finds it hard to realise the existence of the others. 'Poultry-farming is doing well.' That is the wood. Among the trees of that wood are to be numbered the Jewish slaughter house off the Commercial Road and my highly cultured and intelligent young friend's Thursday nights among the blood and excrement.

We had tea in the upper room of a little house in a street of rag merchants, near the St. Katharine Dock. (Rather a melancholy street these days; for rags that used to be worth fourpence a pound will only fetch a farthing now.) My hostess and her sister played Bach Preludes on the piano and sang one or two songs of Schubert. If I had been born and lived my life in this street of rags behind the Docks, should I be playing Bach, I wondered, should I even have heard of Schubert? I felt uncomfortably doubtful. The conquest of poverty demands an extraordinary strength and vitality, a consuming passion for higher things. Most probably, I told myself, I should have succumbed.

On the way back to the Underground I saw a group of male prostitutes, powdered and with scarlet lips, standing round the door of a cheap lodging house.

Moses and poultry; blood, blood poured upon the ground as

water, and modern literature; *Du bist die Ruh*,[1] and rags, and Thursday nights in the slaughter house, and the toccata and fugue in D minor; Karl Marx, and D. H. Lawrence, and plenty of cheap wheat for fattening up the chickens; twenty million bankrupt farmers, and boys with powdered faces, like white masks in the darkness, and blood, blood – 'for the blood is the life; and thou mayest not eat the life with the flesh.'

'Golly!' I said to myself, as I sat in the train travelling westward towards the other London. 'It's a strange world.' And I was proposing to spend the rest of the evening in Bloomsbury – not merely geographically, but also culturally in Bloomsbury. 'Golly!' I said again.

Nash's Pall Mall Magazine, lxxxviii, October 1931, 48–9, 108

---

1 Perhaps the most celebrated of Franz Schubert's Rückert songs (D776), composed in 1823.

A Discussion between Gerald Heard and Aldous Huxley[1]

GERALD HEARD: Well, that was a depressing news bulletin.[2]

ALDOUS HUXLEY: Yes, it looks as though conciliation was over for the time being, and yet I don't see how we are going to settle anything, at this time of day, simply by force.

GH: But force *has* settled things in the past, when argument failed. I know that the Liberals say, 'Force is no remedy'. I am not saying whether it is right or wrong. I am only saying that it can sometimes make a settlement.

AH: I know about all that. People used to say that the blood of the martyrs is the seed of the church. But it is not really true. If you persecute ruthlessly enough you can destroy anything. Look how

1 Huxley first met the scientific journalist and broadcaster Gerald Heard (1889–1971) in 1929. A figure of considerable stature in the 1930s, Heard published a series of influential books: *The Ascent of Humanity* (1929), *The Social Substance of Religion* (1931) and *The Source of Civilization* (1935). He had an exotic taste in clothes, 'was reputed to read two thousand books a year and had an extraordinary flow of information about hygiene, sex, para-normal phenomena and the probable destiny of mankind ... Strangers thought of him, nervously, as a sort of Wellsian supermind or a "man of the future".' P. N. Furbank, *E. M. Forster: A Life*, vol. ii: 'Polycrates' Ring (1914–1970)', London: Secker & Warburg, 1978, 136.

2 Earlier that evening, Brüning, the German Chancellor and Foreign Minister, had issued the following statement in advance of the Reparation and Debt Conference which was to be held at Lausanne at the end of January: 'It is clear that Germany's situation renders it impossible for her to continue political payments. It is equally clear that any attempt to maintain the system of such political payments is bound to lead to trouble not only for Germany but for the whole world.' *The Times*, 11 January 1932, 12.

the Inquisition wiped out Protestantism in Spain.

GH: Then why shouldn't force work today?

AH: Well, in the first place I do not think we are quite so sure of ourselves as the mediaeval Catholics were. We do not believe quite so passionately in the righteousness of our side and the depravity of the other side.

GH: Only eighty years ago we were. I remember meeting Lord Roberts; you could not have imagined a more charming old gentleman; but do you know his letters which he wrote from India as a lieutenant when the Mutiny was being put down, about the way the forces of law and order were re-establishing respect for the Raj? They read like bits out of the Book of Joshua. He did not doubt the rightness of hewing the enemy in pieces.[1]

AH: Well, eighty years is a long time nowadays – a longer time than in the past. Changes take place so quickly. What used to be a year's happenings get telescoped into a month. There has been an immense alteration in the feelings of educated people since the Mutiny. We are not nearly so certain of ourselves.

GH: But some people are still certain of themselves. There are still some people in the world who are afraid to use as much force as possible. Communists and Fascists do not mind using *any* means to make their side win; and it seems, where they have been able to do so, they do win.

AH: Yes, but I do not think it is quite as simple as that. National characteristics come in. We are a people who do not like cruelty. Some races seem to be cruel by nature. The Chinese, for example – even their greatest admirers have to admit they are cruel. And you cannot say that Neapolitans treat animals very well. And, of course, the Russians are much tougher than we are. I heard an amusing story the other day of a Russian who was asked what he thought the

1 Field-Marshal Frederick Sleigh Roberts, first Earl Roberts (1832–1914), was serving with the Bengal Horse Artillery at Peshawar on the North-West Frontier when the Indian Mutiny broke out in May 1857. His letters from this period were published in 1924.

greatest difference between Russia and England was. He said that it lay in the way people treated cats. 'You English,' he said, 'when you see a cat walking in the street, you just let it walk on. In Russia when we see a cat, we simply *have* to go and give it a kick.'

GH: I suppose *we* used to kick them a hundred years ago. That tenderness towards animals is quite a recent thing, isn't it?

AH: Yes. You remember Hogarth's picture of children torturing their animals?[1] It's blood-curdling. And then those cats the furriers used regularly to skin alive because the skin came off more easily when the animal was still living. They threw the flayed animals out into the street still writhing. It was those writhing cats that finally drove Richard Martin to found the R.S.P.C.A. and introduce his first anti-cruelty bill in Parliament. And Peel opposed it, Canning opposed it – many of the most intelligent and eminent men of the day, in fact. All the humanitarians have been voices crying in the wilderness. Take the anti-slavery people: they had public opinion against them for a long time, and it is not more than a hundred years ago that they began to win over general support. It was the same with the prison reformers. And public executions were as popular as cup-finals – up to the very end. Even to-day, when Capital Punishment has been proved to have nothing to do with the prevention of murder, most people are quite willing to let hanging go on; only a tiny body says it must stop. But it is extraordinary what a few people can do if they are sufficiently enthusiastic and determined. All the work against cruelty has been done by isolated individuals or little groups. So far as one can see, the great mass of the people would have been content to go on with the traditional horrors.

GH: So you think that our shrinking from using violence may be due mainly to the squeamishness of the educated? Their education not only makes them doubt their own cause and see the other side; it also makes them feel for the other side. You think the main mass of us would be just as cruel as ever if we were only given the chance?

---

1 Huxley is referring to 'The First Stage of Cruelty', an etching Hogarth made in 1751.

AH: That is a very difficult question to answer. There's that point I mentioned a moment ago, about the English being by nature on the whole less cruel than many other races. But certainly I believe that most of our humanitarianism nowadays is due to the fact that we live in surroundings where cruelty is misplaced and inappropriate. We've made it inappropriate partly by legislation and partly by propaganda. The law now doesn't allow things like public executions and the torture of animals.

GH: But what if there is war? What if there is a revolution? What if there's a general uprising of a subject people as there might be in India?

AH: Ah, well, the moment you change the surroundings, so that cruelty becomes lawful and appropriate – why, then, of course, people start being cruel again, automatically. Think of the French Revolution; think of the Paris Commune, only sixty years ago – the incredible ferocity of the middle classes against the workers! Or if you want something nearer, think of the War. The mildest people did ferocious things then – things they simply couldn't have conceived themselves doing before. Things, what's more, they have never dreamed of doing since. For the moment they got out of the war environment into the peace environment they began behaving in their old humanitarian way – the way they had learnt was appropriate to peaceful conditions. It is really a matter of convention. It's 'not done' to be cruel at home; but it *is* done to be cruel on a battlefield. Just as it's not done to burn white men alive in America; but it *is* done to burn negroes. People can be humane in patches, so to speak – chivalrous to noblemen and ruthless to commoners, like the Black Prince: kind to the rich and harsh to the poor, like nineteenth-century mill-owners. It depends on the prevailing habits of thought and feeling. The alarming thing is that these habits can be changed so easily and quickly.

GH: Yes: it didn't take most men more than a few weeks to adapt themselves to life at the Front.

AH: Quite so. They seem to have got used to the slaughter and the sight of suffering, just as they got used to the bad smells. And when you come to think of it, the two kinds of sensitiveness are rather similar: our physical revulsion from cruelty is very like our physical revulsion from dirt and stink.

GH: That's what Dean Inge is always saying: it's just a matter of squeamishness.[1]

AH: Squeamishness? That's merely a word. Why is a man different from a monkey? Because he's more squeamish. All civilisation is just an increase of squeamishness, if you like to put it like that, and barbarism is a decrease of squeamishness. Habit makes it possible for us to conquer squeamishness. Our ancestors lived permanently in the midst of dirt and stink. They didn't notice these things any more than they noticed the prevailing cruelties. We live in a clean and humane world – at least this corner of it is fairly clean and humane. Result: we're startled by filth, or cruelty; they shock us.

GH: But what I want to get clear in my mind is, can we get on without a certain amount of what I suppose Lord Roberts would have called necessary cruelty? In India, for example, if we don't use the amount of violence, say, that was used by General Dyer at Amritsar, must we clear out?[2]

AH: There's no doubt that men in the past thought that much more violence was needed if public peace was to be preserved. We English have been pioneers in seeing how little violence we can use. For instance, England was the only country in the Middle Ages that did without the use of judicial torture.

GH: Now it's one of the only ones that *does* use torture. We still sentence criminals to be flogged. And what's more, many judges

1 William Ralph Inge (1860–1954), Dean of St Paul's 1911–34, and nicknamed 'The Gloomy Dean' on account of his pessimistic, anti-democratic outpourings in the *Evening Standard* 1921–46.

2 Brigadier-General R. E. H. Dyer (1864–1927). Following an outbreak of violent disorder, in which five Englishmen were killed, Dyer ordered his troops to fire into a large and unruly crowd at Amritsar in the Punjab on 13 April 1919. 379 persons are known to have been killed. Subsequently Dyer issued further orders designed to terrorize and humiliate the native population. After the report of a committee of enquiry, Dyer was forced to resign his commission in March 1920.

and one eminent Recorder have said that without the use of this torture we peaceful citizens wouldn't be safe.

AH: I believe that is all nonsense; it is what is called a rationalisation, a false reason given to cover the real reason. The real reason here is that anger or fear or disgust makes us violent. When we are in a passion we are not averse to torture. We like inflicting pain. But we feel we ought not to like it – so we invent justifications for liking it.

GH: Certainly we have relaxed our punishments in every other direction. But some people think that this is simply sentimentality, and certainly the number of crimes is not decreasing.

AH: But that is because the number of laws is increasing: the more laws the more offences. Moral: have fewer laws.

GH: Still, with public opinion as it is, I sometimes wonder if we shall not have a return to strong and even violent government! Liberalism banked on people responding to trust. But they did not respond as quickly as people had hoped. Today Liberalism is mocked both by the extreme Right and the extreme Left. Liberalism is like Free Trade: it is the best policy, but only if the other side plays the game.

AH: But how do you imagine the strong Government would begin here? I do not see much sign of the force of humanitarianism getting any less. Probably that is why Fascism and Communism make so little headway in this country.

GH: They would very soon make headway if there was another war, or a revolution, or an economic collapse. And what about India? If bad things are done there, English blood may get up.

AH: I do not think that is quite as simple as you seem to fancy. There is another factor that you have left out in this problem of force in India – world public opinion. That is an even newer thing than humanitarianism, but quite as powerful. In every international quarrel nowadays there is a number of onlookers – people not heated by the quarrel and able to give a pretty cool estimate of the rights and wrongs. Japan and China know that, and so does India. Indians are banking on world opinion being on their side.

GH: Propaganda makes it easy for people to throw all the blame on their rulers. In fact, it makes it uncommonly difficult to govern at all. No wonder the Press is not allowed freedom in Italy and Russia. They will not stand this propaganda nonsense.

AH: On the contrary, it is just because Italy and Russia understand the force of propaganda that they make it a State monopoly. In fact, it has become just as important as an army or a navy. I believe myself it is the future substitute for force. If you use it rightly, you do not need to use force. Propaganda can make it psychologically impossible for people to disobey you.

GH: Then you think that force is out of date?

AH: It will be out of date the moment our rulers are educated enough to apply the results of modern psychology to their business of governing. The trouble with politicians is that they are always fifty years behind the times. The technique of mass suggestion exists; but they do not use it. They are the helpless victims of propaganda, not the masters of it. News flies round the world with the speed of lightning and as often as not it is unfavourable to the rulers.

GH: But surely world opinion is a growing force. And surely it must be on the side of law and order? France and Holland and Belgium all have large native populations to control, and the United States know how difficult it is to keep the Philippines quiet and contented. They must understand our problem.

AH: You are forgetting international jealousy. Every nation feels a secret pleasure when it sees another in trouble. Besides, quite apart from this, there is another problem in the use of force by ruling nations today – passive resistance.

GH: It is hardly a new force. It was used successfully by the two greatest religions in the world, at least to get them started, Christianity and Buddhism. I read a remarkable book the other day called, I think, *Non-Violent Coercion*.[1] The author pointed out that it

1 Clarence M. Case, *Non-Violent Coercion: A Study in Methods of Social Pressure* (1923).

only cost some three or four thousand martyrdoms before the Roman Empire capitulated and Christianity, which had been a capital offence, became first tolerated and then, quite quickly, the State religion. You evidently cannot go on killing men if they won't obey you and yet won't resist you. If only the Church had learnt that lesson! Instead of that it forgot the power of passive resistance as soon as it won its victory and took to violence.

AH: That's the trouble with organised religion. It provides so many justifications for violence. It is interesting to reflect that, as a matter of historical fact, humanitarianism has increased as organised religion has declined. For when you think you know what absolute truth is, you feel justified in forcing other people to agree with you; and if your faith is sufficiently strong, you stick at nothing in the way of violent compulsion. Even professional humanitarians have tried to enforce their opinions with cruelty; there was actually a proposal, not so long ago, that people who maltreated animals should be given the cat. The enemies of cruelty advocating torture! It is charming, isn't it? But that is what comes of religious enthusiasm.

GH: But do you think religious people were personally more cruel than others?

AH: No, no. It was only that their religion had provided them with so many occasions when cruelty was appropriate. Though, of course, there is this to remember: there is a real correlation between asceticism and cruelty. Ascetics are people who are hard on themselves; and if you are hard on yourself, you don't mind being hard on other people.

GH: No, I suppose not. But the other extreme is just as bad. Don't forget Tiberius and Nero – they were not ascetics.

AH: No; but modern psychologists have shown that suppressed sex is almost as bad as perverted sex. It tends to make people turn to cruelty. Puritanism has a pretty ugly record. Look at John Knox. Look at Calvin in Geneva. Luckily nobody could accuse the present age of being puritanical! Which is probably one of the reasons why we are more humane than our more pious ancestors.

Perhaps if there is a reaction towards virtue we shall take to torture again.

Broadcast as 'On the 9.20', BBC National Programme,
9 January 1932[1]

1   Published as 'Is Cruelty out of Date?: A Discussion between Gerald Heard and Aldous Huxley', *Listener*, vii, 20 January 1932, 97–8.

Science and Civilisation

There are certain values which we feel to be absolute. Truth is one of them. We have an immediate conviction of its high, its supreme importance. Science is the organised search for truth and, as such, must be looked upon as an end in itself, requiring no further justification than its own existence. But truth about the nature of things gives us, when discovered, a certain control over those things. Science is power as well as truth. Besides being an end in itself, it is a means to other ends. Science as an end in itself directly concerns only scientific workers and philosophers. As a means, it concerns every member of a civilised community.

Our civilisation, as each one of us is uncomfortably aware, is passing through a time of crisis. Why should this be? What are the causes of our present troubles? Most of them are due, in the last resort, to the fact that science has been applied to human affairs, but not applied adequately or consistently. In the past man's worst enemy was Nature. He lived under the continual threat of famine and pestilence; a wet summer could bring death to whole nations, and every winter was a menace. Mountains stood like a barrier between people and people; a sea was less a highway than an impassable division. Today Nature, though still an enemy, is an enemy almost completely conquered. Modern agriculture assures us of an ample food supply. Modern transportation has made the resources of the entire planet accessible to all its inhabitants. Modern medicine and sanitation allow dense populations to cover the ground without risk of pestilence. True, we are still at the mercy of earthquake, flood and the more violent natural convulsions. Against earthquake, flood and hurricane man has, as yet, devised no adequate protection. But these major cataclysms are rare. At most times Nature is no longer formidable; she has been subdued.

Our present troubles are not, then, due to Nature; they are entirely artificial, genuinely home-made. The very arts and sciences which we have used to conquer Nature have turned on their creators and are now conquering us. The present economic disasters are of our own making; we have brought them on ourselves by allowing our mechanical and agricultural science to develop more rapidly than our economic science. We cannot buy what we produce, and are therefore compelled to keep our factories idle and let our fields lie fallow. Millions are hungry, but wheat has to be thrown into the sea. This is where, at the moment, science has brought us.

What is the remedy? Tolstoyans and Gandhi-ites tell us that we must 'return to Nature' – in other words, abandon science altogether and live like primitives or, at best, in the style of our mediaeval ancestors. The trouble with this advice is that it cannot be followed – or rather, that it can only be followed if we are prepared to sacrifice at least eight or nine hundred million human lives. Applied science, in the form of modern industrial and agricultural technique, has allowed the world's population to double itself in about three generations. If we abolish science and 'return to Nature', the population will revert to what it was – and revert, not in a hundred years, but in as many weeks. Famine and pestilence do their work with exemplary celerity. Tolstoy and Gandhi are professed humanitarians; but they advocate a slaughter, compared with which the massacres of Timur and Jenghiz Khan seem almost imperceptibly trivial. No, back to Nature is not practical politics. The only cure for science is more science, not less. We are suffering from the effects of a little science badly applied. The remedy is a lot of science, well applied.

Everyone admits in principle that human activities must be regulated scientifically; but, when it comes to applying this principle, two questions arise. Science, in the present context, is a means to an end: but what end? That is the first question. And (this is the second question) by whom is this instrument to be used? Who is to wield the power which science gives?

Many definitions of the ideal human society have been attempted. That which, I suppose, the majority of modern men and women would find most acceptable is what, for want of a better name, I will call the 'humanistic' definition. The humanist is one who believes that our human nature can, and should be, developed harmoniously as a whole – that the sacrifices which man must always make should be made in his own highest interest, and not in the interest of something external to himself – not in the name of any less or any more than human cause. For the humanist, then, the ideal society is one whose constituent members are all physically, intellectually and morally of the best quality; a society so organised that no individual shall be unjustly treated or compelled to waste or bury his talents; a society which gives its members the greatest possible amount of individual liberty, but at the same time provides them with the most satisfying incentives to altruistic effort; a society not static but deliberately progressive, consciously tending towards the realisation of the highest human aspirations. Science might be made a means for the creation of such a society, but only on certain conditions: that the powers which science confers must be used by rulers who are fundamentally humanist.

Our present crisis is mainly and most obviously economic. The fact is dangerous; for it means that the ends pursued by our rulers, at any rate in the immediate future, will be primarily economic ends. It means that the instrument of science will be used by men primarily interested in economics, and only secondarily, if at all, in the higher humanistic values. I have described the humanist's earthly paradise. What is the economist's ideal society? Briefly, it is one where there is the maximum of stability and uniformity. The economist wants stability because, once you set machinery going, it is hopelessly uneconomic to let it stop or run irregularly. Also industrialists and financiers must be able to look forward with confidence; in a stable world the machine is able to go on running steadily. Again, the economist wants uniformity, because the most profitable form of mechanical production is mass production. The mass producer's first need is a wide market, which means, in other words, the greatest possible number of people with the fewest possible number of tastes and needs.

Now stability and a certain amount of uniformity are essential pre-requisites to any rational plan for improving the quality of civilisation. They are means to ends, not ends in themselves. But it is precisely as ends in themselves that the economist-rulers of the immediate future are likely to conceive them. It is easy to imagine a government of industrialists and financiers using all the resources of science first to secure world-wide stability and uniformity, and then, in the interests of production, to keep the world stable and uniform. The aim of the economist will be to make the world safe for political economy – to train up a race, not of perfect human beings, but of perfect mass-producers and mass-consumers. One of the things economist-rulers would be almost bound to do is to suppress science itself. Once stability has been attained, further scientific research could not be allowed. For nothing is more subversive than knowledge. So long as scientific research goes on, society stands poised above a potential succession of earthquakes. Any day some new discovery may make all existing equipment obsolete, may revolutionise all existing technique, or else, by changing man's physiological habits, radically alter his whole way of thinking and feeling. Having first made use of science, economist-rulers would find themselves forced to destroy it. Even humanist-rulers might often have to forbid the application of certain discoveries. Let us suppose, for example, that a method has been discovered for producing all food synthetically. Humanist-rulers might feel justified in forbidding the application of the discovery on the grounds that agricultural life was humanistically valuable.

But these are remote speculations. Let us try to guess how the resources of science might be used or abused by different types of rulers in the nearer future. I will begin with psychology, the science which concerns us more closely and intimately than any other, the science whose subject matter is the human mind itself. In a rather crude and ineffective way psychological knowledge is already applied to the problems of government. It was shown during the War that propaganda – which is the art of influencing the mind – could become one of the major instruments of national policy. Profiting by war-time experience, the rulers of Russia and Fascist Italy are systematically using this psychological weapon to create new types of civilisation. Even in conservative England our rulers have not disdained to take a leaf out of the Soviet and Fascist book. Systematic mass-suggestion by wireless and poster played a very important part, as we all know, in the last election and during the 'Buy British' campaign of the Empire Marketing Board.

Propaganda is still relatively inefficient even in countries like Russia and Italy, where the State controls all the existing instruments of mass-suggestion, from education to the 'movies' and the Press. But psychological science teaches how it could be made almost irresistibly effective. Freud and his followers have shown how profoundly important to us are the events of the first few months and years of our existence; have proved that our adult mentality, our whole way of thinking and feeling, our entire philosophy of life may be shaped and moulded by what we experience in earliest childhood. Following another line of research, the great Russian biologist, Pavlov, and the American Behaviourists have shown how easy it is, with animals and young children, to form conditioned reflexes which habit soon hardens into what we are loosely accustomed to call 'instinctive' patterns of behaviour. Such are the scientific facts waiting to be applied to the solution of political problems. Rulers have only to devise some scheme for laying their hands on new-born babies to be able to impose on their people almost any behaviour pattern they like. No serious practical difficulties stand in the way of such a plan. One of these days some apparently beneficent and humanitarian government will create a comprehensive system of State *crèches* and baby-farms; and – with a little systematic conditioning of infant reflexes – it will have the fate of its future subjects in its hands. From the baby-farm the already thoroughly-conditioned infant will pass to the State school. He will grow up reading State newspapers, listening to State wireless, looking at State cinemas and theatres. By the time he reaches what is somewhat ironically called the age of reason, he will be wholly unable to think for himself. None but the approved State ideas will ever even occur to him. This will make the overt use of force quite unnecessary. Dictatorship, as a form of government, may have, in the immediate future, a brief spell of popularity. In times of crisis like the present, strong government is probably necessary. But once the position has been stabilised and, above all, once our rulers have been educated up to the point of realising the extent of the power which psychological science has placed in their hands, strong government will cease to be necessary. When every member of the community has been conditioned from earliest childhood to think as his rulers desire him to think, dictatorship can be abandoned. The rulers will re-establish democratic forms, quite confident that the sovereign people will always vote as they themselves intend it to vote. And the sovereign people will go to the polling booths firmly believing itself to be exercising a free and rational choice, but in fact absolutely predestined by a lifelong course of scientifically designed propaganda. Its choice will be determined by an inward psychological compulsion much more powerful than any pressure of physical force from without.

For the economist-ruler, scientific propaganda will seem a heaven-sent instrument. He will use it to train up that race of perfect producers and consumers of which industry has need. He will find it invaluable for producing and preserving that stability and uniformity without which machines cannot be used to their maximum advantage. By means of it, a creed will be inculcated, racial and individual idiosyncrasies as far as possible smoothed out, contentment and conformity incessantly preached. Indeed, scientific propaganda may enable future rulers to do what the mediaeval Popes and Emperors tried but failed to achieve. They may actually succeed in creating a great world-wide community united by common beliefs and aspirations, common wants, tastes and thoughts. It will be a Holy Roman Empire minus the holiness, a Christendom, but without the Christianity – or if nominally Christian, Christian in a way that neither the primitive convert, nor the mediaeval Catholic, nor the later Protestant would recognise as Christian. It will be the kingdom of industry and the machine.

What will be the attitude of the humanist towards scientific propaganda? Fundamentally, I think, he would be opposed to it. For if it were thoroughly scientific and efficient, scientific propaganda would obviously be quite incompatible with personal liberty. Now personal liberty is, for the humanist, something of the highest value. He believes that, on the whole, it is better to 'go wrong in freedom than to go right in chains' – even if the chains are imponderable, even if they are not felt by the prisoner to be chains. Nevertheless, it may be that circumstances will compel the humanist to resort to scientific propaganda, just as they may compel the liberal to resort to dictatorship. Any form of order is better than chaos. Our civilisation is menaced with total collapse. Dictatorship and scientific propaganda may provide the only means for saving humanity from the miseries of anarchy.

The liberal and the humanist may have to choose the lesser of two evils and, sacrificing liberty, at any rate for a time, choose dictatorship and scientific propaganda as an alternative to collapse. Again, the humanist will have to remember that propaganda is a substitute for force in general and war in particular. It would certainly be worth forgoing a great deal of liberty for the sake of peace.

I have dwelt at some length on propaganda because it seems to me that, without it, there can be no large-scale application of scientific knowledge to human affairs. Psychology is the key to science. Many of the possible applications of biology, for example, are so startling that they must be prepared for by a regular barrage of propaganda. Sprung too suddenly on the world, they would be passionately resisted. Let us now consider a few of these possible applications of science, speculating as before how they might be used by the humanist or abused by the economist.

Biologists have collected a very considerable amount of information on the subject of heredity, and are steadily adding to their store. So far as our knowledge goes, negative eugenics – or the sterilisation of the unfit – might already be practised with tolerable safety. On the positive side we are still very ignorant – though we know enough, thanks to Mr. Fisher's admirable work, to foresee the rapid deterioration, unless we take remedial measures, of the whole West European stock.[1] Eugenics are not yet practical politics. But propaganda could easily make them practical politics, while increase of knowledge will make them also purposive and far-sighted politics.

The humanist would see in eugenics an instrument for giving to an ever-widening circle of men and women those heritable qualities of mind and body which are, by his highest standards, the most desirable. But what of the economist-ruler? Would he necessarily be anxious to improve the race? By no means necessarily. He might actually wish to deteriorate it. His ideal, we must remember, is not the perfect all-round human being, but the perfect mass-producer and mass-consumer. Now perfect human beings probably make very bad mass-producers. It is quite on the cards that industrialists will find, as machinery is made more foolproof, that the great majority of jobs can be better performed by stupid people than by intelligent ones. Again, stupid people are probably the State's least troublesome subjects, and a society composed in the main of stupid people is more likely to be stable than one with a high proportion of intelligent people. The economist-ruler would therefore be tempted to use the knowledge of genetics, not for eugenic, but for dysgenic purposes – for the deliberate lowering of the average mental standard. True, this would have to be accompanied by the special breeding and training of a small caste of experts, without whom a scientific civilisation cannot exist. Here, incidentally, I may remark that in a scientific civilisation society must be organised on a

1   Huxley was familiar with R. A. Fisher's *Genetical Theory of Natural Selection* (1930) which recommended the introduction of fiscal incentives to encourage the 'better stocks' to reproduce more numerously.

caste basis. The rulers and their advisory experts will be a kind of Brahmins controlling, in virtue of a special and mysterious knowledge, vast hordes of the intellectual equivalents of Sudras and Untouchables.

What is true of applied genetics is true, *mutatis mutandis*, of applied bio-chemistry and pharmacology. Our knowledge of what can be done by means of drugs is still rudimentary. It may be possible, for example, to modify profoundly men's character, temperament and intelligence by administering suitable chemicals at suitable moments. Yet, once more, the same knowledge will be used by the humanist and the economist in profoundly different ways.

I have neither the time nor the ability to discuss the possible effects on human beings of other scientific discoveries. History shows that almost any new acquisition of knowledge may be made the basis of important practical applications. The abstruse researches of Faraday and Clerk Maxwell have resulted, among other things, in the jazz band at the Savoy Hotel being audible at Timbuctoo. Not a very probable result, you must admit. But then the course of events takes no account of verisimilitude. Fiction has to be probable; fact does not.

And here I should like to make what seems to me an important point. We are unable to foresee what discoveries in pure science will be applied to human life. But equally we are unable to foresee all the results of any given application of science. Certain particular ends may be envisaged by the man who applies scientific knowledge, and these ends may, in fact, be attained. But almost inevitably other ends, not foreseen, will have been attained at the same time. For example, when Bradlaugh and Mrs. Besant spread abroad the medical know-ledge which has been applied as birth control, their intention was that families should be reduced in size.[1] Their action produced its intended effect; but it also produced effects which they certainly did

---

1   Between 1874 and 1885 the freethinking Charles Bradlaugh (1833–91) and the social reformer and theosophist Annie Besant (1847–1933) worked in close association. In 1877 they republished and widely circulated a birth-control pamphlet which had resulted in its previous publisher being sent to gaol.

not consciously intend. For example, it forced architects to build tall blocks of five-roomed flats, rather than long rows of fifteen-roomed houses; and it compelled farmers to breed small cattle, rather than large ones. A century ago prize bulls weighed as much as two tons; today small families require small joints of meat, and prize bulls weigh about half a ton. These unintended effects of birth control are not particularly important or significant; but it often happens that the unintended effects of an action are much more considerable than the intended ones. The application of science to human life has already produced a large crop of unintended effects, some of which are highly undesirable. Science increases our powers of foretelling the future; but we may be quite sure that it will be a very long time before the unintended effect will be altogether eliminated. Nor must we forget that these unintended effects will follow actions undertaken with the highest possible motives. The well-meaning humanist is as likely to give people an unpleasant surprise as the ill-meaning economist. Against unpleasant surprises there is no remedy. Each unexpected situation must be dealt with individually, as it turns up. We can only hope that it will not prove too unpleasant, and that increasing knowledge will permit of more accurate foresight.

I will add a few more words by way of summary and epilogue. Science in itself is morally neutral; it becomes good or evil according as it is applied. Ideally, science should be applied by humanists. In this case it would be good. In actual fact, it is more likely to be applied by economists, and so to turn out, if not wholly bad, at any rate a very mixed blessing. It rests with us and our descendants to decide whether we shall use the unprecedented power which science gives us for good or for bad purposes. It is in our hands to choose wisely or unwisely. Alas, that wisdom should be so much harder to come by than knowledge!

Broadcast on the BBC National Programme, 13 January 1932[1]

1 Published as 'Science — the Double-Edged Tool!', *Listener*, vii, 20 January 1932, [77]–79, 112. Reprinted in a slightly revised form as 'Economists, Scientists and Humanists', in Mary Adams, ed., *Science in the Changing World*, London: Allen & Unwin, 1933, [209]–23.

Dispatches from the Riviera[1]

The late Mr. Kreuger is now, quite definitely, my favourite character in fiction. After the discovery, last week, of those rubber stamps, there could be no doubt of his proper place; it was sublimely among the Micawbers and Stepan Trofimovitches, the Psmiths and Vautrins and Uncle Tobies of this world.[2] *Primus inter pares.*

In admiring imitation I am thinking of having all the signatures of eminent persons in my possession photographically reproduced on rubber. Signed Maugham, or Shaw, or Galsworthy, my little articles will sell, not, as at present, like faintly tepid muffins, but like the hottest of hot cakes. The more I think of those rubber stamps, the better I like them.

I have never had the confidence trick played on me, for the good reason that I do not look like the sort of man who can produce, at a moment's notice, five thousand pounds in bank-notes. If I did look like such a man, and if a genial stranger did begin talking to me about gold mines in Guatemala, should I be taken in? I always imagine that I should not. But then so, beforehand, do all the

1   This piece collates three extracts from the series of 'Notes on the Way' which Huxley contributed to *Time and Tide* magazine at regular intervals in 1932–7. Huxley's contribution for 4 June 1932 appeared under the title 'Politicians and Peoples'.

2   For Kreuger see the Introduction, pp.xix, xx. The Micawbers, Stepan Trofimovitch, Psmith, Vautrin and Uncle Toby are the creations of Dickens (*David Copperfield*), Dostoevsky (*The Devils*), Wodehouse (*Psmith in the City* [1910], *Leave it to Psmith* [1923], etc.), Balzac (*Père Goriot* [1834], *Illusions perdues* [1837–43], etc.) and Sterne (*Tristram Shandy*) respectively.

victims of confidence tricksters. If the genial stranger were genial enough, I should no doubt succumb. Almost all successful swindlers are gifted with irresistible charm. You could not, apparently, meet Kreuger without being completely bowled over. Even bankers and financiers fell in love with him at first sight. Later, when the glamour of success had enhanced his native charm, people fell in love even before first sight.

That the course of the world's affairs should depend to a very great extent on the presence or absence of certain physiological idiosyncrasies – of what Mrs. Elinor Glyn succinctly calls 'it' – must seem to a rationalist somewhat alarming.[1] But there it is, a fact. Some sort of 'body urge' (to use an expressive locution from America) is essential to all who propose to exercise a direct influence on their fellows. Body urge is as valuable to financiers, politicians and clergymen as to movie stars. If the possessor of body urge chooses to abuse the power which his charm gives him, then so much the worse for his fellows. And, in the long run, so much the worse for himself.

Business, the reformers tell us, and after business, government, must be organised in ever larger and larger units. Kreuger was profoundly convinced of this; so was Hatry. Both men, I imagine, were, among other things, far-sighted idealists. In attempting to act on their enlightened convictions, to put their sociological ideals into practice, both were forced into gigantic fraud. It is an odd, ironical story, from which it would be possible to draw a number of mutually contradictory and equally edifying morals.

Competent neutral authorities assure us that, during the war, English propaganda was more effective than that of any other country. Today, if we are to believe Sir Stephen Tallents (and as the head of the Empire Marketing Board, he is particularly well qualified to speak), English peace-time propaganda is, on the

1 Elinor Glyn (1864–1943), English novelist and short-story writer, famous for her highly charged romantic tales. One of her best-known novels was *It* (1927), which was subsequently made into a film. 'It' became a synonym for sex appeal.

whole, the least adequate of the great national selling campaigns. In his lately-published pamphlet, *The Projection of England*, Sir Stephen complains that we are not advertising ourselves properly. Nobody is taking the trouble to 'sell' England and Englishness to the rest of the world. Hence, among numerous other reasons, our present difficulties. Sir Stephen suggests, by way of remedy, the establishment of a 'School of National Projection' – a sort of public utility corporation whose function it shall be to employ all the technical and all the available (or amenable) artistic resources of the country to impress the image of our contemporary England on the world's consciousness. In itself, Sir Stephen's project is excellent. A great exporting country must secure the goodwill and attention of its customers, and to do this, it must use, deliberately and with skill, all the arts of advertisement. A School of National Projection would be a most useful institution, and sooner or later something of the kind will undoubtedly come into existence. So far, so good. The trouble will begin when the School of National Projection has become, by an inevitable process of development, one small department in a great Ministry of Propaganda. The Machiavelli of the mid-twentieth century will be an advertising man; his *Prince*, a textbook of the art and science of fooling all the people all the time. Bayonets, as we all know, cannot be sat on, but good propaganda makes the most reposeful of cushions. An oligarchy which tries to rule by force is doomed to a more or less rapid extinction; but there is no reason why an oligarchy using the science of propaganda should not go on ruling indefinitely. Such an oligarchy can afford to preserve all the forms of democratic government. If it 'projects' itself skilfully enough, the masses can always be relied upon to vote as their real rulers want them to vote. This will doubtless make for peace and happiness; but at the price of individual liberty. A really efficient propaganda could reduce most human beings to a condition of abject mental slavery.

Fortunately, perhaps, (or unfortunately) propaganda is not yet entirely efficient; and even in Russia and in Italy, where the rulers have mobilised all the available machinery of publicity to 'project' their thoughts and wishes on the minds of the ruled, acquiescence is not quite complete. The fault, it seems to me, lies in the machinery of projection rather than in the human mind. If rulers will take the trouble to perfect the first, the second should be (in normal conditions of prosperity and contentment) wholly at their mercy. The trouble about the march of progress is that it is so extremely difficult to call a halt. A School of National Projection would be a wholly admirable thing. But a Ministry of Propaganda, exercising direct or indirect control over newspapers, books, wireless and cinema, would be, at any rate by existing standards of value, wholly odious. But the first must inevitably produce the second. Once the State has started the deliberate peace-time organisation and control of propaganda, it cannot stop until the organisation and the control are complete. Progress marches: that is its essence.

[*From* xiii, 7 May 1932, 514–16]

In the report of the second of Professor Gustav Cassel's recently-delivered Rhodes Lectures there occurred the following phrase: 'We had created systems of unemployment doles calculated to increase the immobility of labour in a very dangerous way.' It set me thinking.

The function of science is to abstract and generalise. Newton's preoccupation was not with the particular apple that fell on his head, but with all apples, all stars and planets, matter in general. Political economy is, or at any rate is trying to be, a science. Political economists must therefore abstract and generalise. Their subject is not my business and your business, but business at large.

Political economy differs, however, from most other sciences, inasmuch as its concern is not with external nature, but with man. The particular cases from which the physicist, the chemist and the zoologist make their abstractions, and upon which they base their generalisations, are without intrinsic significance. The particular cases of the economist, on the contrary, possess this intrinsic significance in the highest degree. Each one is a suffering or enjoying human being.

In terms of the particular – the unescapably significant particular – what exactly do we mean, when we say that 'unemployment doles are calculated to increase the immobility of labour'? Presumably we mean this: that if John Jones and Mary Smith are given enough to keep them from starving, they will not be driven by the gripings of hunger to wander about the country in desperate search of whatever employment may anywhere be offered. In terms of the particular, 'mobility of labour' connotes men with green faces and starting bones, trudging from place to place, sleeping on benches, begging, occasionally stealing; 'immobility of labour' connotes men with merely grey faces lounging at street corners, or squatting on their heels outside cottage doors.

The difference between the things which are Caesar's and the things which are God's is the difference between the general and the particular, between the abstract and the concrete, between the average of many behaviours and each individual behaviour.

Politicians and economists deal with the things that are Caesar's. It is inevitable and necessary. Even in human affairs there must be abstraction and generalisation; if there were not, there would be no seeing the wood for the trees, no seeing the Caesar for the Gods. There must be generalisation and abstraction, yes; but equally, there must be particularisation. Too exclusive a preoccupation with Caesar's things – with abstractions and generalisations – may lead to a ruthless indifference to some of the highest human values. 'Mobile labour' is not, and is not meant to be, an object of compassion; a hungry man, tramping about the country, is. To be compelled to feel compassion, to have the sufferings of others forced upon the imagination, is often disagreeable and incon- venient. That is why we generally prefer to think of human affairs in terms of averages, which evoke no emotion beyond the feeling of satisfaction that comes to us when we have understood something and got it safely pigeon-holed. All men – and particularly 'intellectuals' – are chronically tempted to escape from unpleasant and disturbing particularities into the passionless world of abstraction.

How quickly people contrived, for example, to transmute the horrors of war into smooth abstractions that rolled to and fro in their minds without causing the smallest imaginative irritation! Every non-combatant was a strategist – in self-defence. Men did not want to be too vividly aware of the particular facts of war; and strategy is a science – a system of generalisations and abstractions. Phrases like 'war of attrition' protected the mind from contact with concrete reality and were therefore immensely popular. There was a general retirement of the human spirit to a Platonic world of Ideas. It was the same during the Napoleonic wars. Let Coleridge bear witness:

                        Boys and girls,
And women, that would groan to see a child
Pull off an insect's leg, all read of war,
The best amusement for our morning meal!
The poor wretch, who has learnt his only prayers
From curses, who knows scarcely words enough
To ask a blessing from his Heavenly Father,
Becomes a fluent phraseman, absolute
And technical in victories and defeats,
And all our dainty terms for fratricide;
Terms which we trundle smoothly o'er our tongues
Like mere abstractions, empty sounds, to which
We join no meaning and attach no form!
As if the soldier died without a wound;
As if the fibres of this godlike frame
Were gored without a pang; as if the wretch,
Who fell in battle, doing bloody deeds,
Passed off to Heaven, translated and not killed;
As though he had no wife to pine for him,
No God to judge him![1]

Coleridge's blank verse is (as, alas! it generally is) very blank indeed. It is a pity. A mind-piercing and memorable piece of poetry

1 S. T. Coleridge, 'Fears in Solitude' (1798), ll. 104–23.

on this theme might have exercised a most salutary effect on the thinking of educated people. These lines are too weak to leave more impression on the mind than a corresponding amount of indifferent prose. I quote them, not for their intrinsic excellence, but because they show how, in similar circumstances, psychological history repeats itself. Caesar's world of averages and generalizations and abstractions has always served as a mental refuge from God's all too disquieting world of particular facts and individual character.

[*From* xiii, 4 June 1932, 613–14]

Britain has paid a handsome compliment to the excellence of Russian psychological technique; we now have an official Five Year Plan for Slum Clearance. What will be our next Five Year Plan? For a next one there is sure to be. The idea is too good to neglect. Show people a definite objective and promise them at the same time an indefinite series of rewards for its attainment; give them, for this attainment, a period of time not so long as to transcend the powers of hope or foresight, not so short that they will be tempted to relax their efforts too soon – and you can get an astonishing amount of self-sacrificing work out of them.

The Communists have secularised the eternally popular notion of the Second Advent, made it once more acceptable to the masses of a predominantly materialistic and non-Christian population. Using the myth of the Five Year Parousia, they have persuaded people to undergo immense hardships, not only with resignation, but even with enthusiasm. They have discovered how to exploit the masses in such a way that the masses actually enjoy the process.

It remains to be seen how often the myth can be used, and still retain its powers of stimulation. Men are not like moths that invariably fly towards the candle; the same light now attracts them and now repels. The Five Year Plan stimulus may work very successfully twice, or perhaps three or even four times in succession; but it seems unlikely that it will work more often. 'Positively the Last Appearance' will fill the theatre for a few nights; but it cannot be made the basis for a long run.

England, meanwhile, provides a virgin field for the secular Second Adventists of planning. If it set to work in the right way a government could probably guarantee itself ten or fifteen years of almost unanimous enthusiasm for reconstruction. After that, no doubt, a reaction would set in; (it always does, when the world fails to come to its announced conclusion and the miraculous advent does not materialise). After so much heroic hard work and abnegation, people would be tired and ready for a rest-cure of indifference. But meanwhile a great deal would have been accomplished; and when a new generation had had time to be bored with being bored, the fresh start would be from a higher level of material organisation than exists today.

[*From* xv, 24 March 1934, 370–72]

Industrial Progress and Social Stability

The atom has been disintegrated – not only in the imaginary world of Robert Nichols's and Maurice Browne's very interesting and spirited dramatic fable, *Wings over Europe* [1932], but also in the actual Cambridge of 1932. Lord Rutherford's communication to the press was tantalisingly brief, but he did at least make it quite clear that there is no immediate risk of young physicists from the Cavendish Laboratory posting up to Downing Street and threatening Mr. MacDonald with instant obliteration unless he forthwith inaugurates the millennium. Fortunately, or unfortunately, the fiction of *Wings over Europe* is not yet quite ripe to become accomplished fact. Atomic energy will kill no politicians yet awhile – will not even turn our sewing-machines or mow our lawns for us. And though the transmutation of elements has now actually been achieved, there is no immediate prospect of the world's currency problems being solved by alchemy. The atom is a tough and stubborn little creature, and the process of knocking it to bits is laborious and expensive. 'It is estimated,' write Cockroft and Walton in a letter printed in last week's issue of *Nature*, 'that at 250 kilovolts one particle is produced for approximately 109 protons.' Which means, I take it, that using the existing methods you can disintegrate only one atom in every thousand million. Nine hundred and ninety-nine million, nine hundred and ninety-nine thousand, nine hundred and ninety-nine misses to every hit, seems a fairly high proportion even in the atomic world. The transmutation of metals and the harnessing of atomic energy are not yet commercial propositions.

But because they are not commercial propositions today, it does not follow that the Cambridge discoveries will never be commercially exploitable. The first step has been taken; the next step, and the next, are bound to follow. A thought is like a seed, planted in the right kind of mental soil it is foredoomed to grow – naturally, inevitably, blindly. Yes, blindly so far as our human standards of value are concerned, for thought obeys the laws of its own being, and the laws of thought's being are not the same as the laws of man's being. Logic and the nature of the external universe determine the course of thought's development, which takes place ineluctably, like the development of a tree or a crystal, without any reference to our human wishes and hopes, our fears and our convenience. For the purposes of thought, our minds are simply more or less well-manured plots of ground, more or less thoroughly saturated solutions, in which the acorn is planted or the nucleus of the crystal suspended. To the other plants growing in the garden, to the other objects that may happen to be lying about in the solution, seed and crystal pay no attention. Why should they? Their business is to grow, to become completely themselves; and they do grow often with disastrous results to everything that happens to be in their neighbourhood. History is the record of man's unceasing efforts to adjust himself, first to Nature, and then (a more difficult task) to his own developing thought – or to put it in another way, to the thought that is developing in him.

Developing thought incommodes man in various ways. Embodied as machines or as social organisations it may interfere with an old-established and habitual well-being by altering his physical environment. Unembodied, in the form of new hypotheses about the nature of things, it may disturb his mental and emotional life by undermining his consoling beliefs and making nonsense of his cherished aspirations. There is a technique of scientific discovery. Minds trained in this technique constitute a particularly propitious environment for growing thoughts about the external world. During the last two hundred years an ever-increasing number of good minds have been trained in this technique, and thought about the Universe has developed, in consequence, at an ever-increasing rate. The small seed that was science in Galileo's day is now a gigantic, world-shadowing tree. In recent years this tree has grown so fast, and its growth has so completely altered the conditions of human existence, that men have found themselves quite incapable of adjusting their way of living to the new mental and physical environment created by it. Hence the present crisis in world affairs.

The news of the disintegration of the atom brings into focus one special aspect of the great problem posed by the existence of an incessantly growing corpus of scientific knowledge. It is this: What should society do with such embodiments of developing thought as are calculated, temporarily at any rate, to derange its organisation and imperil its stability? Made commercially exploitable, and duly exploited by private enterprise, the harnessing of atomic energy and the transmutation of elements would cause unspeakable confusion in the world. All the existing sources of energy would be superseded and every type of motor for directing energy would at once become obsolete. The practice of metallurgy would be profoundly modified; the chemical industry would have to change all its methods. Millions of people would be thrown out of work, colossal capital investments would be irretrievably lost. Until the industrial world had adjusted to the new conditions imposed by the new technology, there would be financial and social chaos. On a smaller scale, something of this kind has been going on – and with ever-increasing acceleration – for years. New inventions are continually throwing people into temporary, or, to all appearances, permanent unemployment, are continually reducing expensive plant to valueless old iron. Certainty and stability are the first conditions of industrial activity. One of the chief factors making for the paralysing uncertainties of the present time is an altogether too efficient science.

Thought, as I have said, grows with an inevitable growth. Its development cannot be checked and controlled; nor, of course, is it desirable that it should be. What can be checked and controlled, and what it seems on the whole desirable to check and control, is the embodiment of developing thought in machinery and industrial organisation. My own conviction is that, within quite a few years, governments will find themselves forced to control the industrial application of new inventions. They will have to do it in order to preserve social stability. A community cannot allow its very existence to be jeopardised because some logical process has worked itself out in the mind of some man of science, and because some manufacturer has bought the right to exploit the resulting conclusions.

The principle that the application of new discoveries should be controlled in the interests of society is already clearly recognised. Thus, the transformation of London's telephone system, from manual to automatic, might have been accomplished rapidly, at a single stroke. The Post Office has preferred to do the job slowly and by stages. Why? Because it was not thought desirable to throw a good many thousand girls simultaneously out of work. Similarly, private firms are always buying up patents, not to exploit them, but simply to prevent them being used by anyone else. Why? Because they do not want to lose, at a single stroke, all the capital they have invested in plant which the new invention will render obsolete.

In due time this principle – that social stability is more important than industrial 'progress' and must not be sacrificed to it – will inevitably receive legal sanction and universal application. The commercial rights in all new patents will be acquired by the State, and the exploitation of revolutionary discoveries permitted only under conditions which guarantee the least possible derangement of social stability.

From 'Notes on the Way', *Time and Tide*, xiii, 14 May 1932, 542–4

Sex, the Slump and Salvation

Nothing – not love, not even hate – is safe from the Slump. The latest statistics reveal a twenty-two per cent. decline, during the last year, in the number of American divorces. Judge Joseph Sabath of Chicago, who recently made absolute his fifty-thousandth decree and so may be expected to know what he is talking about, attributes this falling off to the world depression. 'As long as there was plenty of cash for pleasure, husbands were inclined to grow dissatisfied with their wives and wives with their husbands. Now they have more serious things to think about.' Also, he might have added, husbands and wives had more opportunity, when times were good, of meeting and convivially 'getting off with' alternative partners. And the costs of legal proceedings were, to the prosperous, no deterrent.

Wholesale prices have dropped, during the last few years, by about seventy per cent., and, along with wholesale prices, profits from business and dividends. The decline in the divorce rate is only a little over twenty per cent. What does this mean? It means this: the Americans are spending more on divorce than they can afford; they are making sacrifices to get divorced. Which shows how highly they value (a) sexual liberty and (b) respectability. Divorces are common in communities whose members aspire to combine the advantages of a certain promiscuity with those of respectable conformity to rules. Wherever for one reason or another the attractiveness of respectability diminishes, there the number of divorces will decline, even though promiscuity should remain as popular as ever. People who don't want to conform will not go to the trouble of having their liaisons sanctified by Church and State. People, on the contrary, who feel that conformity is worth while, will go to extraordinary lengths to remain respectable. To what lengths is shown by the existence, in America, of what Judge Sabath calls 'gin marriages'. A gin marriage is a marriage between a man and a woman who have met at a drinking party; who fall in love at first sight, or at least at the tenth or eleventh highball; and who hurry out, while love is still at its blindest, to get married by the nearest pastor or magistrate. What an almost unbelievably handsome tribute to respectability! Only people with the most whole-hearted respect for public opinion, the most lively sense of what is socially correct, would remember, when drunk and amorous, that there was such a thing as a church or a register office. Gin marriages, according to the learned judge, are apt to end in divorces. Which shows what a nuisance too much respectability can be. Financial stringency means less gin; less gin means fewer gin marriages; and fewer gin marriages mean fewer divorces. Hence, among other reasons, that twenty-two per cent. decline.

To trace the correlation between the economic life of the community and the emotional and instinctive life of its individual members – between the subject matter of text-books of political economy and the subject matter of novels, plays and poems – is always extremely interesting and instructive. Unfortunately, however, the relevant facts and figures are sometimes simply non-existent, sometimes hidden away in obscure and unlikely places. Thus, it was only by the merest chance that I happened to see in a provincial French paper the annual report of the Monte Carlo Casino Company. This year's profits were some twenty million francs less than last year's. Gambling, at any rate in some of its forms, has been badly hit by the Slump. (The huge success of the Irish sweepstake shows that there are other forms of gambling to which Slump conditions may be actually propitious. Though the chances against winning a prize in the sweep are some hundreds of thousands to one, and the chances against winning at roulette only, at the most, thirty-six to one, the enormously greater value of the reward it offers to success makes the lottery more popular, more imagination-stirring than the game.) How the Slump affects legalised sexual life we have already seen;

the statistics exist and are published. It would be equally interesting to know the influence it has had on illicit sexual activities, such as the white-slave traffic and prostitution in general. No figures, so far as I know, are available. What seems to have happened, however, is this: prostitutes are much worse off than in the days of prosperity; nevertheless, more women have taken to prostitution in order to eke out a living. (So, at least, observers report from the stricken industrial areas of Germany.) Again, a high unemployment rate is said to be to be accompanied by a certain increase in homosexual practices. There is direct homosexual prostitution resorted to by the extremely poor for extremely small rewards; and there are unprofessional *liaisons* between men who have discovered that homosexuality is cheaper, less compromising to personal freedom, than a relationship with a woman. Needless to say, however, there exist on this subject no exact data. They would be well worth compiling.

Verdammte Bedürfnislosigkeit – that was, for a certain German sales-man, the salient characteristic of his Mexican customers (or rather, non-customers). Damned wantlessness. They wouldn't buy – couldn't even be tempted. Electric cigar-lighters and mechanical dish-washers, tinned salmon and depilatory unguents, radio sets and motor cars – to everything that the commercial traveller from an industrialised country can offer, the peon remains, it would seem, completely cold. He is content with what he has and doesn't want more.

In his recently-published volume on Mexico, the American economist, Stuart Chase, has described this wantless civilisation and compared it, point by point, with that of the other America to the north of the Rio Grande.[1] It is a most interesting book. Most apposite, too. 'What shall we do to be saved?' The question is at present on every lip. Mr. Chase shows us how the Mexicans have answered it. Their solution of the problem of economic salvation

1   Stuart Chase, *Mexico: A Study of Two Americas*, London: John Lane/The Bodley Head, 1932.

has the merit of being, for them at least, pragmatically correct: it works. Which is more than can be said for any of our industrial solutions. Nobody is hungry in Mexico – or, at any rate, no hungrier than usual. There are, practically speaking, no unemployed. For the great majority of Mexicans, life goes on as usual; they are unaware that there is such a thing as a world depression. Wherein consists the secret of this happy state of things? In the Mexicans' damned wantlessness. These people live in the age of handicrafts and small-scale agriculture. They have no machines and almost no money. With the exception of cotton cloth, which they import, they make practically everything they need in the place where it is needed. They also grow locally all the food they consume. Each geographical district (with the exception of one or two large cities) is self-supporting. Mexicans are not compelled, like the Danes and the Argentines, to use the things that other people have grown, nor, like the English, to eat what other people have grown, nor. They are independent and free with a freedom and an independence that are not merely political. Theirs is the reality, not the name, of independence. A deluge might drown the rest of the world; Mexico would be able to carry on – and carry on happily, according to Mr. Chase – as though nothing untoward had occurred.

There was a time, not so very long ago, when this was true of England. Now, thanks to industrialism and the wheat lands of the new continents, thanks to artificial manure and steamers and modern hygiene, there are so many Englishmen, and they are so highly specialised to perform particular jobs, that England has lost the last trace of her old independence. Now, if the world were a political unity and its peoples rational and mutually friendly, loss of independence would be no bad thing. As things now stand it is disastrous. But owing to the size of our population we cannot revert to our old condition of life. Moreover, a return would be psychologically all but impossible. Education and advertising have created the wants which the Mexicans are so damnably or so blissfully without.

Mr. Chase seems to think that we can take a leaf or two out of the

Mexican book and bind them up into the chaotically mixed magazine of our Western civilisation. A little handicraft intercalated between the radios and the synthetic ammonia, the picture-papers and the contraceptives. He may be right. Where I should say he was wrong is in supposing that the Mexicans can with impunity take selected leaves from our book and stick them into theirs. Hygiene, for example. They cannot be hygienic without decreasing the death rate. Result, a rapidly-increasing population. But the stability of a handicraft civilisation depends on the growth of population being slow or non-existent. If it increases quickly, the old way of life is thrown hopelessly out of gear, the old leisures and dignities are lost and people are compelled to lead the ant-like existence of modern workers – unceasingly busy in order to get enough to live. There is, of course, a remedy: birth control. But the practice of birth control demands from (and probably creates in) the controllers a way of thinking most unlike the mystical, nature-worshipping, pre-scientific *weltanschauung*, which is the only satisfactory philosophy for wantless handicraftsmen and peasants. As usual, one seems to be up against insoluble problems.

From 'Notes on the Way,' *Time and Tide*, xiii, 21 May 1932, 566–7.

Rational foresight is impossible without knowledge, and we still know relatively very little about psychology, or heredity, or the relations of mind and body. But education is simply applied psychology, applied heredity and applied psycho-physiology. It follows therefore that rational foresight is still, to a great extent, impossible in the sphere of education.

Thus, the most important thing that a Professor of Educational Foresight could do is to foresee the child's future development – what he is likely to do well, what place he can take in the social scheme – to foresee and to plan his training accordingly. It is only on condition of such foresight that our educational system can become really efficient. Mr. J. B. S. Haldane is of opinion that 'if psychologists are allowed anything like a free hand, and co-operate with geneticists' the sorting out of children's abilities and potentialities should become possible 'in the course of the next century'. It is certainly not possible now.[1]

Again, the Professor of Foresight ought to be able to tell us which is the most efficient system of intellectual and moral training.

[1] To mark the tenth anniversary of the BBC, H. G. Wells had broadcast a talk entitled 'Wanted – Professors of Foresight' (reprinted in the *Listener*, viii, 23 November 1932, [729]–730). The *Listener* took up Wells's challenge by inviting Huxley and others to contribute to a 'Professors of Foresight' symposium. Huxley is quoting from J. B. S. Haldane's 'The Inequality of Man', in *The Inequality of Man and Other Essays*, London: Chatto & Windus, 1932, 21. Huxley had reviewed Haldane's book earlier in the month, *Week-End Review*, vi, 10 December 1932, 694.

Literally dozens of methods are at present in the field; but no evidence exists to show which of them is the best. Nor will such evidence exist until it is deliberately made. And the only way of making it is to take a large number of children at present being educated according to different methods and to keep a record of their intellectual achievement, their conduct, their emotional development, throughout the rest of their lives. If the numbers are sufficiently large and if the greatest care is taken to compare only the strictly comparable, then, forty or fifty years from now, it should be possible to come to some fairly reliable conclusion about the relative merits of our competing systems. Lacking this evidence, Professors of Foresight could only do what all parents do today: that is to say, back their fancy and hope for the best.

Those who control the child to a large extent control the man. (Hence the Church's interest in education and hence, in every European country, the determined efforts made by the State to break the clerical monopoly of teaching.) Professors of Foresight would be unable to make plans for education without previous reference to the plans of their colleagues in the department of social organisation. Is the future society to be a communist society or a 'distributive state' of small owners? Is government to be a centralised dictatorship or a federation of small local autonomies? Is the family to be preserved, or is it to be, as far as possible, abolished? Upon the answer to these and similar questions of general policy must depend the attitude of our Professors of Foresight towards education. You cannot make plans for children before you have made plans for men and women.

Some things, however, our Professors could do at once and without reference to anyone. Foreseeing the dangers of war, they could reform the teaching of history, so as to minimise the element of nationalist propaganda. And foreseeing the even greater dangers of superstition and the unscientific attitude of mind, they could make of biology the central theme of all elementary education. Why, it may be asked, biology? Because it is relatively easy, as history shows, to be scientific about what is emotionally remote, very difficult to be scientific about what is emotionally near. If you have been taught to think scientifically about your own vital processes, then you will have little difficulty in thinking scientifically about anything else. Of all the sciences, biology is the least compatible with superstition.

But, like patriotism, a scientific point of view is not enough. For example, a scientific point of view will not kill time. But it is sufficiently clear that, as machinery is perfected, more and more time will have to be killed by more and more people. We are on the threshold of an age of leisure. Indeed, we have crossed the threshold. Even the Government has now officially recognised that, whatever our future prosperity, there must always henceforth be a considerable amount of unemployment. From being what it now is, an unmitigated disaster, this enforced leisure may be converted by a judicious redistribution of wealth into a potential blessing. Potential, I repeat; for leisure, if one does not know how to use it profitably, is by no means an unmixed good. One of the chief tasks of our Professors of Foresight will be to prepare the future generation for its inevitable leisures. Doing nothing is a most difficult profession and requires an elaborate vocational training.

Listener, viii, 21 December 1932, 889

The Prospects of Fascism in England

At the time of the coal strike of 1921 I was living in a boarding-house in North London.[1] My fellow-boarders were salaried small-burgesses, white-collar workers, earning, I suppose, from four to six or seven pounds a week. Politics were discussed across the supper table, and discussed, while the strike was in progress, with a rancour that astonished me. They all hated the miners, passionately, as though they had received some personal injury at their hands. I have never forgotten those conversations; for they first revealed to me a fact which the history of these last thirteen years and my own personal experiences during that time have often corroborated – the fact that the current of class hatred runs more strongly downwards from small-bourgeoisie to proletariat than from proletariat upwards.

The reasons for this state of things are fairly clear. Economically, the small-bourgeoisie has been and is still being progressively proletarised. It is becoming, more and more completely, a class of wage-slaves, no better paid, so far as its lower sections are concerned, than the manual workers on the plane below. And yet, in spite of this economic levelling down, the tradition of class superiority persists. Membership of the bourgeoisie is regarded as a most valuable privilege and the loss of this privilege by degradation

---

1 The strike lasted from 1 April to 1 July 1921. Since it threatened to escalate into a general strike, all armed forces leave was cancelled, reservists were called up, vehicles requisitioned and a special Defence Force created. Huxley was in fact in Italy for the duration of this strike, but was resident at 18 Hampstead Hill Gardens, off and on, during the less portentous coal strike of 17 July to 14 August 1920.

to the ranks of the proletariat seems the worst of disasters. The small-bourgeois lives on the brink of a precipice and in perpetual terror of falling into the proletarian pit beneath. His position is such that he regards every movement in that pit as a personal menace: that chaotic struggling down below may shake him off his perch, those reaching hands are reaching only to drag him down. The proletarian has not very much to lose; but the small-bourgeois has – or (which comes to the same thing) imagines that he has – a great deal to lose, and his fear of losing it is correspondingly intense. Fear begets hate, and, looking down from the precarious verge of his precipice, he passionately loathes the creatures in the pit below. Hence those conversations across the supper table in my boarding-house, and hence, in country after country, the rise of Fascism, which is, among other things, the embodiment and effective social organisation of the downward current of small-bourgeois class hatred.

'Among other things,' I repeat. For Fascism is more than the organised protection of interests and social status. It is also the purveyor of a rich variety of social satisfaction.

Most people desire certainties, feel the need of a faith. Modern education makes religious faith difficult, but has done nothing to undermine political faith. Masses of men and women think them-selves too intelligent and well-informed to believe in miracles or the divinity of Jesus, but find not the smallest difficulty in accepting the infallibility of a Leader. The worship of God is an intellectual impossibility for thousands to whom the worship of a divine being, called the Nation, seems the most natural thing in the world. The old tendencies have not been abolished (they never are); they have merely taken new and, on the whole, less desirable channels. Fascism digs these new channels for worship and provides, in its cult of the divine Nation, a kind of lightning-conductor, upon which thousands of reluctant infidels can discharge the accumulations of their will to believe.

In the second place, Fascism provides a remedy for the complex of inferiority. Political and economic circumstances have, since the war, imposed intolerable humiliations on millions of personally blameless men and women, have reduced whole classes and populations to a state of despair. To these, the doctrine of national or racial superiority comes as an instrument of personal rehabilitation; for it assures the down-trodden individual that, in spite of all the specious appearances of failure, misery and general mediocrity, he is really of the salt of the earth and, in some mystical way, wiser and better than even the best, the strongest, the most talented of other men. At the same time appears the Fascist organiser and enrols him in an army. The principal function of this army consists in bullying the people who do not belong to it. At a single stroke the poor abject recruit finds himself in a position of superiority, promoted from the ranks of the kicked to those of the happy kickers. The last shall be first – nay, already *are* first, in this present world.

Membership of an army provides further satisfactions in the form of exhilarating group emotions (as good, in their way, as the pleasures of drink or of love) and relief from personal responsibility. Nor must we forget the delights of wearing a uniform. A uniform makes a man agreeably conspicuous in a crowd of the un-uniformed and tends to heighten his sex appeal. At the same time, it has some of the charm of a disguise. Putting on fancy dress, we put on a different character and are able to do things which we should never have the nerve to do in grey flannel trousers and a tweed jacket. A coloured shirt and top boots can go a long way to transform the mildest and most timid of Jekylls into a strong and silent Hyde. 'Why do you wear your hair sticking up like that?' was a question asked in those early days when Italian Fascists looked like Struvel Peter. '*Per esser più terribili*,' came the answer.[1] How many of us would like to be, or at least to feel, just a little bit more terrible than in fact we are! In uniform, we can find fulfilment for these ingenuous wishes.

1 'To be more terrible'. Struwwelpeter (Slovenly Peter) first appeared in 1845 as the naughty and unkempt hero of an illustrated book for children by Heinrich Hoffman (1809–94). On the title page of the first edition Struwwelpeter's fair hair 'stands up on end framing a somewhat bewildered-looking face'. Mary Garland, ed., *The Oxford Companion to German Literature*, 2nd ed, Oxford: Oxford University Press, 1986, 875.

Recent events in Austria set one uncomfortably speculating about the prospects of Fascism in England.[1] They are obviously less good, these prospects, than they were in Central Europe at the time of the rise of Hitler and Starhemberg.[2] The small-bourgeoisie of England has suffered, but suffered a good deal less than in Austria and Germany. This means that it has less reason to dislike the proletariat and its policies. The downward current of class hatred is certainly strong; but in most other countries of Europe it was and is stronger. Again, we have not, as a community, had any reason for developing a complex of inferiority. England 'won the war', and, unlike Italy (another winner, but still a victim, for some years, of acute inferiority complex), did not feel that it had been swindled out of any of the 'fruits of victory'. The English have no urgent political or economic reasons for feeling small and humiliated. Therefore they feel no urgent need for rehabilitating doctrines and confidence-restoring armies. In Germany these things were prime psychological necessities; in England they are luxuries, not essential to the life of the community. The English are so circumstanced that they can do without them. Equally, of course, they *could* do without tea and alcohol and tobacco. But having once had experience of these agreeable sedatives and stimulants, few people wish to do without them. When we have sorrows we drown them; in moments of agitation, light a pipe or cigarette. The times are gloomy and nerve-racking; and it may be that the consoling doctrines, the military organisation, the ritual gestures of Fascism will soothe and invigorate the very many individuals who, even in a relatively fortunate country, find the boredom of contemporary existence unbearable,

1 In March 1933 the Austrian Chancellor Engelbert Dollfuss suspended Parliament out of fear of a socialist revolt. In early February 1934 an attack on the socialists ordered by Dollfuss led to five days of civil war before the socialists were crushed. On 12 February 1934 the Austrian Socialist Party was dissolved.

2 Ernst Rüdiger, Prince of Starhemberg (1899–1956). Leader of the Austrian *Heimwehr* (Home Defence Force) from September 1930 and made Vice-Chancellor of Austria in May 1934. Head of the government-sponsored right-wing *Vaterländische Front* (Fatherland Front), 1934–6.

or its strains excessive. The Communists call religion 'the opium of the people'. But Communism is itself a religion, as also is nationalistic Fascism. And religions are not only opium; they are also coca and peyotl, caffeine and even cantharides. Hence, under a variety of forms, their unshakeable persistence.

I have said nothing about programmes or platforms, for the good reason that, in the present context, programmes and platforms are almost wholly irrelevant. People do not follow a Leader because he has a demonstrably sound and workable political plan. They follow him because he is a good public performer and because he knows how to provide them with the psychological satisfactions they need. His programme may be self-contradictory and manifestly absurd; but that makes not the smallest difference. Few people are concerned with logic and not many care very much even about their own material interests. They ask for their daily bread, of course; but for very little more than their daily bread. The wealth they covet is not material, but psychological; they crave emotional satisfactions, they want, in the expressive American phrase, 'to feel good'. A skilful Leader can make them feel superlatively good. Read the chapter 'A Showman of Genius' in Mr. [E. A.] Mowrer's book, *Germany Puts the Clock Back* [1933]; in the light of these descriptions of Nazi propaganda methods it is obvious that, for Hitler, a reasonable and self-consistent programme would have been a hindrance, not a help. The best programme for a politician soliciting the favour of the crowd is a programme of wish fulfilments and consolations. Once he has obtained power and is actually wrestling with the realities of government, the case is altered. Wish fulfilments butter no parsnips, and, if he is to preserve his power, he must adapt his actions to the existing political and economic circumstances. The only circumstances to which the programme of an opposition Leader need adapt itself are the emotional circumstances of his potential followers.

If Fascism comes to be imposed in England it will not be by argument, but by the logic of emotions. Thus, any intensification of the present fear of war or of the present fear of revolution can hardly fail to help the Fascist cause. For, where there is fear of war, nationalistic religion will naturally tend to flourish; and where there is fear of revolution, the downward current of class hatred will flow with unwonted strength. Again, any increase in the present economic stringency may be expected to create a psychological condition favourable to Fascism. For anxiety demands sedatives; and the sense of inferiority, produced by a falling standard of life, requires compensations. An accomplished Leader, as we have seen, knows how to soothe old miseries and create new confidence. Increasing poverty has another effect: it makes the life of the city dweller insufferably boring. Unable to afford any kind of amusement, he does not know what to do with himself. Membership of a well-organised Fascist army is the equivalent of permanent free movies.

Fascism will win, if win it does, on the emotional plane, and it is only on that plane that it can be effectively resisted. The soundest and safest anti-Fascist policy is a policy that will diminish fear, keep up the standard of living and provide people with all the amusements they need to make life seem bearable. The difficulties in the way of finding and applying such a policy are obviously enormous; and even if it were found and applied, it would still provide only an indirect defence against Fascism. Is there not some more direct and inspiring policy of emotional counter-attack? Yes, there is; but though more effective than the indirect defence, it is less safe. The direct defence against Fascism would consist in the establishment of an anti-Fascist religion capable of providing people with as many psychological satisfactions as they derive from Fascism. But to do this is to leap from frying-pan to fire. For any anti-Fascist religion, if it is to be successful, must be at least as intolerant as Fascism itself. At the present moment two important anti-Fascist religions are already in the field – Catholicism and Communism. We are given our choice. Extreme nationalism and a middle-class dictatorship on the one side; and, on the other, the two incompatible internationalisms of the Church and the proletarian dictatorship. On which of these three horns is what remains of liberal democracy to impale itself? As yet, the English and the French have refused to make the uncomfortable choice and are trying to squeeze their way between the spikes. If circumstances are not too unpropitious during the next few years, they may get through.

From 'Notes on the Way', *Time and Tide*, xv, 3 March 1934, 267–9

The scandal of the American airlines, the *affaire Stavisky* in France: the cases are not unique; merely more notorious than all the others, merely the latest and largest of an interminable series of swindles and corruptions.[1] Scandals tend to be rather more numerous and outrageous in France and the United States than in other countries. The reason, I take it, is not that there is more original sin in Paris or New York than in London, say, or Rome or Moscow. It is that the social mechanism for repressing the French or American swindler is inadequate. In the United States the multiplicity of courts provides the rich delinquent with indefinite opportunities for evading the just penalty of his crimes. And in France the law against swindling dates from a time when the financial crook was not in a position to operate on his present enormous scale. In 1810 the careers of company promoters like Kreuger, Hatry and Stavisky were unforeseeable; that is why the French penal code fixes only five years of imprisonment as the maximum penalty for *escroquerie*, and only two years for *abus de confiance*.[2] Most of the large-scale

1 The Stavisky scandal of 1934 brought France to the verge of civil war. Serge Stavisky was accused of issuing fraudulent bonds on the security of a municipal pawn shop in Bayonne. Although Stavisky committed suicide on 3 January, enquiries revealed that he had been protected in other dubious enterprises by government ministers. Serious rioting affected Paris in early February. In the same month, President Roosevelt cancelled the airmail contracts of eleven companies (operating 27,000 miles of airlines) following allegations of irregularities in the way they had been awarded during the Hoover administra-tion (1929–33).

2 Swindling and embezzlement respectively.

French swindlers of recent years have got off with ridiculously light sentences. Where crime is profitable and punishment inadequate, criminals naturally tend to increase and multiply.

But though some civilised countries are more heavily infected than others, all display symptoms of the same disease. Swindling flourishes and the financier everywhere exercises an undue influence on the politician.

Large-scale swindling and more or less definite, more or less criminal corruption of politicians are part of the price that has to be paid for economic progress and democratic government on liberal principles. Inevitably; it is a psychological necessity. Economic progress, liberal government and corrupt practices are three manifestations, in three different spheres of action, of a single type of character.

Let us begin with economic progress. This is made possible by the activities of men remarkable for their ingenuity and resourcefulness, for their interest in external reality and for their readiness to make experiments and welcome change. Only a small minority of human beings belong to this class. The majority are averse from change, take more interest in sentiments than in logic or the external world as it is in itself, have a strong tendency to create and, having created, fanatically to believe in all kinds of metaphysical absolutes. The people of the first class are those in whom (to use Pareto's terminology) the 'instinct for combinations' is unusually strong. In the second category the leading characteristic is the 'persistence of aggregates' of sentiments. Each class has its peculiar strengths and weaknesses. Thus, the strength of a society dominated by men with a pronounced 'persistence of aggregates' lies in its stability and in the violence and the promptitude of the actions dictated by unquestioning faith in an absolute. Its weaknesses are its inability to adapt itself to new conditions and its tendency to economic and mental stagnation. Change all the positives in the foregoing description into negatives, all the negatives into positives, and you have a sufficient account of the strengths and weaknesses for a society dominated by men with a well-developed 'instinct for combinations'.

It was to men of this type that the economic progress of the last two centuries was due. Economic progress made it necessary, in turn, that large numbers of such men should be absorbed into the ruling classes, hitherto mainly composed of individuals of the other type. Now, where the 'persistence of aggregates' is strong, faith is strong; and where faith is strong, men have no hesitation in using violence to enforce conformity to their will. The blood of the martyrs is the seed of the Church; the blood of the heretics is its inevitable fruit. Absolutism in government is correlated with absolutism in philosophy and religion; both are the products of faith, of the persistence of aggregates of sentiments.

Individuals with a highly-developed 'instinct for combinations' have little or no belief in absolutes and, lacking faith, are seldom whole-heartedly prepared to use violence. Called upon to govern, they rely more upon ingenuity and appeals to self-interest than upon force. Liberal principles are the theoretical justification of government by cunning, the condemnation of government by force. Such principles are regularly formulated, whenever economic progress brings men with the 'instinct for combinations' to positions of prominence.

That swindling and corruption should tend, where such men rule, to be as common as liberal principles is only to be expected. A swindle is just one more economic combination, this time on the shady side of the legal barrier. Men in whom the 'persistence of aggregates' is powerful tend to attach a mystical significance to the vetoes of society. Not so the swindler. For him, as for other sceptical 'combiners', social commandments are not supernatural taboos; they are merely tiresome obstacles placed in his way by other men. To circumvent them with impunity is hard; but if one is clever and prudent, it can be done.

Corruption is as natural, in the circumstances of economic progress, as swindling. Lacking faith to use violence, the liberal rulers-by-cunning bribe the electorate at large and, in particular, those individuals who know how to influence the electorate. At the same time a current of corruption flows in the opposite direction from financiers and industrialists in need of favours from the government. (In passing, it should be noticed that, under the present dispensation, many members of governments are themselves financiers and industrialists.)

Swindling and corruption have existed under all political *régimes*, but never on such a scale as during the time when, in so many civilised countries, the ruling classes renounced the use of force for that of cunning. These rulers have doubtless harmed society by their malpractices. But the benefits rendered by them probably outweigh all the mischief they may have done. Their activities have created huge quantities of new wealth and they have made it possible for such people as are capable of thought to think freely.

Liberalism is, unfortunately, a precarious policy. Liberal rulers are reluctant to use force; but among the ruled (and also among the rulers of neighbouring countries) are individuals with faith – people, that is to say, who are prepared to kill for their convictions, to die for their 'persistences of aggregates'. When these are effectively organised and led, liberals stand no chance against them. Sceptical and humane cunning is no match for fanatical force. The history of the last twenty years is a record of the struggle between liberalism and faith, between the ingenious and relatively tolerant 'instinct for combinations' and the believing and therefore ruthless, persecuting and violent 'persistence of aggregates'. Wherever battle has been joined, liberalism has suffered defeat.

In England and France democratic institutions and toleration have survived, partly because circumstances have imposed no unbearable strain on the two societies, and partly because French and English liberalism has never been carried to extremes. The ruling classes in both countries have included among the sceptical and humane exponents of the art of government by cunning a strong minority still possessed of faith. Aggregates of sentiments persist obstinately in the English landed gentry, among peasant proprietors, Catholics and professional nationalists in France. A ruling liberalism, thus leavened with faith, has a chance of surviving and of providing the ruled with the advantages of both systems of government – economic progress and a measure of mental freedom on the one hand, stability, strength and decision in emergency on the other.

In Fascist and Communist countries, 'persistence of aggregates' is encouraged at the expense of mental freedom. It remains to be seen whether these societies can for long enjoy economic progress while systematically repressing the normal psychological activities of those individuals most capable of assuring it.

From 'Notes on the Way,' *Time and Tide*,
xv, 10 March 1934, 306, 308–9

What is Happening to Our Population?

Population is not stable, but varies both in quality and quantity. In Great Britain, for example, there are now more than twice as many people as there were at the beginning of last century; and this quantitative change has been accompanied by qualitative changes, some for the better, some distinctly for the worse.

What have been, and what are likely to be, the effects of such changes upon the destinies of peoples and of individuals? How do they affect national prestige and personal happiness? And, in the event of their influence being undesirable, what are the possible remedies?

Many significant changes in the quality of populations are the result of changes made in the prevailing social environment. Thus, improvements in housing, sanitation, diet and medical services result in improved health and, indirectly, in better opportunities for all to live well and virtuously. Again, education alters and, to some extent, improves men's ways of thinking and feeling. And so on with all the other environmental changes which we call 'social reforms'.

The aim of reformers is to change some particular social situation for the better, in the hope that each improvement will contribute towards general improvement all along the line. Their ultimate aim is the happiness and spiritual amelioration of humanity. They believe that an accumulation of environmental improvements will give men the opportunities for enjoying happiness and will remove many occasions for behaving badly.

But the complexity of society and of human nature is such that it is often very difficult to foresee all the results of a given social change. Reformers frequently discover that, along with much good, they have unintentionally done harm. Hell, alas! is paved with good intentions. This fact does not, of course, excuse us from having good intentions and from resolutely acting upon them. What it does make inexcusable is ill-informed and thoughtless action. A good social reformer should also be a man of science.

The way in which admirable reforms may produce evil as well as good is well illustrated by the recent history of mental deficiency. In 1908 there were in England and Wales, 156,000 mental deficients. In 1929 the Mental Deficiency Committee estimated the number at 300,000. Twenty-five years ago there were between four and five half-wits to every thousand of population; today there are between eight and nine.

Some of this apparent increase is probably due to the fact that the later committee did its work more thoroughly than the Royal Commission of 1908. It looked harder and therefore found more. But when all the necessary discounts have been made, there is still good reason to believe that the number of defectives has increased, within a generation, to an alarming extent.

This increase is primarily due to a decline in infantile mortality – a decline which has affected every class of society, including that from which most defectives spring. This, in its turn, is due to improved sanitation and the wholesale establishment of Maternity and Child Welfare Centres. Mentally deficient children who, in the past, would have died in the cradle are now enabled to reach maturity. An environmental change for the better has resulted, among other things, in a hereditary change for the worse.

This is obviously a very serious matter. National survival depends on national efficiency. But a nation in which the number of half-wits is steadily growing is a nation whose potential efficiency is being steadily impaired. The question is so important that it will be worth while to consider it in some detail.

But first of all what exactly is a mental deficient? For practical purposes mental deficients are divided into three classes: idiots, having a mental age of less than two years; imbeciles, having a mental age of two to six; and the feeble-minded, with a mental age of between six and eight. Five per cent. of defectives belong to the first class, twenty to the second and seventy-five to the third. Practically all the members of the first two classes are in asylums. Of the defectives belonging to the third class more than nine-tenths are at large. In the following paragraphs the words, 'feeble-minded' and 'mentally deficient' always refer to members of the third class.

I have called the spread of mental deficiency 'a hereditary change for the worse'. The phrase is justified by the weight of accumulated evidence. Except in a small number of cases, where it is due to an accident, feeble-mindedness is a heritable defect. Mentally deficient children tend to be born of parents who are themselves either mentally deficient or, if not actually certifiable, of very low intelligence.

Idiots and imbeciles are born at random in all the strata of society. Doctors and lawyers produce as many in proportion to their numbers as do land-owners, farm labourers or pickpockets. But the researches of the Mental Deficiency Committee and, more recently, of Mr. E. J. Lidbetter, have established that the majority of the feeble-minded are the offspring of parents belonging to the so-called 'social problem group'.[1] This group constitutes about a tenth of the total population and includes the greater number of habitual criminals, prostitutes, unemployables, as well as most of the unfortunates who never succeed in emerging from the ranks of casual labourers and slum dwellers.

Sixty years ago there were thirty annual births to every thousand of population. Today there are sixteen. This decline, it cannot be doubted, is largely due to conscious birth-control. Deliberate limit-ation of families seems to have originated among the wealthier bourgeoisie; but the practice has now spread far down the economic

[1] E. J. Lidbetter (1878–1962) gave the Eugenics Society Galton Lecture in 1932. His subject was 'The Social Problem Group as Illustrated by a Series of East London Pedigrees'. This was reprinted in the *Eugenics Review*, xxiv, no.1, April 1932, 7–12. The following year he published *Heredity and the Social Problem Group* (vol.i).

scale. The only class into which it has never penetrated at all is precisely that social problem group from which the majority of mental deficients spring. I cannot do better than to quote, in this context, a few lines from a pamphlet published by the Eugenics Society:

Himes concludes from his analysis of the first 1,000 cases advised at a London birth-control centre that: 'It may be said emphatically that the clinics have been powerless, so far at least, to reach the obviously inadequate, mentally, socially and economically,' and 'to limit the reproduction of those fertile individuals in the community who constitute a serious problem – the feeble-minded, the insane, the chronic paupers and the persistent leaners on the State'. And the Mental Deficiency Report, while making no specific reference to birth control, supports Mr. Himes's conclusion by saying: 'In point of fact, the disparity in the fertility of the normal and sub-normal sections of the population is increasing, the families of the sub-normal group remaining as large as hitherto, while those of the better social classes are steadily diminishing in size.'[1]

In the past, this high birth-rate was compensated by a correspondingly high death-rate. But today, thanks to the philanthropic activities of social reformers, sub-normal parents are helped to rear their sub-normal children to maturity. With the result that there are now eight mental deficients for every four or five that there were a quarter of a century ago.

If conditions remain what they are now, and if the present tendency continues unchecked, we may look forward in a century or two to a time when a quarter of the population of these islands will consist of half-wits. What a curiously squalid and humiliating conclusion to English history! What is the remedy for the present deplorable state of affairs? It

---

1 Huxley is quoting from a pamphlet entitled *Committee for Legalising Eugenic Sterilization*, London: Eugenics Society [1930], 10. It was sent to him by C. P. Blacker, General Secretary of the Society, on 4 December 1933. For further details, see David Bradshaw's 'Huxley's Slump', q.v. Comprising, among others, Blacker, Julian Huxley and R. A. Fisher, the Committee called for voluntary, not compulsory, sterilization.

consists, obviously, in encouraging the normal and super-normal members of the population to have larger families and in preventing the sub-normal from having any families at all.

Eminence in our society is measured almost exclusively in economic terms. Children are expensive; therefore able and ambitious individuals will tend to regard the possession of a large family as a handicap in the race for success. Large numbers of such individuals remain celibate, postpone marriage till late in life, or rigidly limit the number of their children.

In other words, our society is so contrived that many of its most gifted members are condemned to complete or partial sterility. What is the result? Socially valuable stocks tend to die out, while socially indifferent or downright harmful stocks tend to increase.

'The biologically successful members of our society are to be found principally among its social failures ... and classes of persons who are prosperous and socially successful are on the whole the biological failures ... doomed more or less speedily, according to their social distinction, to be eradicated from the human stock.' So writes Dr. R. A. Fisher in his admirable *Genetical Theory of Natural Selection* [1930, 222]. The conclusion is singularly comfortless.

If socially valuable people are to be lured back into the ranks of the biologically successful, the enormous cash bonus which society now automatically hands out to every childless individual must by some means be transferred to the bearers and begetters of children. In certain French factories men doing the same work are paid differently according to the size of their families. To be biologically effective, this system of family allowances should be applied not only to manual workers, but also to all members of those professional classes from which, in the past, so many outstandingly gifted individuals have sprung.

Under the present economic dispensation the machinery for distributing family allowances among professional men and women would be rather hard to devise. But a beginning could be made by increasing the amount of the tax rebate on account of each child. At present, the rebate is absurdly small and bears no sort of relation to the actual cost of a child's maintenance and education.

So far so good. But encouragement of normal and super-normal fertility would do nothing to diminish the fertility of the sub-normal. Mental deficients are congenitally incapable of acting on grounds of enlightened self-interest; nor can they exercise self-control or foresight in the name of an abstract principle, or for the sake of a cause recognised to be good. They cannot be expected, therefore, to limit their own fertility. It follows that, in one way or another, their fertility must be limited for them.

Compulsory sterility is already imposed on idiots and imbeciles, who pass their lives in asylums, where they are prevented from propagating their species. Of the feeble-minded, some twenty-five thousand are in institutions. The rest – about a quarter of a million – are at large.

The Mental Deficiency Committee advised that the accommodation for mental deficients should be quadrupled. But even if this most desirable measure were carried through, about two-thirds of the present population of half-wits would still be at liberty to have children at the expense, biological and financial, of the community as a whole. There is one simple and, so far as it goes, effective way of limiting the multiplication of sub-normal stocks: certified defectives can be sterilised.

Sterilisation is *not* the same as castration. Physical health, character, sexual desires and potency remain unaltered by the operation, which is frequently performed on women for whom child-bearing would constitute a serious danger. As a therapeutic measure, sterilisation is sanctioned by English law. Whether it would be legal if performed for eugenic reasons is uncertain. Even if carried out with the consent of the patient, sterilisation for other than therapeutic reasons might be regarded as a crime under the Offences Against the Person Act. Most doctors are therefore reluctant to perform the operation on eugenic grounds, while those responsible for the policy of the hospitals consistently refuse. In the present uncertainty with regard to their legal position, they are obviously quite right. Eugenic sterilisation has been practised for some time in

America, where it is legal in more than half the states of the Union. In Canada, it is now legal in the province of Alberta. The operation is extensively performed in Switzerland, and in Germany the sterilisation of defectives has been legal and compulsory since the beginning of this year.

In England, a committee of the Eugenics Society has drawn up a Bill legalising voluntary (not compulsory) sterilisation for biological reasons. This, if it became law, would make it permissible for a doctor to sterilise any defective who so desired or for whom, if incapable of speaking for himself, his spouse, parent or guardian had given consent. Safeguards are provided making abuses all but impossible.[1]

The promoters of the Bill do not claim that this very moderate measure will cure all the ills from which the body politic is suffering. Even the sterilisation of *all* certified defectives would not stamp out feeble-mindedness. If no half-wits had children, the number of defectives would probably be reduced by about fifteen per cent. in one generation. This is better than no reduction and a great deal better than the present very large increase.

But obviously it is not enough. The majority of defectives are born of parents not themselves certified, though in many cases certifiable, or only just above the arbitrarily determined frontier separating the normal from the sub-normal. If the amount of feeble-mindedness is to be substantially reduced, the at present disproportionately high fertility of these border-line individuals belonging to the social problem group must somehow be lowered. To devise means for doing so effectively and with a minimum of vexatious State interference will be the task of some future government.

Two classes of people object to eugenic sterilisation: theologians and what I may call mystical democrats. Many influential Anglicans

1 The Bill was reproduced in another pamphlet which Blacker sent to Huxley: The Committee for Legalising Eugenic Sterilization, *Better Unborn*, London: Eugenics Society, [1931], 8–9.

and Non-conformists have expressed themselves in favour of the policy; but the Church of Rome remains resolutely opposed to all eugenic sterilisation, whether voluntary or compulsory – just as it remains opposed to all but two of the numerous forms of voluntary birth-control. To discuss Catholic arguments against sterilisation and birth-control is useless. If you accept the Catholic major premise, you will find these arguments irrefutable.

The arguments of the democrats derive such strength as they have from a powerful and not unworthy sentiment. These people feel that the campaign for sterilisation is just another attempt on the part of the rich to bully the poor; that it is an excuse invented by the ruling class for evading its responsibilities towards people it has itself condemned to a life of degradation. They deny the existence of a hereditary social problem group, and affirm that its members would be just as good as anyone else, if they were only given a fair chance.

Such an attitude is comprehensible and even commendable. It is good for rulers to be reminded that their altruism is always suspect. But the trouble with the extreme democratic position on this subject is that it is not scientific. It ignores two facts: first that the advocates of sterilisation have never proposed to use eugenic methods as a substitute for the improvement of environment, but as a supplement to it; and, second, that defectives do spring very largely from parents belonging to the social problem group. The obvious inference is that such people are members of the group because they are mentally inadequate.

Finally, we may ask mystical democrats how they expect democratic institutions to survive in a country where an increasing percentage of the population is mentally defective. Half-wits fairly ask for dictators. Improve the average intelligence of the population and self-government will become, not only inevitable, but efficient.

I have insisted up till now on the biological arguments in favour of eugenic sterilisation. It can also be justified on humanitarian grounds. Defectives are never fit persons to bring up children. The measure of their unfitness is shown by the following figures.

In every thousand of population there are eight defectives; in every thousand cases of cruelty to children reported to the [N.]S.P.C.C., seventy-five of the culprits are defectives. The defective children of defective parents are greatly to be pitied. But defectives sometimes have normal children. *Their* fate is incomparably worse. What must be the life of a sensitive boy or girl in the hands of parents who have the strength and the passions of adults, combined with the mentality of a child of six or seven? One hates to use one's imagination.

As regards quantitative changes in population, the facts are these. During the nineteenth century the population in Europe, America and to some extent in Asia increased at an (historically speaking) abnormal rate. In most countries the rate of increase has recently declined; so much so, that it looks as though population would soon become stable, or would even diminish.

Most of the increase recorded during the last century has gone to swell the size and number of towns. Out of every hundred English men and women nearly eighty now live in towns. With the exception of Holland, Great Britain is the most highly urbanised of countries; but all have gone far along the same road. Increase of population has meant everywhere a disproportionate increase in the number of town dwellers.

Such are the facts. What are the judgements to be passed upon them? Has the increase been a good thing and should we desire it to continue? Those who regard increase of population as an unmixed blessing do so generally on two grounds, military and economic. That the military prestige and power of a country should tend to rise with its population is to be expected. True, in the past difficulties of transport tended to keep armies relatively small, so that populous countries could not reap the full advantage of their populousness. But the improvement in the means of transport during the nineteenth century made it possible for generals to use indefinite quantities of cannon fodder. This was the epoch of the conscript army, 'the nation in arms' – an epoch which included the Great War and in which many people still believe that we are living.

But there is reason to suppose that the vast conscript army is a thing of the past. Aviation has been vastly developed since 1918, and lines of communication are peculiarly vulnerable from the air. Given the modern aeroplane, the feeding of a nation in arms becomes almost insuperably difficult. The army of the future (for, alas, we are justified in presuming that Europe has as yet no intention of disarming) is likely to be a rather small but highly trained and elaborately equipped professional army. A nation's military prestige will depend on the efficiency of its fighting experts, not on its reserves of cannon fodder. The military reasons for desiring an increase of population are ceasing to be cogent.

As for the economic advantages of a large population, these certainly exist. The trouble is that nobody knows at what point they cease to be advantages and become disadvantages. Economists agree that there is such a thing as the *optimum* population of a country. (Where population is at its *optimum*, the greatest return to industry possible at the given time, in the given place and in the given circumstances, will be achieved. Income will tend to fall off, both where there are too many people, and where there are too few.)

In practice, however, it seems impossible to decide whether a given country is, for economic purposes, over-populated or under-populated. This being so, we had better drop the idea of an economic *optimum* and try to judge the population problem by other standards. Man is not merely economic; he is a mind as well as a stomach. How has the great nineteenth-century increase of population affected him as a mental animal?

The most obvious difference between England today and England in, say, 1750, is a difference in looks. Thinly populated and only slightly urbanised, England was then a very beautiful country. Thickly populated and excessively urbanised, it now reveals itself to the majority of its inhabitants as an extremely ugly country. Town planners promise that this state of things can be remedied; and, obviously, by spending a vast amount of money, we can undo a good deal of the fatal work of the nineteenth century. But can we undo it all? I doubt it. Suppose (which is impossible) that every house in London could be transformed into an architectural masterpiece; London would still contain vast areas of pure dreariness. Repeat even a masterpiece a million times; the result is six hundred square miles of oppressive monotony.

Increase of population has had other distressing results, which I have no time to describe. But I have said enough to make my point clear. The population may or may not have reached an economic *optimum*; there is no means of deciding. That it has gone beyond the aesthetic *optimum* is certain. It has probably also passed the political *optimum*.

A final word about the probable effects of certain temporary fluctuations in population, now beginning to manifest themselves. During the war years – in effect, from 1915 to 1920 – the birth-rate declined sharply in all the belligerent countries. The greatest decline was in France, where the number of births, during this five-year period, amounted to only about half the average. A similar, but less marked, decline was recorded in England and Germany. In the United States, however, nothing of the kind occurred. The immigration figures in 1914 were among the highest on record, and as the fertility of these immigrants was very great, the American birth-rate during all the war years remained high.

From 1934 to 1939 the number of young people entering industry in England, Germany and especially France will be considerably less than in ordinary years. This means that, if other things remain equal, unemployment should decline. In France it is possible that it may temporarily disappear altogether.

All governments in power during this period will obviously take credit for this decline. 'Alone we did it,' they will say in loud self-admiration; whereas it was the non-existent fathers of the war years who did it – or rather, poor devils, who didn't. The automatic decline in unemployment may be expected to achieve, among other things, the consolidation of Nazi power in Germany.

During this same period France will be in a position of unprecedented military weakness. Between 1935 and 1940 only half the usual number of conscripts will come up for their military training. Ingenious schemes for making half a battalion go as far as a battalion are now being discussed. But we may look forward, during this period, to a strengthening of the French professional army so as to make up for the falling off in the conscript reserves.

In the United States, the number of young people entering industry will remain at its present figure for some years to come. This means that there can be no automatic reduction in the number of unemployed. The only improvement that can be expected is an improvement due to a trade revival, to social reorganisation, or to both these things at once. The Administration will not be able to take credit for what are in effect belated war casualties.

Nash's Pall Mall Magazine, xciii, April 1934, 12–13, 76–8

The Worth of a Gift

It is not my purpose this afternoon to tell you the history of Cecil Houses, nor to give you an account of how they are organised, nor even to describe the sort of cases – often indescribably pitiful – with which the organisation deals.

What I want to insist upon is not so much the actual services which Cecil Houses render as the way in which those services are given.[1]

A gift may be intrinsically precious; but the giving may be done with so bad a grace, in a manner so cold and inhuman, that the receiver will not be gladdened by what he gets, but outraged and humiliated. If his need is urgent enough, he will accept the gift – will have to accept it. But the acceptance will be reluctant and resentful. The worth of a gift lies as much in the way it is offered as in its intrinsic value.

Now the way in which the hospitality of Cecil Houses is offered is a wholly admirable way. The homeless, always poor and often actually destitute women who come to them for a night's lodging, are accepted for what they are – unfortunate people in extreme need. They are put through no preliminary interrogation, are asked for no papers or credentials, subjected to no gratuitous disciplinary bullying. If they want to talk, they are sympathetically listened to. If they prefer to be silent, they are left in peace. Everyone who enters

[1] Mrs Cecil Chesterton launched her Woman's Public Lodging House Fund following the publication of *In Darkest London* (1926), in which she recounted her covert 'adventures' among the capital's homeless and destitute women.

is treated with the tact and the simple decency that all men and women have a right to expect – but which, alas, so many hardly ever get in dealings with those in authority. At Cecil Houses one thing is axiomatic – that all who come are human beings. In a single word, Cecil Houses treat their guests as though they were human beings.

Now, this fact is sufficiently remarkable to be insisted upon with a certain emphasis. For the tendency to treat people with very small incomes as though they were not quite human survives, I am afraid, in many quarters even today.

I say *survives*; for there was a time, not so long ago, when it was universally taken for granted that the poor belonged to a different and inferior species. In nineteenth-century novels, for example, the Poor are spoken of as though they were a curious race of African savages – odd creatures with customs that at the best were laughable or quaintly touching, and at the worst were downright repulsive. Some of the Poor, it is true, came rather nearer to being fully human. These were the beings beautifully described as 'the Deserving Poor'. But, alas, the Deserving Poor were few and far between. Most of the Poor were definitely undeserving, and good care was taken by those in authority to see that they got no more than they deserved.

Things are certainly better than they were. But traces of the old mentality still persist. People in official positions, people in any sort of authority, even, in too many instances, the givers of charity feel themselves justified in assuming towards men and women with small incomes an attitude which they would never dream of assuming towards men and women with large incomes. Who ever heard, for example, of the Deserving Rich? And who ever heard of a rich person going round interrogating other rich persons, to find out whether they really were deserving? The thing would be regarded – and rightly regarded – as the grossest impertinence, an infringement of the most elementary rights of spiritual privacy. And yet this sort of infringement is constantly being made upon the rights of people with small incomes. There is a whole class of well-meaning people who still seem to believe that impertinence towards the very poor is not only justifiable, but actually virtuous. How passionately these same people complain whenever, for any reason, they are momentarily treated as though they themselves were poor! Passport formalities, for example, arouse in them a fury which can only find vent in letters to *The Times* and unprintable conversation. These outraged travellers may thank their stars that they are not regularly treated like the very poor and destitute. For the life of the destitute, even on their native soil, is one long succession of passport formalities and interfering impertinences. And, unlike the rich, they have no *Times* to write to.

What I propose to say now is in the nature of a digression – but a digression germane to my theme, which is the humanity and general decency of the way in which the work of Cecil Houses is done. Humanity and decency are impossible without understanding; and understanding is impossible without knowledge and a working hypothesis to act upon. So that what I now propose to say about the psychology of the poor and destitute has a very real relevance to the subject which has brought us together this afternoon.

Some people, I know, will deny that there is such a thing as a psychology of the poor and destitute. And of course it would be absurd to say that all men and women with very small incomes are like one another. They are obviously not. But what does seem to me certain is this: that the conditions of their lives have imposed upon a majority of them certain common traits of character, certain common tendencies towards a particular way of thinking, feeling and acting. It would be surprising indeed if this were not so. If a common way of life can produce national characteristics, it must also produce class characteristics. We recognise that there is an English-eye view of life, a French-eye view, a German-eye view; we must also recognise that there is a Dives-eye view and a Lazarus-eye view.

Perhaps the most striking thing about the psychology of the poor and destitute is patience. Indeed, I should say that the patience of the poor is the most important single fact in history. It is also, for those classes that write indignant letters to *The Times*, the most incredible. For thousands of years the overwhelming majority of the human race have put up with conditions which the minority have always regarded as quite intolerable. And yet — astonishing as it may seem — a century that can show more than five years of large-scale revolutionary activity is an exceptional century. For the most part, the poor have simply accepted the social conditions of their age — accepted them as inevitable, in exactly the same way as we all accept a rainy week-end or a rough Channel crossing. They regard all the things that happen to them, from under-nourishment to the bullying and impertinence of those in authority, as being what the insurance companies call 'acts of God or of the King's enemies'. In this, of course, they are quite wrong. These things are not acts of God or of the King's enemies. They are acts of men and of the King's friends. In other words, they are things under human control. Most of the conditions that the poor and destitute accept with such extraordinary resignation and patience are conditions that can be altered. Cecil Houses represent an attempt, none the less admirable for being on a small scale, to alter at least one of these intolerable conditions.

After patience, perhaps the next most significant characteristic in the psychology of the very poor is a profound indifference to the future. To prosperous people this indifference seems strange. But to people dependent on a very small and precarious income it comes naturally enough. Where wages are paid weekly and contracts can be terminated at a few days' notice preoccupation with the future becomes positively unreasonable.

How far can people with very small incomes confidently look ahead? A few weeks at the most. After that comes the darkness of complete uncertainty. As for the destitute — their future extends, for all practical purposes of foresight, only for a few days, or even a few hours. Whether they like it or no, the very poor are compelled by their circumstances to obey the Gospel precept and take no thought for the morrow. In cases of great destitution, this compulsion is not only psychological; it is also physiological. Chronic under-nourishment leads to a general apathy and indifference, and in particular to a blunting of all interest in anything but the immediate present.

In extreme cases there is a reversion to a mentality which we have learnt to regard as typically oriental – but that may be only typical of underfeeding – a mentality in which the sense of time has been almost completely extinguished. Tomorrow no longer matters, and even today loses much of its significance. Life for the under-nourished is the eternal present of a kind of waking stupor. But this, I repeat, happens only in extreme cases.

To patience and indifference to the future we must add a last characteristic – kindness. This again is a product, in a certain sense, of circumstances. It is not that the very poor are very naturally more benevolent than the prosperous. But the circumstances of their lives are such that they have more opportunities of putting their bene-volence into practice. When the rich need a service, they are generally in a position to buy it. They can hire people to do their housework, to look after their children, to nurse them when they are sick. But when the poor are in need of a similar service, they must rely on their friends and neighbours to do it voluntarily. The rich often have to go out of their way to create opportunities for being kind. Charity with them cannot begin at home, because their homes are so well organised that there is hardly any room for charity and when they want to be charitable they have to go outside their homes. And that so many of them constantly take that trouble is, of course, enormously to their credit. In the case of the poor, the opportunities for kindness are thrust upon them by the circumstances of their lives. Thrust upon them only too frequently, I may add. The response to these constant appeals to good feeling is, in most cases, astonishingly prompt and ungrudging. Most people are potentially a good deal more criminal and a good deal more altruistic than they themselves suppose. Opportunity makes the thief; but it also makes the good Samaritan.

And now, after this digression, we may return to Cecil Houses – return, I hope, with a better understanding and appreciation of what I may call their psychological policy. For that policy is based on a recognition of the facts I have put before you.

It is based, first of all, on the assumption that the poor and destitute women who come to them for a night's lodging are kind and considerate human beings. There is no bullying or regiment-ation, because it is assumed that such things are not needed; and in point of fact the assumption is generally justified. It is found that the number of women who behave in an anti-social and inconsiderate way is very small.

In the second place, this policy is based on the knowledge that the very poor have no future – have nothing beyond the here and the now. Very well then; let the here and the now be as good as possible. Cecil Houses have all the comforts that the available funds can supply. They are bright and cheerful with orange paint and blue curtains; they are physically warm with good fires and emotionally warm with courtesy and friendliness.

And finally the policy of Cecil Houses is based on a recognition of the enormous patience of the very poor – on a recognition of that patience and a steadfast refusal to exploit it. The very poor and destitute will put up with all kinds of bullying and impertinence. The organisers of Cecil Houses know this and have therefore scrupulously refrained from anything in the nature of bullying and impertinence. They have invariably treated their guests, not as members of another species, but as human beings. They have always regarded them as persons, never as mere cases or things.

Evil may be defined as the refusal on the part of the evil doer to regard other men and women as persons. We do evil when we treat others as though they were not persons, like ourselves, but as though they were things. Cruelty, lust, rapacity, domineeringness – analyse any one of the deadly sins; you will always find that its essence consists in this: the treating of a person as though he were wholly or partly a thing. Judge them by this standard, and you must conclude that there is an element of evil even in certain charitable organisations. The good in them outweighs the evil. But the evil is there and should be eliminated. And it can be eliminated. Cecil Houses are there as a proof that it can. No person in a Cecil House is ever treated as a thing. The good it does is quite unmitigated in the doing. That is why I am asking you this afternoon to contribute as generously as you possibly can to help the committee extend its admirable work.

Speech delivered in support of the Cecil Houses Women's
Public Lodging House Fund at Daly's Theatre, London,
16 November 1934[1]

1 Published in the *Seventh Report (1934–1935)* (1935) of the Fund, 16–20.

More clearly than we have done as yet, the Americans realise that anthropology, like charity and good cooking, should begin at home. Systematic research into the 'culture patterns' of twentieth-century America began some six or seven years ago when the Lynds published their exhaustive study of a Middle Western community under the title of *Middletown* – a classic of anthropology worthy to rank with Malinowski on the Trobriand Islanders or Boas on the Kwakiutl Indians.[1] *Middletown* created a precedent and set an example. American anthropologists discovered that their own people were just as much, just as oddly and fantastically, *anthropoi* as the Bantus or the Melanesians. Studies of American folkways in this early aeroplane age are becoming almost common. Future (and for that matter contemporary) statesmen, political theorists and historians are being supplied with scientific documents compiled by field workers trained in the art of making exhaustive 'cultural surveys'.

What is the value of the cultural survey and why is it good to cultivate the anthropological approach to the society of which we ourselves are members? The answer is that it is only in the light of such surveys that we can see ourselves objectively and to some

1 Robert S. Lynd and Helen Merrell Lynd's *Middletown: A Study in Contemporary American Culture* was first published in 1929. In the same year, the private life of the Trobriand Islanders was subjected to public scrutiny in Bronislaw Malinowski's *The Sexual Life of Savages in North-Western Melanesia*. Franz Boas published four book-length studies of the Kwakiutl Indians between 1930 and 1935.

extent, at least, as others see us; it is only by approaching our institutions in the anthropological spirit that we can clearly perceive them for what they are – not God-given, not the expression of some absolute and ultimate Human Nature, but the product of historical circumstances working human nature, and working, we may add, with a surprisingly slight regard for what any reasonable biologist would regard as its fundamental needs and urges. The fact that anthropology brings out most clearly is this: that a viable society can be based on almost any principle that human fancy may choose to invent and human ingenuity to elaborate into a working plan. Our own institutions and habits seem to us to possess a peculiar reasonableness conspicuously absent from those of people belonging to other cultures. But that is due not so much to the intrinsic qualities of the institutions themselves as to the weakness of minds for which the familiar is inevitable and the indigenous the sacred and right. Looking at ourselves anthropologically, we avoid most of the delusions to which this weakness gives rise and so make it possible for our reason to have free play.

Here is an example, to which the recent pepper scandal gives a certain topicality, of the way in which the anthropological approach may help to clarify our views about the nature of existing institutions, legislation and habits of thought and feeling.[1] A few years ago the folkways of Harlem, the coloured quarter of New York, were investigated by a team of working anthropologists. It was observed that even the poorest negroes took a keen interest in the doings of the Stock Exchange. Investment and the various forms of speculation were, of course, entirely beyond their means. For them, it was found, the stock market meant only one thing – the figure for the daily turnover of shares in the Exchange. For the Harlemites had

---

1   On 7 February 1935 a leading article in *The Times* reported that the ''pepper'' holiday . . . is to be prolonged for another day while the brokers and shippers continue to seek a way out of their difficulties. In the meantime the banks, very properly, have decided not to assist the speculators who had hoped by buying on a big scale to be able to force up prices and to unload at a profit.' 'Pepper in the City', 15.

invented a new game of chance and were betting each day on the three last digits of the next day's turnover figure. 'At least,' comments an American anthropologist, 'it cost less than the whites' predilection for gambling in the stocks themselves, and was no less uncertain and exciting. It was a variation on the white pattern, though hardly a great departure.'

In our communities, stockbrokers are honoured citizens; but the people who make bets at street corners are fined or sent to gaol. The Stock Exchange is a place as respectable as a church; but gambling hells (note the implications of the name) are outlawed. Papers which devote a great deal of space to racing news are thought to be low and vulgar; but every high-class journal takes pride in the number and quality of its financial pages. When the Harlemites took to betting on the next day's turnover figures they were partly moved, no doubt, by a desire to appear more socially consequential and important than they actually were. Betting on numbers printed in the financial page of a newspaper must have seemed to them more respectable than betting on the numbers inscribed on a set of dice. We may smile at their ingenuousness; at the same time we have to admit that they had observed the essential facts of twentieth-century social life quite correctly.

I do not know whether there are any human societies in which gambling is unknown. It is very likely, for there are human societies in which war is unknown and even unthinkable, societies which have never heard of fatherhood. The propensity to gambling, which is merely a special case of the more general propensity to work up pleasurable emotional excitements, seems to us profoundly rooted in human nature. But that, as anthropology teaches, is no reason for supposing that gambling is universally practised. Nor, for our purposes, does it matter whether it is or not. What matters to us is that gambling, like war and fatherhood, plays an important part in our own culture as well as in all the more important alien cultures with which we are acquainted. Europe gambles, America gambles, China gambles, India gambles. It is possible that Tierra del Fuego and Easter Island do not gamble; but for our present purposes, I repeat, it doesn't matter.

Gambling, then, is an important element in our culture. But a culture is a whole with a patterned conformation that conditions the significance and the very existence of its parts. If we wished to suppress gambling altogether we should have to modify the pattern of our culture – modify it, moreover, in ways which it would only be possible to determine by large-scale social experiment. This means, in practice, that gambling is likely to persist as a habit and that the only thing the reformer can do about it is to make it as harmless a habit as possible.

Laws have almost always been made by the rich. It is therefore not surprising to find that all the attempts made hitherto to regulate gambling have been attempts to regulate the gambling of the poor. But is the gambling of the poor the most harmful form of gambling? Do the negroes who bet on the last three digits of tomorrow's stock turnover do more mischief to society at large than the whites who speculate in those stocks? If the tree is to be known by its fruits, we must conclude that the stockbrokers and their clients are far more harmful to society than all the dicers, card players, backers of horses and buyers of lottery tickets put together. A hundred million people could play poker continuously for 50 years and produce no effects comparable with those produced by the speculators who prepared the bursting of the South Sea Bubble or the crash in 1929.[1] Financial speculation is probably the most pernicious game of chance ever invented. For, unlike other games of chance, it is played with counters that stand for real objects and, worse, for real living men and women. The roulette player harms only himself and perhaps his family. The speculator in shares may harm vast numbers of innocent investors and workpeople.

It is obviously highly desirable that this power for mischief should be taken away from the speculator. But the propensity to gamble is encouraged by our culture and is not to be suppressed, unless the

1   The speculative South Sea Bubble burst in 1720, ruining many hundreds and prompting mass resignations within the British government, including that of the Chancellor, Aislabie.

pattern of that culture is altered in profound and unforeseeabl[e] ways. Deprived of his opportunities for gambling mischievously th[e] speculator must be compensated by being given opportunities t[o] gamble in a less harmful way. Here Harlem steps in with a sug[-] gested solution. Create an organisation for dealing with investment[s] then tell the rich man to do his betting in some other place than th[e] stock exchanges. If suitable gambling hells do not exist, give hi[m] leave to build them. Fifty casinos will never do as much harm as [a] single bourse.

Meanwhile, of course, the world continues to judge the matter b[y] a hopelessly perverted standard of values. The casino is decried an[d] the bourse respected; the bookie's tout gets sent to gaol and th[e] enriched speculator gets sent to the House of Lords. The anthro[-] pological approach would have preserved us from such dangerou[s] errors of judgment.

Everyman, NS no. 22, 8 March 1935, 525–6

The Next 25 Years

This Silver Jubilee will be having its Silver Jubilee in the year 1960.[1] My son will be forty then, and it is possible that I myself may still be alive. 1960 represents a future sufficiently near to be of real personal concern to us – sufficiently near also to be, not indeed predictable, but at least discussable. What will the journalist of 1960 find to write about the quarter of a century that separates his time from ours?

I will begin, not with a prophecy, but with the expression of a hope – the hope that, whatever else may have happened in the interval, he may not have to write about a war. Indeed, if he has to write about a war, the chances are that he will not be writing at all. I need not repeat the forecasts which sober technicians have given of the probable effects of a large-scale aerial attack with thermite and gas. Sudden death, succeeded by pestilence, famine and anarchy, is their prognosis of the course of the next war. The survivors of such an experience would hardly be likely to take much interest in jubilees.

Let us assume then that what we all hope is actually realised, and that, in spite of everything, Europe is spared the war which its Governments seem quite determined to make inevitable. For the sake of argument we will take it for granted that the twenty-five years from 1935 to 1960 are years of peace. To the retrospective gaze of the writer of our future jubilee article what will have been their most significant features?

[1] I.e. the Silver Jubilee of George V who had ascended the throne in 1910.

He begins, as all rather simple-minded believers in human progress begin, by describing the march of mechanical invention. We read, for example, of the stratospheric air services. London to New York in twelve hours. And when you step out of the airplane at either end and go to your hotel you naturally find television laid on in every bedroom. As for the talkies, they took to colour in the early 'forties and became stereoscopic about nine years later. Producers, our journalist has to admit, found the handling of the new and more complicated medium very difficult; it was some time before results were entirely satisfactory.

His next paragraph deals with synthetic sounds. Pfenninger, of Munich, was already at work on them in 1935.[1] Previously a sound-track could be made only by means of reproduction; the sounds of voices and instruments were projected on to the track in the form of visible undulations. Dispensing with voices and instruments, Pfenninger drew and stencilled novel wave forms of his own invention, had them photographed on to film and, by running the film through the ordinary talkie projector, was able to produce sounds of a kind hitherto unknown. 'By the later 'forties,' we read, 'this technique was so highly developed that musicians had begun to compose directly for the sound film and not for the old-fashioned orchestra.

'At the same time cinema stars took to having themselves fitted with synthetic voices more musical or more noble or more vibrant with sex appeal than their own, or indeed than any other merely human voice. Nor were politicians slow to recognise the potentialities of the new invention. Ministries of Propaganda found that it was possible to supply dictators, monarchs and even democratic Prime Ministers with a brand of synthetic eloquence incomparably more moving than that of the greatest orators of previous epochs. It was in America that the invention was first applied to religion. Revivalists made use of synthetic voices so pathetic and persuasive, so terrifyingly minatory, so suavely unctuous, that they were able to secure mass conversions on a hitherto unprecedented scale.'

1   An imaginary inventor.

Up till now the tone of the article has been on the whole triumphant; but at this point a certain note of bewilderment creeps in. The writer finds himself constantly forced to admit that in spite of progress, even, alas, because of it, things are not quite as they should be. For example, there was the German invention and perfection, during the early 'forties, of an artificial wool, as warm as the natural article and a good deal cheaper; there was that American technique for synthesising a rubber that could be marketed at six cents the pound; there were the new methods, perfected in England, for turning coal into a liquid fuel cheaper than petrol.

Triumphs of applied science! But artificial wool was to devastate Australia. Synthetic motor tyres ruined the rubber planters as completely as, nearly a century earlier, aniline dyes had ruined the indigo planters. And as for the oilfields, all but the most favourably placed of them had been abandoned by 1960. Meanwhile the plant breeders and agriculturists had not been idle, and during the 'forties new methods of treating moorland made possible intensive sheep farming all over Wales and Scotland; in ten years the geneticists were successful in producing several new varieties of soya bean capable of ripening in the climate of Western Europe. By the middle 'fifties all the industrial countries were using soya as their staple food and had considerably reduced their importations of wheat – with the natural result that the wheat-producing countries were able to buy a correspondingly smaller amount of their manufactures.

Meanwhile the average expectation of life had risen, during the period under review, by another three years. The proportion of elderly people in the population was steadily increasing, and with it the number of doctors, nurses, hospitals and clinics required to keep these ageing and ailing members of the community alive. The increase in the numbers of the feeble-minded, which had been so striking between 1910 and 1935, continued with progressive rapidity. In the early 'fifties one person out of every ninety-two was a half-wit. In something like a panic, Parliament passed a series of laws embodying all the principles of negative eugenics.

The later sections of our article deal with social conditions and economics. 'In these fields,' our author insists, 'the outstanding event has been, of course, the decline in the population. After reaching its maximum in 1936, the population remained more or less stationary for a few years, then after 1940 began to decrease. By 1960 it had passed from forty-five to thirty-seven millions; and of these thirty-seven millions more than five millions were over sixty-five years old, while fewer than four millions were under fifteen. In 1960 the number of children in the schools was almost exactly half what it had been in 1935.'

Somewhat inadequately, one feels, our author tries to sum up the results of this decline in the population. 'On the social side,' we learn, 'the decline of population has had certain admirable results. As the supply of houses has overtaken the demand, overcrowding has disappeared and the slum problem has automatically solved itself. Falling land values have made possible the reconstruction of our cities on more rational lines, and the natural beauties of the country are no longer endangered by indiscriminate building. Meanwhile, in the schools the fewer children are being better taught and better looked after. There has also been a great spread of adult education; for the voluntary unemployment centres which already existed in 1935 have been reorganised on a national scale as universities of leisure.'

Circumstances had imposed a kind of State socialism on the country; but owing to the predominance of elderly people in the population, it was an extremely cautious and conservative socialism. And at this point our author is forced to touch upon the new 'generation war', waged by the young against the old. A painful subject, over which he passes as quickly as possible.

The final paragraph deals briefly with foreign affairs. 'The countries of Western Europe,' we read, 'have been driven by circumstances to adopt much the same course as England. Common fear of Asia is unhappily well founded. Luckily the technical resourcefulness of Europeans still seems to be superior to that of the yellow and brown races. Destiny is no longer on the side of the big battalions: it is on the side of good equipment, and the equipment of Europe is still superior to that of Asia.' On this note of tempered optimism our author concludes, and we fall back once more into the present.

The twenty-five years that separate us from 1960 are still in front of us. May we scramble through them with no worse disasters than afflicted the hypothetical world of this imaginary retrospect!

Daily Express, 8 May 1935, 10

The Empire Marketing Board was the first English government department to go into advertising on a large scale. More recently, the Post Office has presented itself with a publicity bureau, and now we are to have an organisation to boost the National Government. Our feet, it would seem, are set upon the road that finally leads to Dr. Goebbels and a Ministry of Propaganda.

Being Englishmen, we shall probably not call the new ministry by anything so vulgar as its own name.

The Ministry of Propaganda, when it comes, will come, no doubt, in some picturesque disguise – as an appendage, for example, to the Lord Chamberlain's office or the College of Heralds. The old names will rumble reassuringly in the public ear, while the new reality of official propaganda is being organised on the most efficient modern lines. Yet once more, we shall enjoy the double satisfaction of being up-to-date and of thinking ourselves traditionalists.

And when we have our Ministry of Propaganda, what then? Shall we all forthwith begin, like good little sheep, to bleat unanimously in chorus with the local Goebbels? Or will there still be stubborn and misguided Britons to insist on thinking for themselves and not as their rulers want them to think? The problem can be stated in more general terms. What precisely is the effect of political and social propaganda on the minds and actions of human beings? How far can the users of such propaganda be sure of moulding public opinion in the way they desire?

These are vital questions and, like most vital questions, are singularly difficult to answer. For though all governments make use of social and political propaganda – some, as in Italy, Germany, Russia, systematically and on a large scale, others, as in France, England, America, only sporadically – I think it is true to say that nobody really knows what that propaganda does, nor how long its effects last, nor which kind of appeal, in any given circumstances, is the best.

An enormous amount of propagandist work is done; but to a considerable extent it is work in the dark. Thousands of men and women in every part of the world pass their whole lives bawling, cajoling, instructing, commanding, wheedling. With what results? They would find it hard to say.

And here, before going any further, I would like to draw a distinction between political and social propaganda and the specialised commercial propaganda which is called advertisement. Advertisers know pretty accurately the potentialities and limitations of different kinds of propaganda – what you can do, for example, by mere statement and repetition; by appeal to well-organised sentiments; by playing on the animal instincts. Advertising, say its practitioners, is a science. This is, of course, an exaggeration. But the fact remains that some commercial propagandists do know their business.

But the problems with which advertisers have to deal are very different from those which confront moralists and politicians. Most advertising is concerned with questions of small importance. Thus, I need soap; but it doesn't at bottom make the slightest difference to me whether I buy Smith's soap or Brown's soap. This being so, I can allow myself to be influenced by such entirely irrelevant considerations as the sex-appeal of the girl who smiles so alluringly from all Smith's posters, the puns and comic drawings that figure on Brown's. In many cases, of course, I don't need the commodity at all. But as I possess a certain amount of spare cash and am possessed by the insane human proclivity to collect unnecessary objects, I succumb easily to anyone who appeals to me to buy superfluous gadgets and luxuries. In either case, nothing serious is at stake. This type of commercial propaganda deals solely with secondary, marginal values.

In a certain number of cases, however, it matters, or at any rate seems to matter, a great deal whether I buy or don't buy. Suffering from some physical pain or discomfort, I read of the extraordinary cures effected by Jones's pills and Robinson's lotion. My necessity is so urgent, that I buy at once. In this case the advertiser has only to make the article persuasively known; the buyer's physical need does the rest.

Social and political propagandists have a very different task. Their business is to persuade people to take actions which are neither indifferent and unimportant on the one hand, nor, on the other, of apparent immediate advantage to the suffering individual. Becoming a member of the Communist party, for example, will not does not even pretend to cure a man of his ailments. Nor is it a matter of indifference, like buying Smith's soap rather than Brown's, or like spending one's spare cash on a superfluous luxury.

But in reality a great many people do treat the most important social and political issues as matters of indifference; and the fact that they do so means that the propagandist has failed at his job, which is the overcoming of indifference. His aim is to secure a permanent 'change of heart', a life-long acceptance of a given set of ideas, a lasting willingness to make sacrifices for his particular 'good cause'. To him, the fickleness and volatility of the public, its rooted aversion to take anything seriously except its own immediate pre-occupations, are the prime enemies. They are enemies by which he is often defeated. In many cases he deserves defeat; for his strategy is bad, he makes disastrous mistakes – the kind of mistakes that any good commercial propagandist might have taught him to avoid.

Thus, in words which I quote from Mr. Raymond Postgate's very interesting book, *How to Make a Revolution*, 'strictly pacifist propaganda and strictly Communist propaganda are equally ill-directed, and up to date have been almost complete failures. This is so, because they take account of what the speaker believes to be absolute truth and not of what the audience is likely to be persuaded is true. The propagandists have failed utterly to follow the most important principles of modern advertising: that the customer is always right.

'Pacifists who tell the uniformed forces that war is an abominable crime and that they are no better than murderers, and Communists who tell them that they are "imperialist lackeys and butchers", have absolutely no chance of a hearing . . . No considerable body of men can ever be convinced that its whole occupation is vile. It may, in certain circumstances, be convinced that it has been tricked and caused to do wrong things; that is as far as it will go.'[1]

Such mistakes as Mr. Postgate describes might, I repeat, be avoided, if social and political propagandists would take a leaf out of the book of their commercial colleagues. But, however excellent their sales talk, the fundamental difficulty of changing people's hearts in any permanent way would remain. Much social and political propaganda is, by the best advertising standards, very good; nevertheless its effects are unpredictable. Sometimes they are good, more often they are unsatisfactory.

The instruments of propaganda are the press, the spoken word (whether heard at short range, as in church or meeting hall, or at long range over the ether) and the cinema, not yet much used by political propagandists outside Russia. Of these, the most immediately effective is the spoken word at short range.

Great orators are able to influence crowds in a way that seems little short of miraculous. Whit[e]field's sermons are unreadable, but when he delivered them, the most hardened sceptics felt convinced of their truth and were moved, temporarily at least, to passionate repentance.[2] Mr. Gladstone's oratory had an almost equally compulsive fascination. The secret of Robespierre's success lay, not so much in what he said, which was almost always remarkably platitudinous

---

1 Raymond Postgate, *How to Make a Revolution*, London: Hogarth Press, 1934, 157–8.
2 George Whitefield (1714–70), renowned for his fervent and emotional Calvinistic sermons.

and dull, as in the beautiful tones in which he said it. Hitler, in spite or perhaps because of a voice like an angry drill sergeant's, can compel a German crowd to feel and believe what he wants it to feel and believe.

On the radio a good deal of the orator's mysterious personal fascination evaporates; but enough remains, however, to make him a very potent force, even at the longest range. But the orator's strength is also the source of his weakness. He can intoxicate his hearers so long as he is actually talking. But when he has stopped, they tend to revert very rapidly to sobriety.

The printed is less thrilling than the spoken word, but possesses several compensating advantages. Its greatest merit is that, unlike the orator's speech, it is always there, and can be re-read again and again. Furthermore, the same theme can be handled in an endless variety of ways by a whole staff of writers, can be stated directly and by implication, and served out day after day to a circle of readers, which the cheapness of wood-pulp, the efficiency of the rotary press and the profitableness of advertising has now extended to include practically the entire population. The press is still the most efficient instrument of adult propaganda, and, accordingly, it is to the press that I shall mainly confine my remarks.

That 'the pen is mightier than the sword' is an aphorism which, since it flatters our vanity, we professional writers are very fond of repeating. But does it happen to be true? And, true or false, is it particularly illuminating? For if 'mightiness' is the quality we are interested in, we are probably mistaken in wishing to award the prize to either of these instruments. History has mainly been written by literary gentlemen with a taste for the picturesque and the dramatic. Hence the importance attributed to books and war.

But, in fact, the tools of the anonymous artisan and the test-tubes of the man of science have probably done much more to shape human destiny than all the pens and swords of the old-fashioned history books. In the long run, the most effective propaganda is the propaganda of social and economic circumstances. This propaganda may be intensified and even, if so desired, nullified, at least for a time, by a judicious use of the sword. The pen only intervenes to consecrate and rationalise the accomplished fact.

Nursed in the belief that the pen is superlatively mighty, politically minded capitalists are ready to spend enormous sums in order to acquire control of the periodical press. In so far as they are capitalists, they often do very well for themselves. But in so far as they are politicians, they are less successful. They buy newspapers in the hope of persuading the electorate to do what they want it to do; but again and again, as recent history makes it abundantly clear, the electorate goes and does something else. Thus the electoral successes of the Liberal Party before the war and of the Labour Party since were won in the teeth of opposition from a newspaper press that was predominantly Conservative.

It can be proved by simple arithmetic that there must be millions of English electors who regularly read a Tory newspaper and regularly vote against the Tories. There is no question of the sword in this case; the pens at the disposal of the press barons are defeated by the ingrained habits, the prejudices, the class loyalties and professional interests of the individual reader and also by the particular circumstances at the time of the election.

Sometimes, of course, these special circumstances may fight in favour of the journalistic pens. They did so, for example, during the khaki election that returned the first Coalition Government [in 1900] and the gold-standard election that returned the National Government of 1931.

Or consider the case of Allied propaganda among the German troops during the war. Until the summer of 1918 this propaganda seems to have been almost perfectly ineffective. During the summer and early autumn of 1918, Lord Northcliffe's balloons dropped twelve million leaflets behind the German lines. Their effect in shaking German *moral* was considerable, but only because increasing hunger and a series of unsuccessful battles had prepared the German soldier to accept their defeatist suggestions. Scattered in March, instead of July and August, the leaflets would have done nothing to stop the German offensive at St. Quentin.

Journalists tend to write badly, and perhaps the pen is mighty only when used with style. But again we find that even the best stylists seem to be largely at the mercy of circumstances. Voltaire exercised a considerable influence on his contemporaries, but largely in virtue of the fact that the educated classes were ready to welcome his attacks on organised religion and his pleas for more rational and democratic government.

Lucian had almost as much talent as Voltaire and wrote of religion with the same disintegrating irony, but his influence upon his contemporaries was for all practical purposes non-existent. The men of the second century were busily engaged in converting themselves to Christianity and a number of other emotionally satisfying religions; Lucian's irony fell on ears that were deaf to everything but preaching, magic and theological metaphysics. Propaganda, it would seem, is fully effective only upon those who are already partly or entirely convinced of its truth.

Let us consider a modern example. Since the war two thoroughly serious and well-written books of propaganda have figured among the very best of bestsellers – [Erich Maria] Remarque's All Quiet on the Western Front [1929] and H. G. Wells' Outline of History [1919–20]. Several millions of people read the German's indictment of war and the Englishman's plea for internationalism. With what results? Goodness knows.

When All Quiet and The Outline were published, post-war fatigue coupled with a measure of economic prosperity favoured the general acceptance of the doctrines they contained. Today internal and external circumstances have changed. All governments foster nationalism in the economic field, because (quite mistakenly) they hope thereby to escape from the world slump. Some encourage it in the military and cultural fields, because they think that by intoxicating the unemployed with nationalistic religious fervour, they may be able to make them forget their miseries. Add to these the apparently natural human tendency to delight in changes of intellectual and emotional fashion, and you will understand why the conversions due to the preachings of

Remarque and Wells were so superficial and short-lived.

And even if most of these conversions had been profound and lasting, would that have made much difference, so long as the world's rulers had remained unconverted? The effectively influential book is not that which converts ten million casual readers; it is the book that converts the one man who succeeds in grabbing power. Marx and Sorel have been immensely influential not because they were bestsellers (they were very bad sellers), but because they were read by Lenin and Mussolini! It may be that some future dictator will grow up with a passion for Wells. In which case *The Outline* will become influential. Today, in spite of its vast circulation, it is not influential.

Up to date, then, conscious propaganda has proved on the whole disappointingly ineffective. (Europe has been subjected to intensive Christian propaganda for the last sixteen hundred years or so; the results, it must be admitted, are not spectacular.) Realising its inadequacy, modern governments are trying to see what can be done to make propaganda more efficient. Hence Goebbels; hence official news agencies; hence the modest beginnings even in England of governmental propaganda.

All governments that undertake the control of propaganda resort to fundamentally the same techniques. I will begin with a brief description of their methods in the sphere of foreign propaganda.

Why rulers should be so extremely susceptible to remarks about themselves and their respective countries made in the foreign press is something I have never been able to understand. So far as I can see, it is a matter of almost total indifference to a government whether its actions are praised or blamed by the journalists of another country. However, rulers evidently think otherwise. (It is extraordinary what terrors that mighty pen inspires!) They react to unfavourable foreign comment as vain and temperamental actresses react to a bad review. But whereas the actress, to avoid further adverse criticism, has no choice but to act better, the ruler can go on acting badly, while bullying, cajoling or deceiving the critics into saying that he is acting well.

The first thing he does is to establish government control over the news agencies. In Europe and Asia all the important news agencies are under more or less complete government control, except the English Reuters, Exchange Telegraph and Press Association, and the French Havas. (This last, however, makes up for lack of government control by mysterious affiliations with heavy industry and finance.)

Now, it is obvious that the correspondents of independent newspapers and news agencies cannot be in more than one place at the same time. It is therefore impossible for them to report all that is happening in the countries to which they are accredited. This being so, a great deal of the news that comes from these countries is news supplied by the local official agencies. To a considerable extent we read what the rulers of those countries want us to read.

In their dealings with foreign correspondents governments use every form of moral and physical pressure to secure a good press. Correspondents who send home favourable reports are bribed with special cable facilities, flattering attentions and decorations. Those who insist on telling the truth even when it is unfavourable are spied upon, threatened and, in extreme cases, imprisoned and expelled, as Mrs. Sinclair Lewis and E. A. Mowrer were expelled from Germany, as the correspondent of the *Manchester Guardian* was expelled from Italy and the correspondent of *The Times* from Turkey.

On the home front the organisation of propaganda is far more elaborate than abroad. The reason for this is obvious; governments have no power outside their own boundaries, but a great deal within them. Desiring love and admiration as well as obedience, they use this power to compel their subjects to volunteer for servitude, to enforce enthusiasm upon them and harry them into willing co-operation. Their ultimate aim is, by means of suitable propaganda, to produce a nation of slaves, but of slaves who believe themselves free, who imagine that their abject obedience is the result of their own choice, who think that the opinions imposed on them by their masters are opinions that they themselves have reached by a process of serious and independent thought.

How far twentieth-century rulers will succeed in realising this grandiose ambition it is as yet very difficult to say. But before I discuss this problem I must describe the methods by means of which they seek to control the minds as well as the bodies of their subjects.

They begin by depriving the press of all liberty of political discussion. 'The press,' says Goebbels, 'must serve the state.' And directly or indirectly, frankly or covertly, it does so in a surprising number of countries. A sober American journalist, Mr. Albin Johnson, computes that, at present, only a quarter of the population of Europe enjoys anything that 'remotely resembles personal liberty and freedom of expression and conscience'.

Press censorship in the dictatorial countries is positive as well as negative. Governments are not content with forbidding newspapers to discuss certain topics, to mention certain names or events; they actually dictate what shall be said. Every word in the political columns, and in other sections of the newspaper as well, is 'inspired'. A man may buy twenty separate journals every morning; but in all of them he will find the same news provided by the official press agencies, adorned with comments inspired from the same august source. Year in, year out, he hears only His Master's Voice.

His Master's Voice bellows out of the loud speakers as well as from the pages of the newspapers. The BBC's praiseworthy attempts at impartiality find hardly any imitators. On important matters, only one opinion is ever expressed by the people who speak from the majority of European broadcasting stations – the opinion of the person who happens to have grabbed supreme power in the country from which the talk is being given.

In the book trade similar conditions prevail. Artists, in Mr. Max Eastman's phrase, are in uniform.[1] In their case, of course, the control is mainly negative. Their work is not susceptible of being 'inspired' in the journalistic sense of the word; but if it contains

1 Max Eastman, *Artists in Uniform: A Study of Literature and Bureaucratism*, London: George Allen & Unwin, 1934.

unsound doctrine, it either fails to get published at all or else, if published, renders the author liable to more or less serious persecution. Even in novels, poems, essays and plays, His Master's Voice must either be heard or, if not actually heard, never shouted down, never contradicted.

How successful are these methods of large-scale and intensive propaganda? No government, so far as I know, has ever issued an official statement on the subject; the relevant statistics are few and far between. Our answer is in the nature of an inference from various known facts. Briefly, it would seem that the results, at any rate so far as adults are concerned, are rather disappointing. Too much propaganda of too violent a kind to a great extent defeats its own object. Thus, when all newspapers print exactly the same news and comments they become so dull that people no longer bother to read them.

Since the establishment of the Nazi regime several hundred German newspapers have had to suspend publication, because they had no subscribers. Similarly, when broadcasting programmes always consist of the same thing, people give up listening-in. For the first year or so after Hitler's rise to power, German broadcasting was the most tedious in Europe. Such time as was not devoted to the frenzied bellowing of political leaders was given up to what was almost worse – the music of politically orthodox contemporary composers. Recently, it is highly significant to note, German programmes have been entirely reformed. Good concerts abound. Listeners are now being bribed by decent music to swallow their daily dose of propaganda without repugnance.

The organisers of the recent electoral campaign in Danzig seem to have made the same mistake of fanatically overstating their case and thus boring people into hostility. Many competent observers attributed the relative failure of the Nazis in the Free City to the fact that they had made too much propaganda.

The governments of dictatorial countries are fond of assuring foreigners that their subjects are absolutely unanimous in favour of the existing regime. And certainly these docile subjects vote as they should and refrain from overt acts of opposition. But is this fact to be attributed to the efficacy of the government's propaganda, or the number and ruthlessness of its soldiers and policemen? My own impression is that the sword, in these cases, is at least as mighty as the pen.

Talleyrand's epigram, that you can do everything with bayonets except sit on them, is really entirely beside the point. For if you are the ruler of a country, you don't have to sit on your bayonets. On the contrary, you jab them into other people's posteriors; and, so far as I can see, this is a pastime that can be continued almost indefinitely. There is a widespread belief that men and women will not put up with intolerable conditions. Alas, this is a complete illusion. If they can be convinced that revolt will entail conditions yet more intolerable (and to most human beings at most times, death and physical pain are more intolerable than even the unpleasantest existence), people will put up with practically anything for practically any length of time.

True, it is among these oppressed masses that propaganda is able to score its greatest triumphs. A good organiser with a simple programme, or policy of revenge and a guarantee of ultimate happiness, can momentarily fuse the inchoate mass of the oppressed into a powerful revolutionary army. But armed revolution against a resolute government possessed of tanks, planes and gas, is foredoomed to failure; the days of the barricades are over. And anyhow, under a vigilant dictatorship, what organiser of revolution would have a chance to spread his doctrines? Wielded with skill and ruthlessness, the dictatorial pen and sword are almost invincible.

So far I have discussed the organisation of propaganda addressed to adults. It is, however, upon the organisation of propaganda for children that the dictators have chiefly concentrated their energies. 'Give us a child', the Jesuit educators used to say, 'from the time he can speak until he is seven years old: we can answer for him for the rest of his life.' And in our own time the psycho-analysts have insisted even more emphatically on the unique importance of childish experience in the moulding of adult character and opinions.

The aim of the dictators is to catch their subjects as young as possible and saturate them so thoroughly with propaganda that the ideology of the local political religion will be incorporated into their very beings and become an integral part of their nature. They believe that children can be 'conditioned' as Pavlov's dogs are 'conditioned' and that the conditioning will last throughout their lives. To the suitable stimulus – fascist slogan or communist watch-word, Nordic boast or Turkish self-glorification, and always and everywhere the identical word of command, the same universally comprehensible kick in the seat of the trousers – the individual who has had the correct conditioning in childhood will automatically respond as he ought to respond, that is to say, as his rulers want him to respond. This is the theory that underlies educational methods in the dictatorial countries.

To describe these methods in detail is unnecessary. Everyone has seen photographs and films of children drilling, children being instructed in the handling of machine guns, children making ritual gestures of devotion before the image of the local boss. (It is interesting to note that the idolatrous emperor-worship prescribed by many Oriental monarchs of antiquity and subsequently by Augustus and his successors at Rome, is now being deliberately revived all over twentieth-century Europe.) We have all read accounts of history *à la mode d'Angora* and anthropology *à la mode berlinoise*;[1] the denunciations of Jewish morality and religion and even of Jewish mathematics, the hysterical self-congratulations of Nordics, Latins, Turks, Japs, Amerindians, Hottentots, and all the rest of them. The hysterical farrago of criminal nonsense that is stuffed into children's heads by dictatorial orders may therefore be taken for granted.

For our present purpose what is important is, not the methods employed, but the results obtained. We want to know whether propaganda applied to children is more successful than propaganda applied to adults. There can be no doubt, I am afraid, that children

1 *Angora*, i.e. Ankara, the Turkish capital.

can be moulded nearer to the heart's desire of the dictators than can grown-ups who have had the advantage of being brought up under a freer regime. But whether, in the conditions prevailing in Europe today, they can be moulded quite as completely as the dictators think and hope, seems to me doubtful. Once more there are no official statements, no relevant statistics. One can only argue from general principles and draw inferences from such facts as can be established.

Anthropologists have shown that, in small, homogeneous, primitive societies, childish 'conditioning' can be completely effective. It is psychologically impossible for a primitive to question his people's fundamental assumptions about the universe, about right and wrong, about the proper organisation of society. A primitive tribe is all of a piece; there are no differences of education and very few differences of occupation. King and slave think and to a great extent act in the same way. Different conditions, as we have seen, dispose to different modes of thought and feeling.

But, conditions in a primitive tribe being similar, primitive thought and feeling will tend to be similar. Fundamental assumptions are questioned only by people whose conditions of life are markedly unlike average conditions. Such people scarcely exist in primitive societies.

Again, primitives have little contact with the outside world; and such contact as they have is mainly with other primitives living in essentially similar conditions and clinging to their fundamental assumptions with a like tenacity.

Finally, primitives are wholly innocent of science – wholly innocent, that is to say, of any technique of systematic enquiry leading to the systematic change of conditions. To a wholly non-scientific mind, social organisations, moral codes, all the habits of thought and feeling instilled during childhood seem realities of the same kind as the weather – given and unalterable.

What the dictators are trying to do is to reproduce primitive conditions of feeling in a modern, technically efficient society. They want their subjects to be, on the one hand, good mechanics, good aeroplane designers, good scientific farmers, good mathematicians and so forth, and on the other hand, blindly obedient, filled with a child-like faith in the government's benevolence and wisdom, drunk with a fanatical crusading enthusiasm for the local political religion, having a savage's contempt and mistrust for the members of other social groups and a savage's sense of absolute, unquestioning solidarity with every member of his own group. In a word, they are trying to make the best of two worlds that are, at bottom, psychologically incompatible.

It is impossible to separate the virtues produced by one kind of social organisation from their complementary defects, nor to pick out for encouragement certain virtues, while rejecting others closely allied to them. A man cannot be an efficient citizen of a large heterogeneous industrial state and at the same time an efficient primitive.

The efforts of the dictators to produce good scientifically minded technicians with the sentiment and convictions of good Melanesians is doomed ultimately to failure. Ultimately, I repeat; but in the interval the systematic application to children of dictatorial propaganda is bound to produce most pernicious effects. In the minds of the children who subsequently undergo a scientific training it can hardly fail to generate a disturbing conflict of values. Science tells them to try all things and to hold fast only to that which seems reasonable; but on the parade ground, in the history classroom, everywhere, indeed, but in the laboratory, representatives of the ruling power are telling them to try nothing and hold fast only to what pleases the boss.

The victims of such divided allegiance have four alternatives before them. Either they can't make up their mind which is right, science or the dictator; in which case they suffer more or less acutely from neurasthenia. Or they decide that science is right, but out of fear continue to express the savage sentiments pleasing to the boss; in which case they lose their moral integrity and live in a state of chronic hypocrisy. Or else they believe that the boss is right and keep boss-worship and science in two water-tight compartments; in which case they lose their intellectual integrity. Or finally, they come to the conclusion that the boss is wrong and act on their conclusion by open rebellion; in which case they are beaten up, shot, or sent to gaol.

In the case of the children who do not receive an intensive scientific training, dictatorial propaganda is likely to be more successful; it will take them longer than the others to discover that primitive sentiments are incompatible with the conditions prevailing in a technicised society. More or less whole-heartedly convinced that the boss is right, they can be used as janissaries to repress the tendencies of the other more highly conscious individuals to rebel against the prevailing tyranny.

In the long run, I repeat, even these untrained people will become aware that their primitivism is out of place in a world where production is scientific and communications are easy. In the long run . . . But, then, in the long run we shall all be dead. What concerns us is the short run; and in the short run, I am afraid, educational propaganda in favour of primitivism can do a great deal of mischief.

Moral: do your best, so long as you still possess political rights and can do anything at all, to prevent your government from organising such propaganda, particularly among the children.

Nash's Pall Mall Magazine, xcv, July 1935, 18–21, 114–16, 118[1]

1   This article was based on Huxley's address to the International Writers' Congress, Paris, on 21 June 1935. A truncated version appeared as 'Naturaleza y limite de la influencia de los escritores', *Sur* [Buenos Aires], no. 11, August 1935, 7–24, and he delivered a paper on the same topic at the Conway Hall, London on 10 January 1936. Revised and reworked, it was published as a five-part article on 'Propaganda' in the *Spectator* between 6 November and 4 December 1936.

Emperor-Worship Up to Date

Let me begin with a quotation. The following lines are taken from a long inscription on a stone set up about 9 B.C. in Asia Minor, to commemorate the birthday of Augustus:

This day has given the earth an entirely new aspect. The world would have gone to destruction had there not streamed forth from him who is born a common blessing . . . The providence which rules over all has filled this man with such gifts for the salvation of the world as designate him the Saviour of us and for future generations . . . By his appearing the hopes of our forefathers are fulfilled . . . The birthday of God has brought to the earth good tidings that are bound up in him. From his birthday a new era begins.

To us who live in the 1930s this early and passionate expression of Roman emperor-worship has a curiously familiar ring. We seem to have heard this sort of thing before, applied to certain of our contemporaries. True, Hitler and Mussolini have not actually been called God by their admirers; the Christian tradition is still too strong for that to be done without arousing indignation and derision. But every other phrase of our inscription in honour of the deified Augustus could be paralleled in eulogies of contemporary dictators. They are, if not themselves God, at least God's vice-regents. Providence has sent them to save their countries, and, if their countries can conquer other countries, the world. They possess every desirable quality of character and intellect. They are infallible. ('Mussolini is always right' is stencilled on a million walls throughout Italy.)

It is not only in their theologies that emperor-worship and modern dictator-worship resemble one another; their practices reveal all manner of similarities. Thus, in Nazi Germany, the *sacramentum*, or oath of allegiance, has taken on all the religious significance it had in Rome under the Empire. The dictator's name and title, like those of the emperor, are used liturgically, as though they had the force of magic spells. Instead of marching to the equivalent of 'left, right, left', Italians now march to '*du-cé, du-cé*'; instead of signing 'yours truly', one finishes one's letter, in modern Germany, with '*Heil Hitler*'. The emperor demanded incense; the dictator is content, by way of homage, with a special salute and a march past at the goose step.

Nor are temples altogether lacking, as anyone can testify who has visited, bare-headed by order, the holy of holies of the Exhibition of the Fascist Revolution at Rome.[1] Suetonius tells us that Augustus's birth-place in the street of the Ox Heads on the Palatine Hill was converted after his death into a chapel. Mussolini's already has its marble plaque, and even during the dictator's lifetime Predappio has become a place of pilgrimage. 'FIVE THOUSAND ON PILGRIMAGE TO MUSSOLINI'S COUNTRY' was a headline that caught my eye in Rome last year. Lenin's shrine in the Kremlin draws its thousands.

Why were emperors and why are dictators worshipped? In many cases, no doubt, the predominating motive is fear. People worship because, if they don't, they will be persecuted. But in most cases, at any rate during the early years of the new religious movement, adoration is not forced, but spontaneous. Fear is only a partial explanation. It would be possible to carry the analysis back to the beginning and discuss why there should be such a thing as worship of any kind. But there is no time for this; nor, in the circumstances, is it necessary. Emperor- and dictator-worship are political phenomena, and their proximate causes are to be found on the political plane.

1 Huxley and his wife visited it during an Easter visit to Rome in 1934.

Emperor-worship was more popular in the provinces of the empire than at Rome itself. Why? Because, in the later Republican period, the provinces had suffered atrociously under the misrule of governors, whose one aim was to extort, during their period of office, the greatest possible amount of ill-gotten wealth. With the civil wars there followed a period of anarchy more distressing than the previous misgovernment. Augustus was the bringer of peace and good administration. Duly grateful, suffering populations worshipped him as a saviour. And in the most literal and material sense of the word, he *was* a saviour.

In our own times dictator-worship has flourished only in the countries most seriously affected by the war and the ensuing peace – in defeated Germany; in an Italy disorganised and, although on the winning side, full of grievances and resentments; in Russia, where the collapse under the strain of war was more complete than elsewhere and the physical sufferings of the people far more intense and long-drawn. In all these countries dictators appeared, promising material blessings and at the same time restoring lost self-esteem and offering the psychological satisfactions of intense group emotion and a shared faith. Gratefully, their followers adored them.

In one particular, emperor-worship and modern dictator-worship are significantly dissimilar. In the time of Augustus people of different race, language and creed worshipped one man. Emperor-worship was a monotheism. Dictator-worship, on the other hand, is polytheistic, in the sense that each country has its own private man-god. The political unification of so many separate States in the Roman Empire made men feel the need for a single religion. Emperor-worship was one of the preliminary phases in a movement towards monotheism and religious unity which finally resulted in the general acceptance of Christianity. The localised worship of dictators is a sign that, in spite of the unifying influence of technology, the tendency of the modern world is towards disruption and separation. The worship of one God persists; but it has a formidable rival in nationalism, of which dictator-worship is the most highly developed form.

How long may we expect the present phase of nationalism and dictator-worship to last? In no circumstances can gratitude be long-drawn. If the benefactor does not fulfil his promise of permanent prosperity for all, he is disliked for his failure; if he succeeds, men take his benefactions for granted and are no longer grateful for them. No single dictator has much hope of being genuinely adored for very long, but in an age of misery and political disruption, each one of a series of separate national dictators might obtain divine honours for a short time.

On the material plane, prosperity and peaceful intercourse are the best cures for fanatical nationalism and dictator-worship. On the plane of thought and feeling, there is no final cure but the general acceptance of a transcendental religion. Socialism may offer a temporary palliative, but the trouble with socialism, as a religion, is that its ideals are largely realisable; and men who have realised their ideals are left hopelessly unsatisfied and empty. Excellent as a temporary counterblast to nationalism, the religion of socialism will ultimately have to be supplemented by some more permanently satisfying faith.

Meanwhile, wherever we look, we see the stupid and dangerous idolatries of nationalism supplemented here and there by the crazy blasphemies of dictator-worship. It is an ugly and disquieting spectacle.

The Star, 11 October 1935, 4

The General Election of 1906 was the first in which I was of an age to take a rational interest. For, of course, my twelve-year-old's enthusiasm for the Liberal cause had very little to do with reason. I was passionately a Liberal because my family was Liberal, and at that period of English history boys of twelve still tended to believe that their families were right.

The election of 1906 was mainly fought on the question of Tariff Reform. The hoardings were covered with pictures of loaves of bread, and with printed asseverations that Protection would (or would not) mean work for all. These I remember only faintly. The election poster that made the deepest impression on my mind was one which represented the face of a peculiarly villainous Chinaman. I cannot remember what were the words that accompanied the image; but the association of this scowling yellow mask with the Conservative policy produced a most powerful emotional effect. Looking at it, one could only feel that the Tories must be extraordinarily wicked people. I now know that this election poster had something to do with the Liberals' protest against the employment of indentured Chinese labour in the Rand Gold Mines – or rather with the Liberals' objection to the indentured Chinese being compulsorily repatriated after their term of service.

That picture of a Chinese bandit was supposed to be a protest against the enslavement of defenceless coolies; in actual fact it subtly suggested that anyone who supported the Tories would somehow be letting his country in for the Yellow Peril in its most criminal form. I have dwelt at some length on these memories of my first General Election; for that sinister Chinaman, whose image impressed itself so deeply on my mind, is wholly characteristic and typical. He made his appearance in 1906. But he might have made it in 1910, 1918, 1931; might make it again in 1935 or 1936.

Voters belong to two main classes; those who either on rational or irrational grounds accept certain political principles or who have decided once and for all that their own private interests will be best served by the victory of a given party; and those who have no particular political faith, don't know which side will bring them the greatest advantages and therefore allow themselves to be stampeded into voting this way or that by appeals, during the election campaign, to their feelings.

No party can win a victory, unless it can persuade the second class of electors to vote for it. Hence that irrelevant and misleading Chinaman, along with all his earlier and later equivalents. Hence those appeals to every sentiment, passion and instinct, from fear to collective vanity, from avarice to hatred, from patriotism to mother-love. Hence all that kissing of babies, that shaking of hands, that perpetually smiling cordiality of the candidates.

A General Election is an event that may have a very considerable historical significance; but for a great part of the population it is also, while it lasts, a most agreeable kind of emotional debauch, something between a Bank Holiday and a prize-fight, between the Cup Final and a Royal Wedding, between Carnival and All Fool's Day. Life is mainly routine, and this routine, to be tolerable, must be punctuated occasionally by orgies, sometimes very disreputable, sometimes more or less respectable, of emotional excitement. A General Election is one of these periodical orgies. But whereas, like virtue, most emotional orgies are their own reward, General Elections have an ulterior purpose and are a means to remoter, non-orgiastic ends. The people who enjoy the gratuitous fun of the election campaign are also voters; and their fun is only a preliminary to an act of choice that may be pregnant with the most momentous consequences to the country as a whole and to every individual within it.

And here a question inevitably propounds itself: what do voters really want, what do they hope to get out of the election? A referendum would show, I suspect, that practically all of them, whether Conservative, or Liberal, or Labour, or without any political principles at all, ultimately desire and hope for one thing: security. Security from the sudden catastrophe of war; security from the creeping disaster of unemployment; security of tenure in what they already possess and, for those who possess nothing, security of tenure in some assured job.

The most perfunctory examination of the propaganda published by the various political parties reveals the fact that the end which all propose is the greatest possible security for the greatest possible number. Each claims to be pre-eminently the advocate of peace, pre-eminently the foe of unemployment and poverty, pre-eminently the friend of higher standards of living and a more assured prosperity. The ends, I repeat, are in all cases the same — or at any rate the avowed ends; for of course there are also ends which it would be most impolitic to avow.

The difference between the parties lies in the means proposed by each for the achievement of those ends. But it is possible that, in practice, the means may turn out to be not quite so different as they appear in theory. Thus, the Conservatives believe in the retention of private enterprise and the incentive of profit; but they are finding already (and the future will doubtless reinforce the lesson of the immediate past) that private enterprise can be retained only in part and on the condition of being largely subordinated to the State; that the incentive of profit can be preserved only if the amount of profit taken be limited. On their side, the Labour Party will probably also be forced to compromise. Labour has never yet polled as much as forty per cent. of the total number of votes cast at a General Election. The majority of electors vote for the bourgeois parties, either because they are bourgeois or else because they would like to be and imagine that their interests are best served by the bourgeois parties.

This being so, Labour will certainly find it very difficult to proceed to the immediate socialisation of the country's entire economic system. To do so at once and violently would be to risk a civil war, from which it is more than possible that the bourgeois would emerge victorious. Nor must we forget that the great Trade Unions are to a considerable extent conservative organisations, interested in preserving their gratifyingly important position in society and the economic advantages which they have secured for their members. For them, almost as much as for the bourgeois with a good professional job, Socialism is two birds in the bush – whereas the present order is definitely one bird in the hand. It is probable that Labour, if it obtained power, would find itself compelled merely to speed up and systematise the policy which the Conservatives are pursuing slowly, reluctantly and piecemeal.

Theoretically, the policies of the socialists and the Conservatives are extremely different. But it looks as though circumstances were going to dictate to both a fundamentally similar course of action – the reorganisation of our economic life by the creation of public utility companies, privately managed, but responsible to the State; permitted to make profits, but only on a strictly limited scale.

Most prophecies are wrong, and there are many ways in which this tentative forecast of mine may be completely falsified. First, there may be a war; and heaven only knows what the result of that would be. Secondly, there may be another sharp decline in economic prosperity; this would tend to inflame class antagonism and to make any process of constitutional reform extremely difficult. Thirdly, a sweeping Labour victory might frighten the middle-classes into a wholesale adoption of Fascist methods. A thoroughly scared bourgeoisie might easily organise itself into an army for the purpose of violently resisting all economic and social change, however reasonable and desirable. Nor must we forget the possibility of a more gradual, more discreet, but none the less effective growth of Fascism under the auspices of a Conservative Party – successful indeed, but only just successful, at the polls and disturbed in mind about the future.

In this case there would be no nonsense about black shirts and banners and Nazi salutes; the method employed would be that

which the English (like the Romans before them) have regularly
employed throughout their history – the method that consists in
preserving the names of ancient institutions while completely
changing their substance. Thus, on paper, our monarchy is all and
more than all that it was in the time of Henry VIII. The resounding
names and titles are still there; but the substance of political power
has departed. Hitherto this curious political method has been
chiefly used for reconciling the new facts of political liberty with the
old traditions of absolutism. There is no reason, however, why the
direction should not be reversed, so that the honourable names of
long-established free institutions should cover the facts of a new
tyranny. Augustus was in fact the absolute ruler of Rome; but he
assumed no titles except those which had belonged to the officers of
the defunct republic. It is not difficult to imagine an analogous state
of things coming about in twentieth-century Britain.

Whether in fact the ruling and propertied classes will seriously
attempt, either openly or surreptitiously, to create a fighting organisation for the defence of their interests remains to be seen. In
England, hitherto, these classes have had the sense to see that half a
loaf is better than no bread; they have preferred giving up part of
their power and privileges to risking the chance of losing them all in
an open struggle. Perhaps they will do the same now. Perhaps, on
the other hand, they may feel that, this time, they will have to give
away too much and that it is worth while fighting for what they have
– all the more worth while since modern weapons such as planes,
tanks and gas give their possessors the complete certainty of victory
over those who do not possess them. Thanks to mechanical invention, the twentieth-century world is a place where (except when
used between nations, each of which is as well armed as the others)
violence pays much better than it did in the recent past.

With regard to the outcome of the approaching election, it would
be mere folly to prophesy.[1] Here, for what they are worth, are a few

1   The General Election was held on 14 November and was won by the Conserva-
    tives, thus confirming the National Government in another term of office.

siderations which a prophet would have to take into account. The floating army of unaffiliated electors on whom the result of the contest depends will certainly have two sound psychological reasons for voting against the National Government. First, the desire for change: the National Government has been in power long enough for people to be bored with it. And second, the tendency present in all human beings to 'blame the Government' for everything unpleasant that may happen to them: the National Government is now governing and so inevitably gets blamed. There is every reason, therefore, to suppose that the Conservatives and their allies will lose a considerable number of votes.

Now the English electoral system is peculiar and singularly undemocratic – which is probably the reason why our English democracy has worked as well as it has. Each constituency returns only one member; whose majority over his rival may consist of only one vote. In any given constituency half the voters minus one may be completely unrepresented in Parliament. This means that a small change in the number of votes cast for a given party may result in a very large change in the number of its representatives in Parliament. In 1931, for example, Labour polled about thirty per cent. of the total number of votes cast instead of the thirty-six per cent. it had polled at the previous election. Not a very heavy decline. But, light as it was, it entailed for Labour the loss of two hundred and fifteen seats in the House of Commons. A correspondingly slight movement of the electors in the opposite direction may mean as heavy a loss to the supporters of the National Government. Whether this loss of seats will be so great as to entail the actual loss of a majority in Parliament, it is, of course, impossible to guess.

Every Government in office inspires dislike, just because it is the Government, and also, if it has been in office for long, weariness and disgust. But it possesses one great compensating advantage: it can go to the country at the moment that suits it best. Circumstances may arise which will work so strongly in the Government's favour that the electors may forget their natural boredom and dislike, and vote, if they are given a chance, in its favour. A fortunate Government finds such circumstances ready-made; a prudent one does its best to produce them artificially. Will the National Government be skilful enough to manufacture its own good luck? It will be interesting indeed to see.

Artists Against Fascism and War

The work in this exhibition is being shown as a protest against Fascism and War. Personally, I should have preferred to 'Fascism' the more general term 'dictatorship'; for I am convinced that, however admirable the ends proposed by the dictators, any form of dictatorship is intrinsically bad. Good ends never justify bad means for the simple reason that, in the process of being used, the bad means change the good ends, so that what in fact is reached is not the goal originally proposed, but some other and worse goal. Good ends, on the whole, are less important than good means. If the means are good, the end reached will also be good. This truth is constantly being illustrated in the arts. Fine ends get you nowhere; what the artist needs is adequate means. Benjamin Robert Haydon, for example, had as his end the revival of 'historical art', by which he meant the sort of art produced by the masters of the Italian High Renaissance. Unhappily, his means for producing pictures were inadequate and often (artistically speaking) downright vicious. Haydon's ambitious compositions were and are without the smallest value or significance. His bad means had corrupted his noble ends.[1] What is obviously true of art is a little less obviously, but no less certainly, true of politics.

The practice of art is a discipline, but a discipline freely accepted by the artist. The good artist is, so to speak, a special case of the

Huxley wrote an Introduction to Tom Taylor's edition of *The Autobiography and Memoirs of Benjamin Robert Haydon* (1926) which was reprinted in Huxley's *The Olive Tree* (1936).

The Hidden Huxley

good citizen; in his studio and while painting, he is self-controlled, scrupulous, conscientious – he practises, in a word, the virtue which, practised in all circumstances, make the ideally good citizen. War-lords and dictators have no use for such self-discipline. All that they require from their victims is a passive obedience; which they are able to extort because they have previously imposed on them a mechanical discipline from without. There is a very real sense in which the whole activity of the self-disciplined artist is standing protest against war and dictatorship. It is also a standing protest against that pacific liberalism which is merely soft and self-indulgent. The artistic life is not identical with the good life, but it is certainly an image of it, a deeply significant emblem.

Foreword to the catalogue of an exhibition mounted by Eric Gill,
  Duncan Grant, Augustus John, Laura Knight, Henry Moore,
  Paul Nash and the Artists International Association at 28 Soho
  Square, London, 13–27 November 1935, under the banner
  'Artists Against Fascism and War'

Total War and Pacifism

he argument between those who think that capital ships are still
ful and those who think that they are not, continues with unab-
ed vehemence in articles and letters to the press. Meanwhile, an
ficial assurance has been given that the air defences of capital
ips are now satisfactory. There is, however, no evidence that
sts comparable even to those carried out some years ago by the
nited States Navy have ever been repeated here. These tests
emed to show that heavy bombs falling, not even on, but near a
ip could inflict serious damage and even sink it. Battleship-
vers behave like Don Quixote with his helmet. His first repair to
e vizor he tested by giving it a blow with his sword; the vizor was
roken. Laboriously, Don Quixote mended it again; but this time
e risked no dangerous and disturbing experiments. He assumed
at his handiwork was sound, because he wanted it to be sound.
he optative had actually become the indicative tense.

Most stupidity is not due to congenital defects in the thinking
echanism; it is due to will. We are stupid, in a majority of cases,
ecause stupidity is to our advantage. Sometimes this advantage is
easurable in terms of cash. More often the gains we seek, the
sses we try to avoid, are purely personal and subjective. Why, for
ample, do we refuse to change our opinions, even when chang-
g circumstances have made nonsense of them? Not on account
f some native imbecility, but because it is intolerable to us to have
admit that we are no longer right. It is a point of honour, a
atter of prestige. In other words, it is a point of pride, a matter of
ersonal vanity. Logic has little or no effect on those who have a

personal interest in remaining unconvinced by it.

The lovers of light warships and planes attack the lovers of battleships with facts and inferences logically derived from these facts. In vain. The battleship-lovers are far less vulnerable than their own ironclads. They have always believed in capital ships and they refuse to stop believing in them. To admit that one is wrong is a humiliation which very few people are prepared to accept.

Neither side seems to perceive that, sinkable or unsinkable, not only battleships, but also cruisers, destroyers, submarines and all the rest are now almost completely irrelevant to the realities of the day. From a military point of view, a fleet is valuable for enforcing or resisting blockades, or for permitting the transport overseas of an army. But the next European war will not in all probability be fought by armies; nor will blockade be enforced out at sea, but from the air, by the destruction of harbours and docks. No modern strategist is going to risk the safety of his planes and pilots by sending them to attack elaborate pieces of floating ironmongery which, intact, can do him no harm and whose destruction can do him very little good. No, he will order the bombardment of the enemy's towns, not of the hostile fleet. If the towns can be badly damaged and the surviving population reduced to panic, starvation and anarchy, nothing else matters. The fleet may safely be allowed to steam about and let off its big guns until fuel and ammunition are exhausted. Then it will have to go home – only to find that there is no home. In any future European war that it is possible to foresee, it seems simply not to matter whether the fighting ships are large or small, nor even whether they are on the surface of the water or at the bottom.

In regard to air armaments, ardent nationalists and League of Nations idealists agree as to the consummation to be desired. It is this: that there should be such overwhelming air power available that would-be aggressors will see that aggression doesn't pay. The differ only in their views regarding the right means for achieving that desirable consummation. The nationalists want the available air power to be exclusively national. This means that we must adopt a two-power or, if necessary, an n-power standard of air armament

The idealists are shocked by the doctrines and policies of undiluted nationalism. Their demand is for a more modest increase in our bombing fleet, accompanied by collective security – that is to say, by the collaboration of all national bombing fleets against an aggressor nation.

What is the probability of either of these policies having the good effects expected of them? Let us try to answer. First of all, populations which have to think they have a grievance (the subjective are more important than the objective facts) are seldom if ever put off from fighting for what they consider to be their rights by considerations of risk. Nor do considerations deter the dictator. If he is crazy, he doesn't perceive the risk. If he is coldly Machiavellian, he sees that in desperate circumstances he personally may risk less by going to war than by submitting to the threats of foreign governments. Second, we are not alone in regarding our neighbours as potential aggressors; they return the compliment. Any increase in our national air armaments must inevitably lead to a corresponding increase in other people's air armaments. And any increase in the air armaments of the powers allied for the purpose of 'collective security' must inevitably lead to corresponding rearmament on the part of those powers who remain outside the collective system or who, though nominally within it, feel that they are likely to be picked out as aggressors. Armament races are exhausting competitions; the moment one side feels that it is reaching the breaking point, it will strike.

In the light of such conclusions the policy of threats, whether made by individual nations or by groups of nations, seems foredoomed to failure. As for the moral consolations derived by the idealists from the words 'collective security' – these turn out, upon examination, to be less consoling than they appeared to be. For what, as a matter of actual and contemporary fact, is collective security? It is the name we now give to an alliance binding a certain number of great powers (the small ones, from a military point of view, don't count) to collaborate for the purpose of destroying peoples whose governments are considered by the allied governments to have committed an act of aggression. But mass murder is as wrong when it is called 'police action in defence of collective security' as it is when it is called war. And the physical, economic and psychological after-effects of the two processes are identical. New presbyter is but old priest writ large. A bomb dropped by a pilot belonging to one of the powers which, when in alliance, constitute the police force of the League, kills and mangles just as many people and leaves just as bitter a memory of wrong among the survivors, as does a bomb dropped by a pilot belonging to the same power, when fighting on its own account. And a system of military alliances labelled 'collective security' is indistinguishable, morally and in fact, from a system of military alliances designated by any other name. A system of collective security based upon a policy of threatening and in the last resort using military sanctions is the best system as yet proposed by 'practical politicians'. Its defects would seem to be these: (a) there is no likelihood of its working and (b) its use of militaristic methods makes it morally and as a matter of concrete, personally experienced fact, indistinguishable from any other system devised for the waging of war. 'The idea that you have solved any problem of practical life in modern societies by saying that X or Y is bad, and that you will, therefore, have nothing to do with it, may sound extremely fine and attractive, but is really either a doctrine of despair or just silliness.' So writes Mr. Leonard Woolf in the paragraph devoted to the Pacifist Position in his recently published pamphlet, *The League and Abyssinia*.[1] If this in fact were the pacifist position, he would be quite right in regarding pacifism as a policy of despair and silliness. But the pacifist does not dream of saying that he will have nothing to do with evil. His policy is to be a realist and to deal with evil in the only way that is effective. To deal with it by means of more evil is demonstrably unpractical. An evil act always produces further evil acts, however good the intentions of the actor and however evil the person against whom he is acting. True, the effect of evil-doing may be neutralised by a striking act of reparation and restitution. English

1 Leonard Woolf, *The League and Abyssinia*, London: Hogarth Press, 1936, 29.

policy in South Africa after the Boer War provides a case in point. The pacifist would short-circuit the process by cutting out the evil act, for which reparation must be made, and using intelligent generosity at the beginning instead of at the end of the drama. It may be very difficult to prevent certain European nations from attacking their neighbours. What is quite certain is that threatening them with war if they do so or making war upon them, even with a collective bombing force, will not achieve what is desired. Whereas it is possible that even at this late hour the summoning of a conference and the frank discussion of grievances, the sincere and genuine effort to settle outstanding differences in an amicable way might be successful in allaying the present madness.

From 'Notes on the Way', Time and Tide, xvii, 7 March 1936, 325–6

'We have not attempted to meet the views of those who, instead of desiring more coherent design in our political and social system, are content to trust rather to improvisation.

'There are those who virtually assume that man cannot control his economic future, or master the forces making for war by rational, constructive and collective effort; those who . . . desire to reverse the whole trend of recent development, or else to "muddle through" by successive improvisations as each emergency occurs, with a mystic faith in the ability of natural forces or instinctive human action to reinstate a workable order.

'On the other hand, there are those who believe that we can and must master international anarchy . . . and that the community can and must deliberately plan, direct and control . . . the economic development to which innumerable individual activities contribute. These believe that the State, and other institutions associated with the State, must be increasingly active partners, both in encouraging and directing economic enterprise.' So write the framers of the programme put forth by 'The Next Five Years' Group'.[1] And they go on to affirm their belief in planning. 'The present situation,' they conclude, 'offers at once a new challenge and a new opportunity. The democratic system of government is on its trial. It will only

[1] Huxley is quoting from the Introduction to *The Next Five Years: An Essay in Political Agreement*, London: Macmillan, 1935, 6–7. Those involved in the Next Five Years project included Gerald Heard, Julian Huxley, Siegfried Sassoon and H. G. Wells. A 'Next Five Years' Group' of 150 persons was formalized the following year.

survive if it can produce a policy equal to the problems of our time, and a leadership capable of evoking the co-operation and enthusiasm necessary to carry it through.'

Most of us will agree that a policy of improvisations and muddling through is no longer a practical policy. It worked in the distant past, because society was simple and therefore capable of withstanding very rough treatment. You can take an ox wagon over roads that would destroy a Rolls-Royce. Muddling through also worked during the nineteenth century, when society was already extremely complex. It worked, because the population was rapidly increasing and because a rapidly-increasing population provides automatically a solution to the major problems of economics. In a world where markets are continually expanding, one does not have to give much thought to questions of technological unemployment or insufficiency of purchasing power. New inventions throw men out of work; but they are re-absorbed into industry almost immediately, because of the steadily increasing demand for the products of industry. At the same time, inadequacy of individual purchasing power hardly matters, because the number of individuals is continuously growing. A people which breeds hard has almost no need to think about its economic problems. But now comes a moment when people cease to breed. Population increases less and less rapidly, ceases to increase at all, and finally starts to decrease. At the same time scientific and industrial progress goes on at an ever accelerating speed. What is the result? Technological unemployment and deficiency in individual purchasing power become the most serious of problems. A population which practises birth-control can no longer leave its economic problems to be solved automatically. A world which has stopped breeding must begin to think. Our world has chosen to combine a personal policy of birth-control with a national policy of high tariffs. Customs duties aggravate the economic effects of contraceptives. Result: we must think yet harder. Hence the necessity for those co-ordinating plans; hence the danger in persisting in a policy of improvisation and muddling through.

Members of the Next Five Years' Group are not, of course, the only people to have realised the necessity for large-scale and long-range planning. The Communists and the Fascists have been in the field before them. Where they differ from these planners is in their insistence that planning shall be combined with democratic institutions. The thing they are most anxious to avoid is 'a despairing lapse' on the part of England 'into the tyrannical and barbaric methods' which have been employed by planners in other countries [p.8].

That planning should be undertaken democratically is, of course, extremely desirable. The difficulty will be to realise this ideal in practice. For it is in the very nature of a comprehensive plan that it does not lend itself easily to being carried out democratically.

England has been hitherto the home of improvisation and muddling through. We have made any number of reforms without ever accepting the principles underlying them. The King's titles are still what they were four hundred years ago; we still talk of our devotion to individualism, in spite of the fact of much State and municipal control. Large-scale planning has always been absent from English politics; and English politicians have tended to refrain from thinking in terms of first principles. One of the results of this state of things is that English politics have been on the whole very good-natured. We have been content to deal with emergencies as they arose, to avoid first principles and reduce each successive political conflict to a particular piece of haggling. Now hagglers may lose their tempers, but do not normally regard one another as fiends in human form. But this is precisely what men of principle and systematic planners find it all but impossible not to do. A principle is by definition *right*; a plan *for the good of the community*. It logically follows that those who disagree with you and will not help you to carry out your plan are enemies of truth, goodness and humanity. They cease to be men and women and become incarnations of evil. People hesitate to kill men and women, even when they insist on haggling; but to kill fiends is a duty and a pleasure. Hence the Holy Office, the Committee of Public Safety, the Ogpu, the Gestapo.

Men with strong religious and revolutionary faith, men with well-thought-out plans for improving the world, have been more systematically and cold-bloodedly cruel than any others. Thinking in terms of first principles has generally entailed acting with swords and rubber truncheons. A government with a comprehensive plan for bettering the lot of its subjects, either in this world or in the next, is too often a government that uses torture. Contrariwise, if you never consider first principles and have no comprehensive plan, but are content to deal with situations as they arise, piecemeal, you can afford to have unarmed policemen, freedom of speech and *habeas corpus*. Admirable. But what happens when an industrial society learns, first, how to make technological advances at an ever-accelerating speed and, second, how to prevent conception? The answer is that it must either plan itself or break down. But governments with principles and plans have generally been tyrannies making use of terrorism. Intelligent co-ordination has been achieved by means of enslavement and torture.

Breakdown on the one hand; secret police rule on the other. It is a horrible dilemma. The Next Five Years' Group seems to think we can pass between the horns if only we can produce 'a leadership capable of evoking the co-operation and enthusiasm necessary to carry ... through' [p.7] a comprehensive plan. But however successful the leader, is it likely that he will be able to arouse enthusiasm in, and obtain co-operation from, all the individuals in the community? Hitler and Mussolini seem to be about as successful as any leader can reasonably expect to be; but even they have had oppositions to deal with. English leaders will have their opposition; and this opposition will be bitter in proportion as the plan opposed is comprehensive and the political and economic principles involved are fundamental. We know how oppositions have been dealt with in the other highly-planned countries of Europe. What will be the fate of the English opposition to planning? The ideal of our planners is a co-ordinated society democratically controlled. A noble ideal. But in practice how far is co-ordination (if it is to be brought about in so short a period as five years) compatible with democratic methods? That is the uncomfortable question.

From 'Notes on the Way', *Time and Tide*, xvii, 14 March 1936, 357–8

If We Survive

Four and a half years of homicidal and suicidal mania were followed by seventeen of more or less acute neurosis during the last reign. At the start of a new reign our civilisation is showing symptoms of physical and mental disease even more alarming than those which were discernible before 1914. The new reign opens upon a momentous question: will the disease be allowed to run its course, or shall we decide that it is time to begin a new epoch of history and try to cure the present symptoms and prevent their recurrence?

The situation is at once a good deal worse than when George V came to the throne and a good deal better. Worse, because, thanks to technological progress, a lunatic world is in a position to do itself much more harm than it could do a quarter of a century ago. It is worse also, because the physical condition of the patient is less satisfactory than it was before 1914. It is better, because self-satisfaction has disappeared and increasing numbers of men and women have begun to realise more or less clearly what is wrong.

The disease from which our civilisation suffers may be described in a few words. Since the accession of Queen Victoria there has been enormous and accelerating technological progress. Machines and the arts of organisation have been developed out of all recognition. But, unfortunately, we and our fathers before us have persisted in regarding technology as the Pharisees regarded the Sabbath. We have behaved as though man were made for technology, not technology for man. In the first half of Queen Victoria's reign, technology was a kind of Moloch to which human beings were sacrificed in the most brutal way. In mine, factory and slum, the lives of countless thousands of men, women and children were offered up to industrial progress. We have come to be shocked by such manifest immolations and think that the claim made by technology to feed on broken human bodies is altogether excessive – at any rate, in time of peace; for we still think it right that progress should have its fill during war-time.

It is only recently, however, that we have, as a nation, begun to see that man's mind is no more made for technology than is his body, and that, conversely, technology is valuable only in so far as it helps men to cultivate sanity and goodness as well as bodily health. Moreover, we now begin to suspect that many technological advances hitherto regarded as wholly beneficial may have their bad as well as their good side. For example, technicians have made possible the multiplication of many kinds of novel amusements and distractions, from the modern newspaper to television. People enjoy these distractions. But that does not mean that they are, humanly speaking, altogether good. People also enjoy hashish and opium, when these are made available. It seems possible that we are paying a heavy spiritual price for our new-found amusements.

And what are we paying, as individuals and as a species, for some of the recent advances in pharmacological and medical technique? The market is flooded with new drugs. Is this one of the reasons why the number of doctors has doubled since the beginning of the century, while the population has increased by only about a fifth?

As for the doctors, they are engaged in activities which are in the main of obvious immediate benefit to individuals. But what of the long-range effects of their activities? Eminent authorities have warned us that wholesale inoculation against infectious diseases will probably result in the survival and increase of those human strains which have no congenital resistance to the disease in question. This may mean that we are now preparing the ground for future epidemics on a scale hitherto undreamed of. No less immediately beneficent is our present medical policy of preserving weakly and disease-prone infants, who would otherwise have died. But what will be the results of that policy a generation or two from now? Time alone can give the answer; but meanwhile there are many who look forward to that answer with profound apprehension.

Again, what price is being paid for the urbanisation which science and industry have made possible? Does a place like London offer its inhabitants an environment fit for fully human beings? Or consider modern transport. It saves us from using our muscles; creates and then allows us to satisfy a nervous craving for going somewhere else and being in a crowd; it carries us so swiftly from place to place that we cannot observe the details of the intervening landscape. What price, physiological and psychological, are we paying for railways, cars and planes? Factory production makes possible the multiplication at a cheap rate of innumerable objects. But is even the best factory a proper environment for fully human beings? And is there any sense in encouraging human beings to complicate their lives by possessing ever increasing numbers of unnecessary bits of matter? This brings us to a series of yet more fundamental questions. What is the price of industrial prosperity? What psychological states are correlated with different incomes? What is the price we pay for a philosophy which exalts what Hitler calls 'the heroic conception of wealth' – in other words, the idea that money must be made for its own sake, merely as a symbol of power?

It is because such questions were never answered, and, indeed, hardly ever asked, that the new civilisation which grew up so rapidly under Victoria and Edward VII came so near to perishing under George V. What will happen during the reign of Edward VIII? Shall we at last decide that technology is made for man, not man for technology? If we do this, and begin to put the principle into practice, the reign should be a happy one. If we prefer to go on as we are going now, there is no saying what may happen.

'What is needed is immediate co-operation on certain practical issues.' So write the authors of the first pamphlet issued by the People's Front Propaganda Committee; and they go on to urge the leaders of the Labour Party to drop their 'regrettable prejudice against a People's Front', to abandon their present 'unwillingness' to work with men and women belonging to other organisations, to forget that 'these men and women [often] differ from them on [some] points of Labour policy and as to the ultimate goal of Socialism', and only to remember that they are at one with them in a desire for peace, democracy and particular measures of social and economic reform.[1]

A People's Front, composed of members of all the progressive parties co-operating on certain specific issues, is desirable for two distinct sets of reasons. It is desirable for what we may call short-range reasons – because the present situation at home and abroad is so threatening that progressives must either hang together or hang separately. It is also desirable for long-range reasons – because concentration on practical problems tends to unite, whereas pre-occupation with words and theories foments divisions and hostilities. A People's Front would have this great merit: it would possess

1 Huxley is quoting from *People's Front for Britain*, no. 1, 1936, 6, published by the People's Front Propaganda Committee. The PFPC was organized by the ex-Communist John T. Murphy to bring about the defeat of the National Government. Murphy defined the Front as consisting of 'a coalition of all parties and organisations, irrespective of class, on the basis of an agreed programme of immediate demands concerning foreign and home policy.' John T. Murphy, *New Horizons*, London: John Lane/The Bodley Head, 1941, 318.

the minimum of ideology and the maximum of practical policies. Ideologies are one of the major causes of persecution and war. Those who think of social relations in terms of some speciously simple political or religious theory, always tend to regard their fellow men and women, not as human beings, like themselves, but as the representatives of a principle regarded as being, *ex hypothesi*, divine or diabolical. When they meet as human beings, people generally behave towards one another with remarkable consideration and decency. When they meet as representatives of principles formulated by the abstracting mind of an ideologist, they often behave towards one another like fiends. Political propaganda has only one aim – to persuade one set of people that certain other people are not concrete human beings, but walking abstractions. For minds obsessed by an ideology, Jones and Smith are no longer Jones and Smith, but emblems of Communism, Fascism, Popery, Heresy, Non-Aryanism, Hunnishness, or whatever the local principle of evil may be. Hence it follows that Jones and Smith must be not understood, not persuaded, not restrained, if need be, from behaving in an undesirable way, but liquidated – painfully, if possible, as befits vermin or devils. Ideologies are incitements to, and philosophical justifications of, personal sadism and organised persecution, domestic murder, and international war. Any move that will induce people to forget their ideologies for a little and settle down to the solution of specific practical problems is a move in the direction of the things for which our organisation stands – peace, tolerance, liberty. The formation of a People's Front would be, I believe, precisely such a move.

For Intellectual Liberty Bulletin No.1, November 1936, 14–15

How to Improve the World

This is not a political article. It makes no propaganda for any kind of coloured shirt or flag or symbol; it outlines no grandiose plans, suggests no constitutional or economic reforms.

Not that reforms are unnecessary or plans superfluous: in a world that is poised upon the brink of war, a world in which statesmen can find no better remedy for unemployment than rearmament, a world the majority of whose inhabitants do not earn enough money to buy the things that they themselves produce — in this nightmare world of ours we are in sore need of coherent planning and intelligent reform. But the literature of the subject is already too copious; there is no need for me to add to it. Besides, our world is marred by a number of defects which would not necessarily be eliminated by even the most drastic changes in our political and economic systems. We might adopt Communism, or Fascism, or State Socialism, or Anarchism; the defects I am thinking about would not thereby be remedied.

For these defects are not directly due to shortcomings in our economic or political methods. They are due to inefficiency in other spheres — to a lack, in the particular circumstances of each case, of forethought or consideration, to the conservatism that makes us cling to old habits of thought and action long after they have ceased to be useful, to plain cussedness and stupidity.

In this article I have listed a few of the defects which would not be eliminated by a change of government or even a change of social system. Each one of them affects us intimately and, given a certain amount of good will and intelligence, each one is remediable. The world we live in is largely a world of our own making; there are very few features of it, which cannot be modified if we so desire.

The fact is at once encouraging and depressing. Encouraging, if we think of all that it is in our power to do in the future; depressing, if we consider how absurdly little we have troubled to do in the past. We can only hope that tomorrow we shall be different from what we were yesterday and are today.

Let us begin where all terrestrial life begins and ends – with our bodies. In obedience to the ridiculous customs of our civilisation, we treat these precious and irreplaceable instruments with a stupidity that is almost criminal. Learning accumulates; science advances. But where our long-suffering bodies are concerned we are for the most part like savages playing with a chronometer. Worse than savages, indeed. Savages have the excuse of ignorance. We are stupid in spite of the fact that we know quite well how to behave intelligently.

Take, for example, the all-important matter of diet. A science of nutrition exists, but are its precepts followed? They are not. Half the population is too poor to be able to feed itself properly. (The remedy for this is in the hands of the economic planners.) The other half possesses the means, but neglects the available knowledge and eats either excessively or mistakenly.

Open any popular newspaper: you will find that about a third of the advertising space is filled with propaganda for laxatives, cold-cures, pain killers and pick-me-ups. All these drugs are more or less harmful, but most of them are able to palliate at least for a time the disagreeable symptoms induced by faulty nutrition. We poison ourselves with the wrong food, then try to mitigate the painful consequences of our folly by poisoning ourselves still further with drugs. After which we wonder why it is that life should seem so little worth living and proceed to blame the Government.

Not long ago I visited one of the largest drug factories in Europe.[1] A magnificent building made of glass and concrete, and about twice

1 This was the Boots factory in Nottingham, which Huxley visited with Victor Rothschild in March 1936.

as large as St. Paul's Cathedral. Thousands of workers. The very latest machines. Vast cellars, in which hundreds of tons of tonics and aperients lay in store. Waggon-loads of frozen pancreas coming in at one end and tiny phials of insulin going out at the other. Working conditions wholly admirable; production enormous. A model factory. But my admiration for the really astonishing achievement of those who had designed the buildings and the machines, for those who had worked out the techniques of manufacture and organisation, was somewhat tempered, I must confess, when I asked myself the simple question: what is the purpose of all these beautifully co-ordinated efforts?

The purpose is to produce, in huge quantities and at a very cheap rate, a large variety of more or less poisonous substances, capable of temporarily counteracting the effects of other poisons. How much better it would have been for everyone concerned (except perhaps the shareholders of the drug company) if the energy and ingenuity put into the manufacture of these palliative poisons had been applied to the task of making the use of them unnecessary!

It is characteristic of human beings that, when anything goes wrong, they should always begin by thinking out some ingenious device for masking the superficial symptoms. The idea of going to the root of the matter and finding means for preventing the trouble from ever breaking out seems to occur to them only as a kind of afterthought. To think in terms of prevention rather than of cure is a sign of great mental sophistication, and it is a most encouraging fact that this idea should now be making such headway among us. True, we will still go on trying to whitewash the symptoms of maladjustment, but we do at least have a disquieting feeling that our behaviour is futile and that what we ought to be aiming at is not the appearance of cure but the solid fact of prevention. Meanwhile the patent medicine factories are working overtime, and we still refuse to apply such knowledge of nutrition as we already possess.

It is the same with physical training. We know that the body needs a certain amount of exercise and we know, thanks to the practical work of Alexander and the theoretical work of Magnus, how the body ought to be trained so as to get the whole organism functioning harmoniously.[1] Do we apply the knowledge? We do not. Millions of us pass our working lives sitting still, and such exercise as we take is spasmodic and ill chosen. St. Paul was a tent-maker as well as a preacher and philosopher. How much healthier and happier we should all be if we arranged our lives so that we could switch over periodically from sedentary to manual work and back again! As things are we are tied to our office chairs by the snobbery that despises muscular labour and to our bad habits of exercise by mere inertia and conservatism.

It is the same story with clothes. We know that it is good for the body to be exposed as much as possible to the air, and we know that our garments ought to be clean. Women have applied this knowledge much more completely than have men. But for a few trifles like high-heeled shoes, their clothing is now almost rational. With us men the case is sadly different. Even in the hottest weather, we muffle ourselves up to the chin and down to the wrists and ankles.

Worse, we are at pains to be dirty. Our outer garments are all made of materials that cannot be washed; between dry cleanings, weeks and even months may elapse, during which we accumulate all the variegated filths and infections of the cities in which we live. The introduction of cotton fabrics at the beginning of the eighteenth century marked an immense step forward in the cleanliness of the European nations. Before that time most garments had been unwashable and even (owing to the absence of benzine and acetone) uncleanable. After it, cleanliness became a luxury which

1 Frederick Matthias Alexander (1869–1955) was the originator of the Alexander Technique of physical and mental re-education. He had written three books to date, *Man's Supreme Inheritance* (1910), *Constructive Conscious Control of the Individual* (1923) and *The Use of the Self* (1932). He is the original of Miller in *Eyeless in Gaza* (1936). Alexander had a profound effect on Huxley after he began to visit the Australian therapist on a daily basis in the autumn of 1935. Sir Henry Irving and G. B. Shaw were among many others who consulted Alexander.

Rudolf Magnus (1873–1927) investigated the complex integrative reflex system by which the brain stem and spinal cord control musculature. His life's work culminated in *Die Körperstellung* ['Posture'] (1924), a classic work of reflex physiology.

even quite poor people could afford. It is time that the happy revolution begun by our ancestors two centuries ago was carried to its logical conclusions. Only when we are dressed in clothes all of which can be regularly washed, shall we be entitled to call ourselves a genuinely cleanly race.

Not only do we fail to apply the useful knowledge we already possess; we also fail to search in any systematic way for new knowledge. An example: our bodies are capable of suffering an almost indefinite amount of pain. By living in a sensible way, we can suppress many of the existing sources of pain, but it is impossible in the nature of things that we should ever succeed in suppressing them all. There will always be a need for analgesics and anaesthetics. In view of this, it would be only reasonable for the State or some learned society to undertake large-scale, systematic researches for the purpose of discovering the most effective and least harmful methods of producing insensibility to pain. In fact, nothing of the kind is done. New anaesthetics and pain killers turn up from time to time, but the researches of the chemists and physiologists are not co-ordinated.

Still less is there any question of systematic research into the resources of psychological analgesia. In the 'forties of last century Esdaile and other surgeons were performing major operations on patients anaesthetised by means of hypnotic suggestion. The introduction of chloroform, coinciding as it did with the birth of modern spiritualism, cut short this immensely promising development. Hypnotism was annexed by the mediums and thus became discredited in the eyes of sober physiologists. At the same time doctors found it less trouble to asphyxiate their patients with chloroform than to remove their sensibility to pain by means of hypnosis.

The things we need to know – the things that a systematically organised research should be able to tell us are these: the number and the nature of the cases in which analgesia can be produced by psychological means; the best and most easily learned techniques for inducing insensitiveness to pain in oneself and in others; and finally the extent to which chemical and psychological methods can be used in conjunction. (It has already been shown that, given a small and relatively harmless dose of scopolamine and chloral, patients sink into a state of complete suggestibility and that they will subsequently carry out in waking life the orders given to them while under the influence of the drug. There would seem to be enormous potentialities, for evil as well as for good, in such combinations of chemical and psychological methods of treatment.)

A problem closely allied to that of analgesics, and no less important to us as suffering and enjoying beings, is the problem of intoxicants, stimulants and sedatives. Everywhere and at all times men have felt the need of taking an occasional holiday from the common round of every-day affairs – a holiday from the world and from themselves. It is difficult to procure reliable figures, but I should guess that, at the present time, the inhabitants of our planet spend nearly ten per cent. of their total income on intoxicants, stimulants and sedatives. Some of these – tea, for example, and tobacco – are very mild; others, such as alcohol, opium and cocaine, are exceedingly powerful drugs. But the purpose served by all of them is the same; people take them in order to escape from the boring or unpleasant reality of their own characters and the surrounding world.

Now it is obvious that the desire to take holidays from reality will tend to diminish in proportion as the individual is well adapted to his surroundings and in proportion as he leads a life which he feels to be interesting and valuable. Like all the rest, the problem of intoxicants, stimulants and sedatives can best be tackled at the source – by prevention rather than by cure. If we can arrange our world in such a way that most people's lives will seem to them worth living, there will be a smaller demand for pick-me-ups and stupefacients, for booze and dope.

There is no reason, however, to suppose that the need for occasional holidays from self and surroundings will ever be wholly eliminated. This being so, we should take a realistic view of the matter and proceed to search systematically for the most efficient and least harmful forms of chemical holiday-givers. It ought not, for example, to be impossible to discover some sort of booze that shall make glad the heart of man without giving him sclerosis of the liver – to invent a substitute for the Indian weed that shall not stink out our trains and theatres nor ruin our digestions and discolour our teeth.

At the same time all the psychological and chemico-psychical techniques for holiday-making should be carefully investigated. Here our lack of foresight has been truly appalling. We teach our children none of the techniques of mental concentration and meditation, by means of which it is possible for the individual to escape, by purely psychological means, from the distractions of ordinary life, to forget for a moment and even permanently to transcend the shortcomings of his character. And at the same time we permit irresponsible individuals to use all the resources of applied science in order to tell us lies and to fill our minds with ideas which are either ignoble or idiotic.

We can take holidays from reality in the films and the popular press, but these holidays from reality are also, to a considerable extent, holidays from truth, from good sense, from a fully human standard of values. In democratic countries, the techniques of modern propaganda are used by rich men in their own political or financial interests. In dictatorial countries, they are used by the ruling oligarchy. Bad though it be, the first of these two dispensations is preferable to the second. The rich men who control the news in democratic countries have different interests, so that the suppressions of fact are different in each paper; their quarrels permit a good deal of truth to make its way into the open. Moreover, the tripe served up as popular art has no marked political tendency; all that its purveyors are out for is money. In the dictatorial countries, on the contrary, all the papers tell the same lies and suppress the same facts, and all the popular art is tendentious as well as bad.

Between these two repulsive extremes there is a middle way. The nature of that way has been indicated in England by the BBC. This institution is far from perfect, but it does at least suggest the sort of use that ought to be made of the enormous resources which modern technology has placed at the disposal of the journalist and the popular artist.

Like electric power, transport and wireless entertainment, our news, our films and our popular periodical literature should be supplied by a public utility corporation. Under the charter of this corporation, all its newspapers should be compelled to print all the news and the comments of writers belonging to all the political parties. News would be charged to rates and taxes, like street lighting or domestic water. This means that papers would not have to depend for their very existence upon the advertisers. It would become possible for editors to pick and choose their advertisements, and the propaganda for worthless or downright harmful products which now disfigures even the most respectable journals would be effectively checked.

With the purification of news would go an improvement in the standard of popular drama and literature. Nobody can deny that the BBC has done much to popularise good music and intelligent talks. It should be possible for a similar, financially independent corporation to persuade large numbers of people that films and stories need not be half-witted or sub-human in order to be interesting. In this way – and only in some such way as this – it would be possible to use the gifts of technology for the spiritual benefit of human beings instead of, as now, for the purpose of deluding and vulgarising them.

The Sabbath was made for man; but from the dawn of history down to the present day human beings have gone on behaving as though man were made for the Sabbath. True, we have got rid of a good many of the senseless and often iniquitous conventions and taboos to which our ancestors systematically sacrificed themselves. But in the place of the gods and demons who used to tyrannise over human life, we have installed new masters in the shape of badly applied science and misdirected technology.

In an age of scientific progress the sensible thing to do would be to examine each new discovery as it appeared, with a view to making it serve some worthy human end. Instead of which we have allowed the new techniques to develop, like cancers, according to the law of their own being, and have subordinated our human interests to those of the cancerous growths.

To make matters worse, we are inconsistent. Our love of novelty is strangely combined with conservatism. We welcome technical changes and at the same time refuse to alter the old habits of thought and action which those changes have rendered meaningless or even dangerous. Thus, we have welcomed the automobile, but have obstinately insisted on making it run on roads that were made for pedestrians and horses. The result is a yearly casualty list that would have done credit, in the old days, to a first-class war.

It will be instructive, in this context, to consider the other items in the price we pay for the internal-combustion engine. The motor-car satisfies a longing for change and movement – a longing that is partly natural and spontaneous, partly the fruit of intensive propaganda. It has also (largely owing to propaganda) become a symbol of social superiority. To possess a car is the first ambition of an ever-increasing number of civilised men and women. But cars – even cheap cars – cost a lot of money. Under the present dispensation it is all but impossible for the majority of car owners to support more than a very small family. The choice is between babies and an internal-combustion engine. Ninety-five out of a hundred choose the engine. At the present rate of decrease in the birth rate, the white race will be extinct in a few generations.

Once again we have displayed our inconsistency and lack of foresight. We have fostered the mass production of novel and entertaining objects, such as the automobile; we have used all the resources of propaganda to persuade people to buy these objects, but we have refused to change our old methods of distributing purchasing power. It is obvious that, if we want people to keep the factories running at capacity and at the same time to produce enough children to ensure the survival of the race, we shall have to change these methods.

In one way or another, people will have to be paid what their children cost them. If they are not, the internal-combustion engine will put an end to us within a couple of centuries. Unless, of course, it puts an end to us within the next ten years. For the most exorbitant item in the price we are paying for the fun of jaunting about the country in cars is modern armaments and the prospect of another war, incomparably more destructive than the last. Once more we have shown ourselves thoughtlessly conservative and at the same time thoughtlessly receptive of novelty. We have accepted modern technology, but we refuse to change the political systems evolved long centuries before modern technology was even dreamed of. Our international politics are those of the bronze age, but our weapons are aeroplanes and tanks, thermite and vesicants.

These few examples must suffice. They show clearly enough that what is wrong with the world is almost exclusively ourselves. Ingenious and systematic in small things, we are hopelessly stupid, improvident and inconsistent in large ones. We will take infinite pains to perfect a machine, but when it comes to thinking out the best way of using that machine for the benefit of the human race, we simply can't be bothered.

Most of us are good but stupid – or clever but slack – or kindly but irresolute. Only those who combine good intentions with energy, and a strong will with intelligence, can hope to improve the world.

Nash's Pall Mall Magazine, xcviii, December 1936, 84–8

The Man without a Job

Unemployment Centres and clubs were called into existence for a particular purpose – to provide men and women condemned to the miseries of enforced idleness with purposeful and useful occupation, with places where they could meet for talk, work and play, with opportunities for learning and being entertained.[1] The best of them have performed their function very well. Indeed, they have performed it so well that it is becoming apparent that their significance is more than merely local and contemporary. Even if the circumstances which produced them were to disappear, they would still be of value. In other words, the Unemployment Centre or something like it would still be needed, even if there were no unemployment. In the process of making life a little less unbearable for those who have neither work nor money, the Centres have found themselves compelled to seek solutions for two of the most vital problems of the present and the immediate future – the problem of leisure and the problem of the organisation of work.

The problem of leisure is, first of all, a psychological problem. But since individuals do not live in isolation, since they are producers and consumers and must earn and spend money, it is a social problem;

1 The first Ministry of Labour Government Training and Instructional Centres came into being during the winter of 1925–6. Under the provisions of the Unemployment Act of 1934 eight new Training Centres were opened. However, as the historian C. L. Mowat observed, 'the state's efforts were dwarfed by those of a voluntary character. Unemployed clubs, community service clubs, occupational centres sprang up by the score, both in the smaller towns and in the large cities.' C. L. Mowat, *Britain Between the Wars 1918–1940*, London: Methuen, 1984, 488.

also an economic and industrial problem.

Let us consider it, very briefly, in all its aspects. To be able to do nothing and yet be happy one must either be exceptionally stupid or else exceptionally gifted and specially trained. The exceptionally stupid person can behave like a contented animal and doze away the intervals between meals; the exceptionally gifted can draw on his own inner resources and fill empty time with intense mental activity. But for the vast majority of us, neither of these courses is possible. We are too intelligent to pass our time like cats before the fire; and we lack those powers which enable a few rare spirits to live as self-sufficient philosophers or contemplatives. We need something to do and we like to do it in company. For most of us, more than a certain amount of leisure is a burden. Our nature abhors a vacuum.

The leisured rich, who are not paid to do anything, themselves pay for the privilege of filling their vacuum with active occupations or passive diversions. Sport in all its varieties, alcohol and elaborate eating, love-making, theatre-going, card-playing – these are some of the activities and diversions with which the rich can afford to fill up the aching void of their leisure. By means of such distractions they contrive to keep boredom and melancholia at bay. Not always, it is true, with complete success. In spite of shooting and cabaret shows and cocktails, the enemy persistently breaks through. But at least the vacuum is partially filled. To the onlooker, the leisures of the rich may not provide a particularly uplifting spectacle; but for the rich themselves unemployment is not intolerable. A poor man, living at subsistence level, can buy no opiates or stimulants. For him, the vacuum of leisure is complete. He is exposed to the full force of boredom and depression. He is never able to forget, as the rich man can forget in the whirl of his distractions, the futility of a life deprived of sense or purpose and contributing nothing to the greater life of society at large. The effects of prolonged and unmitigated leisure are appalling. Slowly and insidiously it tends to reduce its victims to a kind of living death.

The Unemployment Centres were created in order to bring relief to the victims of too much leisure. Their aim has been to supply the unemployed with at least the psychological rewards of work. These psychological rewards are of two kinds. There is, first of all, the pleasure that all human beings feel in doing a job well, the pleasure that springs from the exercise of skill and ingenuity and the over-coming of difficulties – the pleasure, in a word, of being, on however small a scale and in however humble a way, creative.

Secondly, there is the satisfying consciousness that what one is doing has a point and is worthwhile. Under the present economic dispensation the unemployed are completely deprived of both these satisfactions. And if things continue to move as they are moving now it seems likely enough that a proportion even of the employed will come to find the psychological rewards that every man has a right to demand from his work progressively decreasing. Indeed, it is prob-ably true to say that, in many cases, this decrease in the psychologi-cal rewards of labour has already begun. Technological progress and the hierarchical authoritarian organisation of industry are the two factors responsible for taking the satisfaction out of work. About the organisation of work and the light which the experience gained in certain Unemployment Centres throws upon this impor-tant subject I shall speak in another article.[1] In this place I shall mention it only incidentally and shall deal mainly with the effects of technological progress.

Looking forward, it is possible to foresee a not so very distant time when technological progress will permit of so substantial a reduction in working hours that the greater part of the ordinary man's life will consist – not of labour, but of leisure. But more than a certain amount of leisure is a source of misery rather than of satisfaction – a vacuum too considerable to be adequately filled with mere distractions and amusements and demanding some kind of creative activity.

The shortening of working hours is for the future. Meanwhile, technological progress, combined with the authoritarian organisation

1 I.e. the one which follows in this volume, 'Pioneers of Britain's "New Deal" '.

and the excessive division of labour, is making work increasingly monotonous. The new mechanical devices save not only muscular labour, but also intelligence; at the same time the authoritarian structure of industry increasingly limits the use of initiative in the interior economy of the factory. An incredible amount of skill and ingenuity is concentrated in the designing of machines, which then relieve their users from the necessity of thinking or even putting forth any manual dexterity. An almost equal quantity of ingenuity goes into the working out of elaborate plans of industrial strategy, tactics and drill – plans which emanate from above and effectively prevent workers, already deprived by the machine from the chance of using their wits on the job itself, from using them on the organisation of the job.

Not long ago I visited an extremely efficient bicycle factory.[1] Out of its 4,000 workers, nearly 3,000 were boys and girls between the ages of 14 and 20. The machines were so perfect that they could be worked by children fresh from school. No training was needed, and no special skill had to be shown. All the young people had to do was to repeat an identical process once every five or six seconds throughout the day. By no means all industrial work is of this nature. Nevertheless, the fact remains that more and more processes which used to be within the capacity only of highly skilled and intelligent workmen are coming to be performed by machines that can be operated by untrained boys and girls. Within the next few years technological progress will have made it possible for numerous industries to carry on almost entirely with children. One can look forward to a time when, in a good many factories and a great many offices, nine-tenths of the staff will consist of boys and girls – all under sentence of dismissal the moment they reach the age of 21 and qualify for an adult's wages.

Whether we like it or no, circumstances will compel us to undertake a complete reform of the existing arrangements for distributing

1 This was the Raleigh factory in Nottingham, which Huxley toured on the same occasion that he visited the Boots plant with Victor Rothschild in March 1936.

purchasing power. Meanwhile, however, the problems raised by technological progress will remain, whatever may happen to the economic and political systems. Leisure will be increased and repetitive work in front of a machine will tend to become more boring as the machine becomes more perfect and the division of labour is carried to still further lengths. It is true, of course, that unsatisfactory relations existing between workers and an authoritarian management are a more fertile source of discontent than the unsatisfactory relations existing between workers and their tools. The man-machine relationship is secondary; the relationship of primary importance is that of man to man. By altering the man-to-man relationship one can, if not abolish, at least mitigate the unsatisfactoriness of the man-machine relationship. (I shall have more to say on this subject in the next article.)

Meanwhile, the fact remains that no amount of re-organisation can prevent increasingly ingenious machines from making the work performed by the people whose job it is to look after them increasingly uninteresting. The pleasure that comes from the exercise of skill and ingenuity is one of the principal psychological rewards of work. But the better the machine, the smaller, in general, is the psychological reward. Those who have been deprived of these rewards will feel a growing need for opportunities to exercise their creative faculties. In other words, they will come to feel a need for the opportunities at present provided by the Unemployment Centres. Even if there were no unemployment, there would still, I repeat, be a place for the Unemployment Centre.

Inadequate funds and the urgent needs of those who use them have naturally limited the scope of the existing centres. Most of them can offer only a small variety of opportunities for creative work. Carpentering, cobbling, stocking-making, dress-making, dress-repairing, such are the staple handicrafts of the average urban Centre. In Centres on the land these are supplemented by different kinds of agricultural work. Here and there more ambitious workshops have been set up, and men have exercised incredible skill and patience in producing, with absurdly inadequate equipment, the most surprisingly elaborate pieces of mechanism.

To these opportunities for creative work must be added the opportunities given in a great many Centres for creative entertainment. Where instruments can be procured, music is studied and performed. Plays are produced. Debating societies hold discussions. And so on. Limited as they are, these opportunities are yet sufficient to make life worth living for a great many people who would otherwise find it barely tolerable. Furthermore, they have made it possible for men and women hitherto ignorant of their own potentialities to discover what they are capable of. Our civilisation offers more opportunities than any civilisation has ever offered before. If so few of us ever take these opportunities, it is because we are specialists. In every walk of life there is specialisation. Our world is immeasurably wide; but we are all on rails, predestined to one particular course. Men are turned into the mere embodiments of social or economic functions. Their profession (which in most cases they have not chosen but have had forced upon them by accident and economic necessity) confines them to thinking, feeling and acting in one particular way and in one way only.

The Unemployment Centres have performed a great service in giving people opportunities to realise their own hidden potentialities. Here, for example, is an unemployed plumber, who goes to live at a settlement on the land, and makes the discovery that his real vocation, the job he can be perfectly happy in, is the tending of animals. Here is a city clerk who realises, as a result of an experiment at the Centre, that he has a remarkable gift for wood carving. Such instances could be multiplied indefinitely. The great majority of us, I suspect, live in more or less complete ignorance of what we could do if we tried. The reason is simple: we never have the opportunity of trying.

The world would be a vastly happier and more interesting place if something like a glorified Unemployment Centre were at the disposal of every member of society – if there were places in which people could explore themselves and discover, by a process of trial and error, the full range of their personal potentialities; where they could find out what kind of creative activity brought them the completest fulfilment; where they could experience, if they were 'intellectuals', the pleasure that comes from thinking with one's hands, or, if they were manual workers, the pleasures of speculation and knowledge. What is needed, in a word, is a kind of university of common life – a university with colleges and laboratories scattered all over the country, where it should be possible for men and women of all ages to study and experiment with the art of living in all its aspects, personal, social and professional.

It is from the Unemployment Centres that such colleges and laboratories could most easily be developed. But there are also many other organisations – clubs, institutes, local societies and the like – which contain within them some of the germs of our hypothetical university. In some other countries the impulsion towards the development of such an institution has come from the central authority. The after-work organisations, which flourish in Germany and Italy, have their good points; but unfortunately all are marred by a grave defect. They are official institutions whose primary aim is not to give individuals opportunities for experimenting with the art of life, but rather to give the totalitarian state opportunities for influencing individuals even in their hours of leisure. They take their place as a part of that elaborate machinery, by means of which the central authority aspires to discipline all its subjects into obedience and like-mindedness.

Our aim should be the creation of schools of liberty, not of slavery to the powers that be; and for this reason it is desirable that these universities of common life should be as far as possible autonomous, that the State should exercise a minimum of control over them.

Pioneers of Britain's 'New Deal'[1]

At the Grith Fyrd camp for unemployed men you will find, in the New Forest, what is almost a replica of an American backwoods settlement of a century ago. In a clearing among the trees stands a cluster of log cabins. Sleeping cabins, with bunks around the walls. A cabin that serves as dining and assembly room; and another that serves as a workshop. This last contains a carpenter's bench and tools, two hand looms, an old knitting machine, and a small printing press. A few hundred yards away is a patch of land where the men grow potatoes and vegetables, and keep chickens, pigs and goats.[2]

Life in the camp is co-operative, and in the fullest sense of the word, communistic. The unemployment benefit drawn by the men living in the camp is pooled; all the food they produce is shared equally among them or, if in excess of their immediate needs, bartered for anything that may be required and can be got. The other products of their labour become the property of the camp and are used by the community as a whole. So far as material equipment

1 The New Deal is the broad term for the social and economic reforms initiated under President Franklin D. Roosevelt's first and second administrations. The first New Deal programme (1933–5) was aimed specifically at financial recovery and relief of unemployment.

2 Grith Fyrd means 'peace army', in Old English. The camp Huxley visited was at Godshill in the New Forest. This, and another camp in Derbyshire, had been set up by the Order of Woodcraft Chivalry in 1932. See John MacMurray et al, The Grith Fyrd Idea, 'The Woodcraft Way' Series, no. 19, Godshill: The Order of Woodcraft Chivalry, 1933, and 'Grith Fyrd Camps', in S. P. B. Mais, S.O.S. Talks on Unemployment, London and New York: Putnam, 1933, 245–6, 312–15.

is concerned the camp is primitive. There is nothing slick or modern or machine-made about it. Its primitiveness is the sign that the men who made it, and are still making it, have had to rely on their own personal resources. Its relatively high efficiency proves how great those personal resources were, and how well they have been used.

Here are men who go out from some industrial town into the equivalent of an undeveloped wilderness, where they set to work to construct, from the ground upwards, and with almost no resources beyond those of their own minds and muscles, a new self-supporting community: it will be surprising, indeed, if these men do not discover in the process all sorts of new and interesting facts about their own characters, if they do not unearth buried talents and develop new interests.

The centres are not only schools of leisure; the best of them are also laboratories in which men are carrying out experiments in the all-important field of social and industrial organisation. In what follows, I propose to discuss some of the useful lessons that may be learnt from these experiments.

Self-government is one of the rules in these co-operative farms for the unemployed which are beginning to spring up at different points all over the country. In each farm there is, of course, a permanent secretary to do the executive work; but the co-operators themselves frame the rules, in accordance with which work is done and the produce of work distributed. Experience has shown very clearly that it is advisable to keep such co-operative, self-governing groups rather small. Thus, it has been found that about 20 is the best number for a co-operative farm. Where groups are large, contact between members is less intimate, and their knowledge and understanding of one another less complete. The sense of solidarity – the feeling each man has that what matters is not so much himself as the whole community – suffers in consequence.

This seemingly trivial question of numbers is in reality of the greatest significance. Human beings, it would seem, are so constituted that they do their best co-operative work and experience the greatest enthusiasm for a cause when they are organised in groups between the size of a boat's crew and a rugger team.

This profoundly important psychological fact has been almost completely neglected by the organisers of modern industry. In a thoroughly 'efficient' modern factory, where the division of labour has been carried to extremes, and where every worker's programme is arranged for him in its minutest details by an all-competent authoritarian management, the individual is merely one of a great crowd. One of a crowd, and yet completely isolated. In industries which permit of the complete atomic division of labour he has no relations with his fellow workers; the 'efficient' management has so ordered matters that it is quite unnecessary for him to have any relations with them. Everything is so arranged that he cannot, while working, participate in the life of a group. All he has to do is to perform his particular function and pay no attention to anyone else. In the crowd he is a solitary unit. Physically, he stands close to other people; psychologically, he stands alone. In the name of 'efficiency' he is robbed not only of the right to use intelligence and initiative but also of the right to co-operate with his fellows. He has no voice in deciding what he shall do or how he shall do it; he merely receives orders. In a word, everything that can be done to eliminate co-operation within an industry, everything that can be done to destroy that life in common which is the foundation and almost the condition of morality, is done. 'Efficiency', as even the practitioners of it are beginning to discover, is rather less efficient than it seems.

From the experiments which have been carried out in a number of Unemployment Centres – particularly agricultural centres – we may draw several very interesting and important conclusions. First: co-operative, self-governing groups can be constituted, and will actually hold together. Second: provided that the group be reasonably small, it is not difficult for co-operators to come to a satisfactory arrangement about the distribution of produce or profits. Everyone understands the principles of justice; but where large numbers are involved and the situation is confused it may be very hard to see how those principles should be applied. In a small group this difficulty hardly arises. Furthermore, the sense of solidarity most intense in a small group. All its members come to feel a certai[n] responsibility for one another. Hence the tendency for members o[f] such groups to be not only just but actively generous. The sma[ll] co-operative group is a school of the highest social ethic.

Our third conclusion is that such groups are often remarkab[ly] efficient. Men who co-operate freely and who themselves hav[e] helped to make the rules controlling their activity tend to wor[k] intelligently and with energy. If slave labour had been as efficient a[s] the labour of free men the chances are that slavery would still b[e] with us. But slavery was demonstrably less efficient than freedo[m.] The religious and humanitarian objections to slavery wer[e] reinforced by powerful economic considerations. Work in a facto[ry] managed on authoritarian principles — where the workers ar[e] expected to behave like Tennyson's Light Brigade and obey orde[rs] without ever reasoning why — is not very far removed from slaver[y.] It is therefore (in spite of the perfection of the machinery employe[d] and in spite of the inventiveness of the experts in organisation) a good deal less efficient than it might be.

The experiments made by unemployed men in self-governin[g] co-operation are extremely significant in this context. Their succes[s] is a tribute, among other things, to the high cash value of freedo[m.] The experts have achieved a considerable degree of mechanic[al] efficiency by means of the division of labour. What is now needed i[s] an increase in human efficiency; and that increase will not b[e] achieved except by an increase in liberty and co-operation. Libert[y] and co-operation are supremely desirable in themselves. But the[y] also possess this incidental advantage, that they pay.

The results of the experiments undertaken by the unemploye[d] have been confirmed on a number of occasions under norma[l] working conditions. In New Zealand, for example, it has for som[e] time been the practice for co-operative groups of workmen t[o] contract for particular jobs of railway construction. The grou[p] treats with the company through its elected officials. Experience ha[s] shown that work is done more expeditiously and economically b[y]

These self-governing groups than by workmen organised in the traditional way.

Again the men employed at the Government printing works have for many years been organised in co-operative groups which contract to do particular jobs for a lump sum, and which themselves decide the terms upon which their members shall work.

There seems to be no reason why methods such as these should not be applied to a great many industries. Instead of being an isolated unit in a crowd, under the orders of an overseer appointed from above, the worker could become a member of a small co-operative and nearly autonomous group functioning in the same factory with other autonomous groups. As a member of the group he would help to make the laws governing the group's activity. He would take part in elaborating, and from time to time improving, the methods of work used within the group. He would have a say in making equitable arrangements for distributing the product of the group's co-operative labour.

So far as one can see, this is the only way of getting rid of the present highly unsatisfactory relationship between worker and management. In a thoroughly efficient modern factory the man-machine relationship is bad enough; but when to this bad relationship is added a relationship between man and man that is equally bad, or worse, the position becomes intolerable.

In the self-governing, co-operative group the unemployed have made a discovery – or, if you like, a rediscovery – of something that is destined, I believe, to play a very important part in the life of all civilised men.

Sunday Chronicle [Manchester], 27 December 1936, 6, 11

Acknowledgements

Copyright in Aldous Huxley's published and unpublished writings owned by the Aldous L. Huxley Estate. I am grateful for permissio to quote from this material, and would especially like to thank Dor Halsey for her advice and support.

I am also grateful to my colleagues the Provost and Fellows Worcester College, Oxford, for granting me a period of sabbatic leave which enabled me to prepare this book for the press.

I am indebted to the following libraries, institutions, individua and company for allowing me to quote from unpublished or copy right material in their possession: Bodleian Library, Oxford; Con munist Party Archive, London; Enoch Pratt Free Library, Baltimor Harry Ransom Humanities Research Center, University of Texas Austin; House of Lords Record Office (Strachey Papers); Lac Huxley; National Library of Wales; Random House UK Ltd.; Ra Books and Manuscripts Division, The New York Public Librar Astor, Lenox and Tilden Foundations; Mr Raglan Squire; Depar ment of Special Collections, University Research Library, Universi of California at Los Angeles.

In addition, the following individuals were particularly helpful one time or another during the preparation of this volume: Mrs Ann Borg, Mr Montague Bream, Dr Keith Gore, Mr Colin Hawkins, D Tony Hunt, Mr Arnd Kerkhecher, Mr Julian Loose, Mr Georg Matthews, Dr Clare Ratliff, Dr John Stevenson, Ms Sylvia Vanc and Mr Edward Wilson.

Having acknowledged my various debts I must no less readi accept sole responsibility for any errors or deficiencies which mig be found in this book.

D.B.

Index